The History of the Origins of Christianity
Christianity
Book III - Saint Paul

By Joseph Ernest Renan
Edited by Anthony Uyl

Devoted Publishing

Woodstock, Ontario, 2017

The History of the Origins of Christianity Book III - Saint Paul

By Joseph Ernest Renan

Member of the French Academy.

Edited by Anthony Uyl

Originally Published by:
London: MATHIESON & COMPANY

What kind of philosophies do you have? Let us know!

Contact us at: devotedpub@hotmail.com
Visit us on Facebook: @DevotedPublishing
Get more products via our website: www.devotedpublishing.com

Published in Woodstock, Ontario, Canada 2016

For bulk educational rates, please contact us at the email address above.

ISBN: 978-1-988297-71-2

Table of Contents

INTRODUCTION

CRITICISM OF ORIGINAL DOCUMENTS

The fifteen or sixteen years of religious history comprised in this volume in the embryonic age of Christianity, are the years with which we are best acquainted. Jesus and the primitive Church at Jerusalem resemble the images of a far-off paradise, lost in a mysterious mist. On the other hand, the arrival of St Paul at Rome, in consequence of the step the Author of the Acts has taken in closing at that juncture his narrative, marks in the history of Christian origins the commencement of a profound darkness into which the bloody glare of the barbarous feasts of Nero, and the thunders of the Apocalypse, cast only a few gleams. In particular, the death of the Apostles is enveloped in an impenetrable obscurity. On the contrary, the era of the missions of St Paul, especially of the second mission and the third, is known to us through documents of the greatest value. The Acts, till then so legendary, become suddenly quite authentic; the last chapters, composed in part of the narrative of an eye-witness, are the sole complete historical writings which we have of the early times of Christianity. In fine, those years, through a privilege very rare in similar circumstances, provide us with documents, the dates of which are absolutely authentic, and a series of letters, the most important of which have withstood all the tests of criticism, and which have never been subjected to interpolations.

In the introduction to the preceding volume, we have made an examination of the Book of Acts. We must now discuss seriatim the different epistles which bear the name of St Paul. The Apostle informs us himself, that even during his lifetime there were in circulation in his name several spurious letters, and he often took precautions to prevent frauds. We are, therefore, only carrying out his intentions in subjecting the writings which have been put forth as his to a rigorous censorship.

There are in the New Testament fourteen of such epistles, which it will be necessary at the outset to divide into two distinct categories. Thirteen of these writings bear in the text of the letter the name of the Apostle. In other words, these letters profess to be the works of Paul, so that there is no choice between the following two hypotheses: either that Paul is really the author, or that they are the work of an impostor, who wished to have his compositions passed off as the work of Paul. On the other band, the fourteenth epistle, the one to the Hebrews, does not bear the name of Paul in the superscription) [1] ; the author plunges at once in medias res without giving his name. The attribution of that epistle to Paul is founded only on tradition.

The thirteen epistles which profess to belong to Paul may, in regard to authenticity, be ranged into five classes:--

1. Epistles incontestable and uncontested. These are the Epistles to the Galatians, the two Epistles to the Corinthians, and the Epistle to the Romans.

2. Epistles that are undoubted, although some objections have been taken to them. These are the two Epistles to the Thessalonians, and the Epistle to the Philippians.

3. Epistles of a probable authenticity, although grave objections have been taken to them. This is the Epistle to the Colossians, to which is annexed the note to Philemon

4. Epistle doubtful. This is the epistle addressed to the Ephesians.

5. Epistles false. These are the two Epistles to Timothy, and the Epistle to Titus.

We have nothing to remark here in regard to the epistles of the first category; the most severe critics, such as Christian Baur, accept them reservedly. We shall hardly insist on discussing the epistles of the second class either. The difficulties which certain modern writers have raised against them, are merely those slight suspicions which it is the duty of the critic to point out frankly, but without being determined by them when stronger reasons should sway him. Now, these three epistles have a character of authenticity which outweighs every other consideration. The only serious difficulty which has been raised against the Epistles to the Thessalonians, is deduced from the theory of the Anti-Christ appended in the second chapter of the second Epistle to the Thessalonians,--a theory which seems identical with that of the Apocalypse, and which consequently assumed Nero to be dead when the books were written. But that objection permits of solution, as we shall see in the course of the present volume. The author of the Apocalypse only applied to his times an assemblage of ideas, one part of which went back even to the origins of Christian belief, while the other part had reference to the times of Caligula.

The Epistle to the Colossians has been subjected to a much more serious fire of objection.. It is undoubted that the language used in that epistle to express the part played by Jesus in the bosom of the divinity, as creator and prototype of all creation, trenches strongly on the language of certain other epistles, and seems to approach in style the writings attributed to John. In rending such passages one believes oneself to be in the full swing of Gnosticism. The language of the Epistle to the Colossians is far removed from that of the undoubted epistles. The vocabulary is a little different; the style is more emphatic and more round, and less abrupt and natural. At points it is embarrassed, declamatory and overcharged, similar to the style of the false Epistles to Timothy and to Titus. The ideas are hardly those with which one would expect to meet in Paul. Nevertheless, justification by faith occupies no longer the first place in the predilections of the Apostle. The theory of the angels is much more developed; the æons begin to appear. The redemption of Christ is no longer simply a terrestrial fact; it is extended to the entire universe. Certain critics have been able to discern in many passages either imitations of the other epistles, or the desire of reconciling the peculiar bias of Paul to the different schools of his own (a desire so apparent in the author of the Acts), or the inclination to substitute moral and metaphysical formulas, such as love and science, for the formulas of faith and works which, during the first century, had caused so many contests. Other critics, in order to explain that singular mixture of things agreeable to Paul, and of things but little agreeable to him, have recourse to interpolations, or assume that Paul confided the editing of the epistle in question to Timothy. It is certain that when we sift this epistle to the bottom, as well as the one to the Philippians, for a continued account of the life of Paul, we are not quite so successful as in the great epistles of certain authenticity, anterior to the captivity of Paul. In the latter, the operation furnished, so to speak, its own proofs; the facts and the texts fit the one into the other without effort, and seem to recall one another. In the epistles pertaining to the captivity, on the contrary, more than one laborious combination is required, and more than one contradiction has to be silenced; at first sight, the goings and comings of the disciples do not agree, many of the circumstances of time and place are presented, if we may so speak, backwards.

There is, nevertheless, nothing about all this which is decisive. If the Epistle to the Colossians is, as we believe it to be, the work of Paul, it was written during the last days of the life of the Apostle, at a date when his biography is very obscure. We shall show later on that it is quite admissible, that the theology of St Paul, which, from the Epistles to the Thessalonians to the Epistle to the Romans, is so strongly developed, was developed still further in the interval between the Epistle to the Romans and that of his death. We shall show likewise, that the most energetic expressions of the Epistle to the Colossians were only a short advance upon those of the anterior epistles. St Paul was one of those men who, through their natural bent of mind, have a tendency to pass from one order of ideas to another, even though their style and their manner of perception present sentiments the most fixed. The taint of Gnosticism which is to be found in the Epistle to the Colossians is encountered, though less articulated in the other writings of the New Testament, in the Apocalypse, and in the Epistle to the Hebrews. In place of rejecting some passages of the New Testament in which are to be found traces of Gnosticism, we must sometimes reason inversely, and seek out in these passages the origin of the gnostic ideas which prevailed in the Second Century. We may, in a sense, even say, that these ideas were anterior to Christianity, and that nascent Christianity borrowed more than once from Gnosticism. In a word, the Epistle to the Colossians, though full of eccentricities, does not embrace any of those impossibilities which are to be found in the Epistles to Titus and to Timothy. It furnishes even many of those details which reject the hypothesis as false. Assuredly of this number is its connection with the note to Philemon. If the epistle is apocryphal, the note is apocryphal also; yet few of the pages have so pronounced a tone of sincerity; Paul alone, as it appears to us, could write that little master-piece. The apocryphal epistles of the New Testament--those, for example, to Titus and to Timothy--are awkward and dull. The Epistle to Philemon resembles in nothing these fastidious imitations.

Finally, we shell soon show that the so-called Epistle to the Ephesian is in part copied from the Epistle to the Colossians, which leads to the supposition, that the compiler of the Epistle to the Ephesians firmly regarded the Epistle to the Colossians as an original apostolic. Note, also, that Marcion, who is in general so well informed in his criticism on the writings of Paul,--Marcion who so justly rejected the Epistles to Titus and to Timothy,--admits unreservedly in his collection the two epistles of which we have just been speaking.

Infinitely more strong are the objection. which can be raised against the so-called Epistle to the Ephesians. And first of all, note that this designation is nothing if not certain. The epistle has absolutely no seal of circumstance; it is addressed to no one in particular; those to whom it was addressed occupied for the moment a smaller place in the thoughts of Paul than his other correspondents. Is it admissible that Paul could have written to a Church with which he had so intimate relations, without saluting anybody, without conveying to the brethren the salutation of the brethren with whom they were acquainted, and particularly Timothy, without addressing to his disciples some counsel, without reminding them of anterior relations, and without the composition presenting any of those peculiar features which constitute the most authentic character of the other epistles?

The composition is addressed to converted Pagans; now the Church at Ephesus was, in great part,

Judæo-Christian. When we remember with what eagerness Paul in all his epistles seized on and invented pretexts for speaking of his ministry and of his preaching, we experience a lively surprise in seeing him throughout the course of a letter addressed to these same Ephesians--"that for the space of three years he did not cease, night and day, to exhort with tears"--lose every opportunity presented to him of reminding them of his sojourn amongst them; in seeing him, I say, obstinately confining himself to abstract philosophy, or, what is more singular, to the lifeless formulas least suited to the growth of the first Church. How different it is in the Epistles to the Corinthians, Galatians, Philippians, and Thessalonians, even in the Epistle to those Colossians, whom, however, the Apostle even only knew indirectly. The Epistle to the Romans is the only one which in this respect resembles somewhat the epistles in question. Like them, the Epistle to the Romans is a complete doctrinal expos'; whilst in regard to the epistles addressed to those readers who had received from him the Gospel, Paul supposes always the basis of his teaching to be known, and contents himself with insisting upon some point which is related to it. How does it come about that the only two impersonal letters of St Paul are, in the one case, an epistle addressed to a Church which he had never seen, and in the other, an epistle addressed to the Church with which he had the most extended and continuous relations!

The reading of the so-called Epistle to the Ephesians suffices, therefore, to awaken the suspicion that the letter in question had not been addressed to the Church at Ephesus. The evidence furnished by the manuscripts changes these suspicions into certainty. The words en Epheso, in the first verse, were introduced about the end of the fourth century. The Vatican manuscript, and the Codex Sinaiticus, both of the fourth century, and whose authority, at least, when they are in accord, are more important than that of all the other manuscripts together, do not contain these words. A Vienne manuscript, the one which is designated in the collection of the Epistles of Paul by the figures 67, of the eleventh or twelfth centuries, presents them erased. St Basil maintains that the ancient manuscripts which he was able to consult did not have these word. Finally, the testimony of the third century proves that at that epoch, the existence of the said words in the first verse was unknown. If then everybody believed that the epistle of which we are speaking had been addressed to the Ephesians, it was in virtue of the title, and not in virtue of the superscription. A man who, in spite of the a priori dogmatic sprit which is often carried into the correction of the holy books, had frequently flashes of true criticism, Marcion (about 150 A.D.), contended that the so-called Epistle to the Ephesians was the Epistle to the Laodicæans, of whom St Paul speaks in the Epistle to the Colossians. That which appears the most certain is, that the so-called Epistle to the Ephesians was not addressed to any special Church, and that if it belongs to St Paul, it is a simple circular letter intended for the churches in Asia which were composed of converted Pagans. The superscription of these letters, of which there are several copies, might present, according to the words τοις οὖσιν, a blank destined to receive the name of the Church to which it was addressed. Perhaps the Church at Ephesus possessed one of these copies of which the compiler of the letters of Paul availed himself. The fact of finding one such copy at Ephesus appeared to him a sufficient reason for writing at the head Πρὸς Ἐφεσίους. As it was omitted at an early date to preserve a blank after οὖσιν, the superscription became: τοῖς αγίοις τοῖς οὖσιν, χαὶ πιστοῖς, a rather unsatisfactory reading which may have been rectified in the fourth century, by inserting after οὖσιν, in conformity with the title, the words ἐν Ἐφέσῳ.

This doubt in regard to the recipients of the so-called Epistle to the Ephesians might be very readily reconciled with its authenticity; but critical reflection upon this second point excites new suspicion. One fact which confronts us at the very threshold, is the resemblance which is to be remarked between the so-called Epistle to the Ephesians and the Epistle to the Colossians. The two epistles are copies of one another. Which is the epistle that has served for the original, and which is to be considered as an imitation? It looks indeed as if it were the Epistle to the Colossians which has served for the original, and that it is the so-called Epistle to the Ephesians which is the imitation. The second epistle is the most fully developed; the formulas in it are exaggerated; everything that distinguishes the Epistle to the Colossians among the epistles of St Paul is more pronounced still in the so-called Epistle to the Ephesians. The Epistle to the Colossians is full of special details; it has a dictum which corresponds well with the historical circumstances in which it must have been written; the Epistle to the Ephesians is altogether vague. We can understand how a general catechism might be drawn from a particular letter, but not how a particular letter might be drawn from a general catechism. In fine, the 21st verse of chapter vi. of the so-called Epistle to the Ephesians takes it for granted that the Epistle to the Colossians was previously written. As soon as it is admitted that the Epistle to the Colossians is a work of St Paul's, the question then may be stated as follows:--How could Paul waste his time in counterfeiting one of his own works, repeating himself, to make an ordinary letter out of a topical and special letter?

This is not altogether impossible; but it is not very probable. The improbability of such a conception is diminished if we suppose that Paul delegated that task to one of his disciples. Perhaps Timothy, for example, may have taken the Epistle to the Colossians so as to apply it, and to make of it a general composition which could be addressed to all the Churches of Asia. It is difficult to speak with assurance on this point: for it is also supposable that the epistle may have been written after the death of

Paul, at an epoch when people set about seeking out apostolic writings, and when, seeing the small number of such writings, people were not over scrupulous in producing new ones--imitating, assimilating, copying, and diluting writings previously held to be apostolic. Thus, the second general Epistle of Peter was manufactured out of the first epistle, and out of the Epistle of Jude. It is possible that the so-called epistle to the Ephesians owed its origin to the same process. The objections which have been raised against the Epistle to the Colossians, both as regards language and doctrines, are addressed principally to the latter. The Epistle to the Ephesians, in respect of style, is sensibly different from the undisputed epistles; it contains favourite expressions, gradations which only belong to it; words foreign to the ordinary language of Paul, some of which are to be found in the Epistles to Timothy, to Titus, and to the Hebrews. The sentences are diffuse, feeble, and loaded with useless words and repetition, entangled with frivolous incidents, full of pleonasms and of encumbrances. The same difference is apparent in the ideas. In the so-called Epistle to the Ephesians Gnosticism is plainly manifest; the idea of the Church conceived as a living organism, is developed in it in such a way as to carry the mind to the years 70 or 80; the exegesis is foreign to the custom of Paul; the manner in which he speaks of the "holy Apostles" surprises one; the theory of marriage is different from that which Paul expounded to the Corinthians.

On the other hand, it must be said that the aim and the interest the counterfeiter might have had in composing this piece is not altogether apparent, inasmuch as it adds little to the Epistle to the Colossians. It seems, moreover, that a forger would have written a letter plainly addressed and circumstantial, as was the case with the Epistles to Timothy and to Titus. That Paul wrote or dictated this letter is almost impossible to admit; but that some one may have composed it during his lifetime, under his eyes, and in his name, is what cannot be declared as improbable. Paul, a prisoner at Rome, is able to charge Tychicus to go and visit the Churches of Asia and to remit several letters--the Epistle to the Colossians, the Note to Philemon, and the Epistle, now lost, to the Laodicæans; he could, besides, remit to him copies of a sort of circular letter in which the name of the destined Church was left in blank, and which could be the so-called Epistle to the Ephesians. On his way to Ephesus, Tychicus may have shown this open letter to the Ephesians; and it in permissible to suppose that the latter took or retained a copy of it. The resemblance of this general epistle to the Epistle to the Colossians was, as if that a man who had written several letters at intervals of a few days, and who, being pre-occupied, with a certain number of fixed ideas, had relapsed, without knowing it, into the same expressions; or, rather, as if that Paul had charged either Timothy or Tychicus in composing the circular letter to make it fit in with the Epistle to the Colossians, and to exclude everything of a topical character. The passage, Colossians iv. 16, shows that Paul sometimes caused the letters to be carried from one Church to another. We shall see presently that a similar hypothesis must be made use of to explain certain peculiarities of the Epistle to the Romans. It appears that, in these last years, Paul adopted encyclical letters as a form of writing well adapted to the vast rural ministry that he had to fulfil. In writing to one Church, the thought occurred to him that the things which he indited might be suitable for other Churches, and he so arranged matters that the latter might not be deprived of them. We come in this way to regard the Epistle to the Colossians and the so-called Epistle to the Ephesians, taken together, as a pendant to the Epistle to the Romans, as a sort of theological exposition, which was destined to be transmitted in the form of a circular letter to the different Churches founded by the Apostle. The Epistle to the Ephesians had not the same degree of authenticity as the Epistle to the Colossians; but it had a more general application, and it was preferred. In very early times it was taken for a work of Paul's, and for a writing of high authority. This is proved by the use which is made of it in the first epistle attributed to Peter, a treatise whose authenticity is not impossible, and which, in any case, belongs to the apostolic period. Among the letters which bear the name of Paul, the Epistle to the Ephesians is probably the one which was the first cited as a composition of the Apostle of the Gentiles.

There remain the two Epistles to Timothy and the Epistle to Titus. The authenticity of these three epistles presents some insurmountable difficulties. I regard them as apocryphal productions. To prove this, I would point out that the language of the three writings is not that of Paul. I would take note of a series of turns and expressions either exclusively peculiar, or particularly dear to the author, which being characteristic, ought to be found in similar proportions in the other epistles of Paul, or, at least, in the proportion desired. Other expressions, which bear in a kind of way the signature of Paul, are lacking in this. I would particularly point out that these epistles embrace a multitude of inconsistencies, both as regards the supposed author and the supposed recipients. The ordinary characteristic of the letters fabricated with a doctrinal intention is, that the forger sees the public over the head of the pretended recipient, and writes to the latter about things of which he is entirely conversant, and to which the forger desires the public to listen. The three epistles under discussion partake in a high degree of this character. Paul, whose authenticated letters are so particular, so precise; Paul, who, believing in the near end of the world, never supposed that he would be read in after ages. Paul was herein a general preacher, just enough interested in his correspondent to make sermons to him which had not relation to himself, and to address to him a small code of ecclesiastical discipline in view of the future. But these arguments, which of themselves ought to be decisive, I can afford to pass over. I shall only, in proving my thesis, make use of reasonings which are more or less material. I shall attempt to demonstrate that there is no possible means of putting these into the known frame, or even into a possible frame of the life of St Paul. A very important preliminary observation is the perfect similarity of these three epistles, the one to the other--a similarity which compels the admission that either all three are authentic or all three must be rejected as apocryphal. The particular features which separate them widely from the other epistles of St Paul are the same. The odd expressions in the language of St Paul, which are to be remarked in them, are to be discovered equally in the three. The defects which render the style unworthy of St Paul are identical. It is a curious enough fact that each time St Paul takes the pen to write to his disciples he forgets his habitual mannerisms, falls into the same looseness, the same idioms. The ground-work of the ideas gives rise to a similar observation. The three epistles are full of vague counsels, or moral exhortations, of which Timothy and Titus, familiarised by daily intercourse with the ideas of the Apostle, had no need. The errors which are combatted in them are always a sort of Gnosticism. The predilections of the author in the three epistles do not much vary; we see the jealous and anxious care of an orthodoxy already formed and of a hierarch already developed. The three narratives are sometimes a repetition of one another, and copies of the other epistles of St Paul. One thing is certain, namely, that if the three epistles had been written at the dictation of Paul, they belong to the same period of his life--a period separated by long years from the time when he composed the other epistles. Any hypotheses which place between the three epistles in question an interval of three or four years, for example, or which placed between them some one of the other epistles which are known to us, ought to be rejected. To explain the similarity, the one to the other, of the three epistles, and their dissimilarity to the others, admits of but one possible construction, and that is to suppose that they were written in a space of time somewhat short, and a long time after the others--at an epoch when all the circumstances which surrounded the Apostle had been changed, when he had become old, when his ideas and his style had undergone modification. Certainly one might succeed in proving the possibility of such an hypothesis, but that would not resolve the question. The style of a man may change; but from a style the most striking and the most inimitable that ever existed, one cannot fall into a style, prolix and destitute of vigour. In any case, such an hypothesis is formally excluded by what we know for certain of the life of Paul. We proceed now to demonstrate this.

The first Epistle to Timothy in the one which presents the fewest individual traits, and nevertheless, did it stand alone, we would not be able to find in it an incident in the life of Paul. Paul, when he was reputed to have written this epistle, had, for a long time, left Timothy, for he had not written to him since he went away (i. 3). The Apostle quitted Timothy at Ephesus. Paul at that same time had departed for Macedonia. Not having time to combat the errors which had begun to spread at Ephesus, the chief advocates of which were Hymenæus and Alexander (i. 20), Paul had left Timothy in order to combat these errors. The journey which Paul made was to be of short duration; he calculated to return soon to Ephesus (iii. 14, 16; vi. 13).

Two hypotheses have been proposed in order to include this epistle in the contexture of the life of Paul, each as those which are furnished by the Acts, and confirmed by the certain epistles. According to the one, the journey from Ephesus into Macedonia, which separated Paul and Timothy, is the one which is narrated in Acts xx. 1. That journey took place during the third mission. Paul remained three years at Ephesus. He left in order to see once more his churches in Macedonia, and those in Achaia. It was, it is said, from Macedonia or Achaia that he wrote to the disciple whom he had left in Ephesus, giving him full powers. This hypothesis is inadmissible. First, the Acts inform us (xix. 22) that Timothy had gone in advance of his master into Macedonia, where in fact Paul joined him (2 Cor. i. 1). And then is it probable that, almost on the morrow of his departure from Ephesus, Paul should have given to his disciple the instructions of which we read in the first Epistle to Timothy? The errors which he singled out in it he had himself been able to combat. The turn of the verse (1 Tim. i. 3) is not compatible with a man who is about to depart from Ephesus after a long sojourn. Besides, Paul announces the intention of returning to Ephesus (iii. 14; iv. 13); but Paul, in quitting Ephesus, had the fixed intention of going to Jerusalem without passing again through Ephesus (Acts xix. 21; xx. 1, 3, 16; 1 Cor. xvi. 4; ii. 1, 16). Let us add, that if we suppose the epistle to be written at that moment, everything about it becomes awkward; the defect of the apocryphal letters, which are anything but precise, in which the author holds up to his fictitious correspondent things au courant of what was about to be; such a defect, I say, is carried so far as to be absurd.

In order to avoid this difficulty, and above all to explain the intention announced by Paul of returning to Ephesus, some have had recourse to another explanation. It is supposed that the journey from Macedonia, mentioned in the verse (1 Tim. i. 3), is a journey not recounted in the Acts which Paul would have made during his three years' sojourn at Ephesus. It is certainly permissible to believe that Paul was not all that time stationary. It is supposed, then, that he made a journey into the Archipelago, and through there, at the same sweep, a link was designed to be attached to the Epistle to Titus in a manner more or leas conformable to the life of Paul. We do not deny the possibility of such a journey, although the silence of the Acts presents, it is true, a difficulty: yet, we cannot deny that it is here where the embarrassments begin which are found in First Timothy. By accepting this hypothesis, we understand less than if we had adopted the former one as to the meaning of the verse i. 3. Why does he tell Timothy what he already knows quite well? Paul had just passed two or three years at Ephesus, and he will soon again return there. What signifies these errors he has suddenly discovered at the moment of departure, which he leaves Timothy at Ephesus to settle? By the latter hypothesis, moreover, the first Epistle to Timothy should have been written about the same time as the great authentic epistles of Paul. What! is it on the morrow of the Epistle to the Galatians, and on the eve of the Epistles to the Corinthians, that Paul could have written such a milk-and-water amplification? He must have dropped his habitual style in setting out from Ephesus; he must have found it again on returning there, in order to write the letters to the Corinthians, excepting on one occasion, a few years after, when he took up again the pretended style of the journey for the purpose of writing to the self-same Timothy. The second to Timothy, by the admission of everybody, could not have been written before the arrival of Paul at Rome, a prisoner. Accordingly, there must have elapsed several years between the first Epistle to Timothy and that to Titus, on the one hand, and the second to Timothy, on the other. This could not be. The three narratives have been copied the one from the other; but how are we to suppose that Paul, after an interval of five or six years, in writing to a friend, should make extracts from old letters? Would that be a proceeding worthy of a master of the epistolary art, one so ardent and so rich in ideas? The second hypothesis is then, like the first, a tissue of improbabilities. The verse (1 Tim. i. 3) is a maze from which the apologist cannot extricate himself. That verse raises an impossibility in the biography of St Paul. We must find an instance where Paul, in going into Macedonia, could only have touched at Ephesus; that instance has no existence in the life of St Paul previous to his imprisonment. Let us add, that when Paul is reputed to have written the epistle in question, the Church of Ephesus possessed a complete organisation of elders, deacons, and deaconesses; this Church even presents the usual appearances of a community already grown old with its schisms and errors, nothing of all of which is applicable to the time of the third mission. If the first to Timothy was written by Paul, we must throw it into an hypothetical period of his life posterior to his imprisonment, and beyond the scope of the Acts. This hypothesis, involving also the examination of the two other epistles of which we have just been speaking, will be reserved by us, till later on.

The second Epistle to Timothy furnishes many more facts than the first. The Apostle is evidently in prison at Rome (i. 8, 12, 16, 17; ii. 9-10). Timothy is at Ephesus, (i. 16-18; ii. 17; iv. 14-15, 19), where the false doctrines continue to increase through the fault of Hymenæus and Philetus (ii. 17). Paul has not been long at Rome and in prison, when he gives to Timothy, in the form of news, certain details about a journey into the Archipelago he had just made; at Miletum he has left Trophimus sick (i. 11, 20); at Troas he has left several things with Carpus (iv. 13), and Erastus remained at Corinth (iv. 20). At Rome the Asiatics, among others Phygellas and Hermogenes, have abandoned him (i. 15). Another Ephesian, on the other hand, Onesiphorus, one of his old friends, having come to Rome, sought him out, and found him, and cared for him in his captivity (i. 16-18). The Apostle is filled with a presentiment of his near end (iv. 6-8). His disciples are far removed from him. Demas has forsaken him to pursue his worldly interests, and is departed unto Thessaloncia (iv. 10); Crescens to Galatia (ibid.), Titus unto Dalmatia (ibid.); and he has sent Tychicus to Ephesus (iv. 12); only Luke is with him (iv. 11). A certain Alexander, a copper-smith from Ephesus, did him much harm, and opposed him actively; this Alexander has set out again for Ephesus (iv. 14-15). Paul has already appeared before the Roman authorities; on this occasion no one has assisted him (iv. 16), but God has aided him, and delivered him from out of the mouth of the lion (iv. 17). In consequence of this, he begs Timothy to come before the winter (iv. 9, 21), and to bring Mark with him (iv. 11). He gives him at the same time a commission, which is, to bring him his cloak, the books, and the parchment which he left at Troas with Carpus (iv. 13). He recommends him to salute Prisca, Aquila, and the household of Onesiphorus. He sends to him the greetings of Pudens, of Linus, of Claudia, and of all the brethren (iv. 21).

This simple analysis suffices to point out some strange incoherencies. The Apostle is at Rome; he has just made a journey of the Archipelago, he gives to Timothy the particulars of it, as though he had not written to him since the journey. In the same letter he speaks to him of his prison and of his trial. Will any one say that this journey into the Archipelago was the journey of Paul the captive, narrated in the Acts? But in this journey Paul did not traverse the Archipelago, neither could he go to Miletum, nor to Troas, nor, above all, to Corinth, since at the elevation of Cnide, the tempest drives the vessels upon Crete, then upon Malta. Will any one say that the voyage in question was the last voyage of St Paul, a free man, his return voyage to Jerusalem in company with the deputies charged with accusing him? But Timothy was in that voyage, at least from Macedonia (Acts xx. 4). More than two years rolled away between that voyage and the arrival of Paul at Rome (Acts xxiv. 27). Can we conceive that Paul would recount to Timothy as being news, things which took place in his presence a long time before, when, in the interval, they had lived together, and had hardly been separate? Far from being left sick at Miletum, Trophimus followed the Apostle to Jerusalem, and was the cause of his arrestment (Acts xx. 29). The passage, 2 Tim. iv. 10, 11, compared with Col. v. 10, 14, and with Philemon -- 24, forms a contradiction not less serious. How could Demas have forsaken Paul when the latter wrote the second to Timothy, seeing that epistle was posterior to the Epistle to the Colossians and to the Epistle to Philemon? When writing these last two epistles Paul has Mark near him; how, in writing to Timothy, could he therefore say,--"Take Mark and bring him with thee; for he is profitable to me for the ministry?" On the other hand, we have established the fact, that it is not allowable to separate the three letters; but in the manner it has been treated by some there would be three years at least between the first and the second to Timothy, and it is necessary to place between them the second to the Corinthians and the Epistle to the Romans. One single refuge then remains here for the first to Timothy, and that is to suppose that the second to Timothy was written during a prolongation of the life of the Apostle of which the Acts makes no mention. This hypothesis may be demonstrably possible, but a multitude of inherent difficulties to the epistle would still remain. Timothy is at Ephesus, and (iv. 12) Paul says dryly, "I have sent Tychicus to Ephesus," as if Ephesus was not the place of destination. What could be more barren than the passage 2 Tim. iii. 10-11? Nay, what could be more inexact? Paul was only associated with Timothy in the second mission, but the persecutions which Paul underwent at Antioch in Pisidia, at Iconium, and Lystra took place during the first mission. The real Paul writing to Timothy would have had many other mutual experiences to put him in mind of. Let us add, that he would not have dreamt of losing his time in recalling them to him. A thousand improbabilities rise up on every side, but it is useless to discuss them, for the hypothesis itself is in question, and according to which our epistle would be posterior to the appearance of Paul before the council of Nero. This hypothesis, I say, ought to be discarded, as we shall demonstrate when we come to discuss, in its turn, the Epistle to Titus.

When Paul wrote the Epistle to Titus, the latter was in the island of Crete (i. 5). Paul, who had just visited that island, and had been very much dissatisfied with the inhabitants (i. 12, 13), left his disciples there, in order to complete the organisation of the churches, and to go from city to city to establish presbyteri or episcopi (i. 6). He promised Titus to send him soon Artemas and Tychicus; he begged his disciples to come, when he had received these two brethren, to rejoin him at Nicopolis where he calculated to pass the winter (iii. 12). The Apostle next recommends his disciple to bring diligently Zenas and Apollos, and to take great care of them (iii. 13).

And here, again, with every phrase, difficulties present themselves. Not a word for the faithful Cretians--nothing but hurtful and unbefitting severity (i. 12, 13)--fresh declamations against errors, the existence of which the churches recently established had not dreamt of (i. 10 et suivi)--errors Paul, absent, saw and was better acquainted with than Titus who was on the spot--details which presumed Christianity to be already old and completely developed in the island (i. 5, 6)--trivial recommendations bearing upon points quite clear. Such an epistle would have been useless to Titus, as it did not contain a single word that he ought not to have known by heart. But it is by direct arguments, and not by plausible inductions, that the apocryphal character of the document in question can be made clear.

If it is wished to connect this letter with the period in the life of Paul known through the Acts, the same difficulties are experienced as in those which precede. According to the Acts, Paul only touched at Crete once, and that was when shipwrecked. He made but a very short stay there, and during the stay he was a captive. It is surely not at this moment that Paul was able to commence the founding of churches in the island. Besides, if it were the voyage of Paul as a captive which is related (Tit. i. 5), Paul, when he wrote, ought to be a captive at Rome. How could he say from his prison at Rome that he intended to pass the winter at Nicopolis? Why did he not make, as wan his custom, some allusion to his being in the condition of a prisoner?

Another hypothesis has been tried. It has been attempted to connect the Epistle to Titus and the Epistle to Timothy the one with the other. It has been premised that these two epistles were the results of the episodical voyage, which St Paul might have composed during his sojourn at Ephesus. No doubt this hypothesis may go a very little way to explain the difficulties in the first to Timothy, but we most investigate it to see whether the Epistle to Titus can lend it any support.

Paul was at Ephesus for a year or two. During the summer he formed the project of making an apostolic tour, of which the Acts has made no mention. He left Timothy at Ephesus, and took with him Titus and the two Ephesians, Artemas and Tychicus. He went first into Macedonia, then from there to Crete, where he founded several churches. He left Titus in the island, charging him to continue his work, and to repair to Corinth with Artemas and Tychicus. He made there the acquaintance of Apollos, whom he had not seen before, and who was on the point of setting out for Ephesus. He begged Apollos to go a little way out of his straight route so as to pass through Crete, and to carry to Titus the epistle which has been preserved. His plan at that moment was to go into Epirus, and to pass the winter at Nicopolis. He sends to inform Titus of that plan, announces to him that he will see again Artemas and Tychicus in Crete, and begs him, as soon as he shall have seen them, to come and rejoin him at Nicopolis. Paul then made his journey into Epirus. He wrote from Epirus the first to Timothy, and charged Artemas and Timothy to take it with them; he enjoined them likewise to pass through Crete, so as to give at the same time the notice to Titus to come and join him at Nicopolis. Titus repaired to

Nicopolis, and the Apostle and his disciple returned together to Ephesus.

With this hypothesis we can in a fashion give an account of the circumstances contained in the Epistle to Titus, and the first to Timothy. Nay, more, we obtain two apparent advantages by it. It serves to explain the passages of the Epistles to the Corinthians, from which it appears, at first glance, to result that St Paul, in going to Corinth at the end of his long sojourn at Ephesus, went there for the third rime (1 Cor. xvi. 7; 2 Cor. ii. 1; xii. 14, 21; viii. 1); it serves further to explain the passage in which St Paul pretends to have preached the Gospel as far away as Illyrium (Rom. xv. 19). There is nothing substantial about these advantages, nor anything to compensate for the injuries done to probability in order to obtain them!

First, this pretended episodical voyage, so short that the author of the Acts did not judge it proper to speak of it, must have been very considerable, since it embraced a journey into Macedonia, a voyage to Crete, a sojourn at Corinth, and wintering at Nicopolis. This must have taken almost a year. Why, then, does the author of the Acts say that the sojourn of Paul at Ephesus extended over three year. (Acts xix. 8, 10; xx. 31)? Doubtless these expressions do not exclude short absences, but they exclude a series of journeys. Besides, in the hypothesis we are discussing, the voyage to Nicopolis should have taken place before the second Epistle to the Corinthians. Yet, in that epistle, Paul declares that Corinth is, at the date when he wrote, the extreme point of his missions towards the west. Finally, the itinerary which has been traced of the journey of Paul is not very natural. Paul went first into Macedonia--the text is formal (1 Tim. i. 3)--and thence he repairs to Crete. In going from Macedonia into Crete, Paul must have cruised about the coast, either at Ephesus--in which case the verse, 1 Tim. i. 3, is denuded of meaning--or at Corinth, in which case we cannot conceive why he wanted to return there immediately after. And how is it that Paul, in desiring to make a journey from Epirus, speaks of the winter which he must pass, and not of the journey itself? And this sojourn at Nicopolis, how is it that we do not know more about it? To suppose the Nicopolis in question to be the one in Thrace, on the Nestus, only adds to the confusion, and does not possess any of the apparent advantages of the hypothesis discussed above.

Some exegites think to remove the difficulty by modifying a little the journey required by this hypothesis. According to them, Paul went from Epirus into Crete, from there to Corinth, then to Nicopolis, then to Macedonia. The fatal verse, 1 Tim. i. 3, is opposed to that. Let suppose a person starting from Paris, with the intention of making a trip to England, following the banks of the Rhine in Switzerland and Lombardy. Would that person, having arrived at Cologne, write to one of his friends in Paris: "I have left you at Paris, and am going to Lombardy?" The conduct of St Paul, in any of these suppositions, is not less absurd than the route of such a one. The journey of Tychicus and Artemas into Crete is not susceptible of proof. Why did Paul not give to Apollos a letter for Timothy? Why did he delay writing to him through Tychicus and Artemas? Why did he not fix a time with Titus when he should come to join him, seeing that his projects were arrested? These journeys from Corinth to Ephesus, all made by way of Crete, for the lack of an apology, are not at all natural. Paul, in this hypothesis of the episodical journey, in whatever manner we may regard the itinerary, gives and holds back perpetually; he does things without due consideration; he extracts only from his wanderings a portion of their advantages, reserving for future occasions that which he could very well accomplish at the moment. When these epistles are in question, it seems that the ordinary laws of probability and of good sense are reversed.

All attempts to include the Epistles to Titus and Timothy in the work of the life of St Paul traced by the Acts are tainted with insoluble contradictions. The authentic epistles of St Paul explain, suppose, and permeate one another. The three epistles in question may be compared to a small round which has been punched out by a severe critic; and this is so much the more singular when two of them, the first to Timothy and the one to Titus, should happen just in the middle of that whirl of affairs, so very consecutive and so well known, which have reference to the Epistle to the Galatians, the two to the Corinthians, and that to the Romans. Several also of the exegites who defend the authenticity of these three gospels have had recourse to another hypothesis. They pretend that these epistles ought to be placed at a period in the life of St Paul of which the Acts makes no mention. According to the latter, Paul, after having appeared before Nero, as is implied in the Acts, was acquitted, which is very possible, nay, even probable. Set at liberty, he resumed his apostolic career, and went into Spain, which is likewise probable. According to the critics, of whom we are speaking, Paul, at that period of his life, made a fresh journey to the Archipelago--the journey which is referred to in the Epistles to Timothy and Titus. He returned again to Rome, and was there made prisoner a second time, and from his prison wrote the second to Timothy.

All this, it most be owned, resembles much the artificial defence of an accused person who, in order to answer objections, is driven to vent an assemblage of facts which have no connection with anything that is known. These isolated hypotheses, without either support or force, are in the eyes of the law a sign of culpability, in criticism the sign of apocryphy. Even admitting the possibility of that new voyage to the Archipelago, it would take no end of pains to bring into accord the facts related in the three epistles; these goings and comings are susceptible of very little proof. But such a discussion is useless. It is evident, in fact, that the author of the second to Timothy knew well how to speak of the captivity mentioned in the Acts, and to which allusion is made in the Epistles to the Philippians, Colossians, and Philemon. The similarity of 2 Tim. iv. 9-22 with the endings of the Epistles to the Colossians and to Philemon, proves it. The personnel which surrounded the Apostle is nearly identical in both cases. The captivity, from the midst of which Paul is reputed to have written the second to Timothy, finishes with his liberation (2 Tim. iv. 17-18). Paul in this epistle is full of hope; he meditates new schemes, and is pre-occupied with the thought, which, in fact, he is full of during the whole of his first (and only) captivity, namely, to perfect evangelical preaching--to preach Christ to all nations, and in particular to peoples of the far west. If the three epistles were of so far advanced a date, we cannot conceive why Timothy should always be spoken of in them as a young man. We are able, besides, to prove directly that the voyage to the Archipelago, posterior to the sojourn of Paul at Rome, did not take place. In such a voyage, indeed, St Paul would have touched at Miletum (2 Tim. iv. 20). Now in the fine discourse which the author of the Acts attributes to St Paul at the end of the third mission, while passing through Miletum, he makes Paul say, "And now, behold, I know that ye all, among whom I have gone preaching the kingdom of God, shall see my face no more" (Acts xx. 25). But it is not argued that Paul was deceived in his previsions, so that he had to change his opinions, and to see again a church to which he thought he had said a final adieu. This is not the question, however. It matters little to us whether Paul may or may not have uttered these words. The author of the Acts was well acquainted with the routine of Paul's life, although, unfortunately, he has not judged it proper to inform us of it. It is impossible that he could have put into the mouth of his master what he knew very well could not be verified.

The letters to Timothy and to Titus are therefore refuted by the whole contexture of the biography of Paul. When they are forced into it by one party, they are thrust out of it by another party. Even if an express period in the life of the Apostle were created for them, the result would not be any more satisfactory. These epistles refute themselves; they are full of contradictions; the Acts and the authentic epistles would be lost if we could not succeed in creating another hypothesis to uphold the epistles of which we are speaking. And may it not be alleged that a forger could not have thrown a little more sprightliness into these contradictions? Demo of Corinth, in the second century, has a theory not less chimerical in regard to the journeys of St Paul, inasmuch as he makes him arrive at Corinth and to depart from Corinth for Rome in the company of St Peter--a thing utterly impossible. There is no doubt that the three epistles in question were fabricated at a period when the Acts had not yet gained full authority. Later, the canvas of the Acts was embellished, like as did the author of the fable of Theckla about the year 200. The author of our epistles knew the names of the principal disciples of St Paul; he had read several of his epistles; he had formed a vague idea of his journeyings; justly enough, he is struck by the multitude of disciples which surrounded Paul, and whom he sends out as messengers in every direction. But the details which he has invented are false and inconsistent: they always represent Timothy as being a young man; the imperfect notion he has of a journey Paul made into Crete makes him believe that Paul had founded churches there. The personnel which he introduces into the three epistles is peculiarly Ephesian; we are tempted at moments to think that the desire to exalt certain families of Ephesus and to depreciate some others belonging to it was not altogether singular in a fabricator.

The three epistles in question, were they apocryphal from one end to the other? or were they made use of for the purpose of composing authentic letters addressed to Titus and to Timothy, that they should have been diluted, in a sense, to conform with the ideas of the times, and with the intention of leading the authority of the apostles to the developments which the ecclesiastical hierarchy took? It is this that is difficult to decide. Perhaps, in certain parts, at the close of the second to Timothy, for example, letters bearing different dates have been mixed up; but even then it must be admitted that the forger has given himself plenty of scope. Indeed, one consequence which is derived from what precedes, is that the three epistles are sisters, that, to speak accurately, they are one and the same work, and that no distinction can be drawn between them in anything that regards their authenticity.

It is quite otherwise with the question of finding out whether some of the data of the second to Timothy (for example, i. 15-18; ii. 17, 18; iv. 19-21) have not a historical value. The forger, though not knowing all the life of Paul, and not possessing the Acts, might have, notably in the last days of the Apostle, some original details. Especially do we believe that the passage in the second of Timothy (iv. 19-21) has much importance, and throws a true light upon the imprisonment of St Paul at Rome. The fourth gospel is also, in one sense, apocryphal; yet we cannot say that on this account it is a work destitute of historical importance. As to that which it possesses of chimera, according to our ideas of such supposititious works, it must, on no account, be discarded from the New Testament. This ought not to occasion the least scruple. If the pious author of the false letters to Timothy and to Titus could be brought back and made to assist amongst us in the discussions of which he has been the cause, he would not be forbidden; he would respond, like the priest of Asia, author of the Romance of Theckla, when he found himself pressed into a corner: convictum atque confessum id se amore Pauli fecisse.

The time of the composition of these three epistles may be placed about the year 96 to 100. Theophilus of Antioch (about the year 170) cited them expressly. Irenæus, Clement of Alexandria, and Tertullian admitted them also. Marcion, on the contrary, rejected them, or did not know them. The allusions which are believed to have been found in the epistles attributed to Clement of Rome, to Ignatius, to Polycarp, are doubtful. There were floating about at that epoch a certain number of hemitetic phrases, all facts; the presence of those phrases in a writing does not prove that the author has borrowed them directly from some other writing in which he has found them. The agreements which we remark between certain expressions of Hegesippe and certain passages in the epistles in question, are singular; one does not know what consequence to draw from them, for if, in those expressions, Hegesippe has in his eye the first Epistle to Timothy, it would seem that he regarded it as a writing posterior to the death of the Apostles. However that may be, it is clear that when he had collected the letters of Paul, the letters to Titus and to Timothy, he enjoyed full authority. Where were they composed? Probably at Ephesus; probably at Rome. The partisans of this second hypothesis may say that, in the East, people do not commit errors which are remarked on. Their style bristles with Latinisms. The intention which prompted the writing, to wit, the desire of augmenting the force of the hierarchical principle, and of the authority of the Church, in presenting a model of piety, of docility, of "ecclesiastical spirit," traced by the Apostle himself, is altogether in harmony with what we know of the character of the Roman Church from the first century.

It only remains for us now to speak of the Epistle to the Hebrews. As we have already said, that epistle does not belong to Paul; but it ought not to be put in the same category as the two epistles to Timothy and the one to Titus, the author not seeking to pass off his work for a writing of Paul. What is the value of the opinion which is established in the Church, and according to which Paul is the author of this maudlin epistle? A study of the manuscripts, an examination of the ecclesiastical tradition, and a searching criticism of the work itself, will enlighten us on that point. The ancient manuscripts bear simply at the head of the epistle, Πρὸς Εβραίους. As to the order of transcription, the Codex Vaticanus and the Codex Sinaiticus representing the Alexandrine tradition, place the epistle among those of Paul. The Græco-Latin manuscripts, on the contrary, exhibit all the hesitation which still remained in the West during the first half of the middle ages, as to the canonicity of the Epistle to the Hebrews, and, by consequence, its attribution to Paul. The Codex Boernerianus omits it; the Codex Augiensis gives it only in Latin after the epistles of Paul. The Codex Claramontanus puts the epistle in question outside the list, as a sort of appendix, after the stichometry general of the writing, a proof that the epistle was not found in the manuscript from which the Claramontanus was copied. In the aforesaid stichometry (a very ancient composition) the Epistle to the Hebrews does not appear, or, if it appears it is under the name of Barnabas. In fine, the errors which abound in the Latin text of the Epistle of the Claramontanus are sufficient to awaken the suspicion of the critic, and prove that that epistle was only included gradually, and as if surreptitiously, in the canon of the Latin Church. But there is uncertainty even as to the tradition. Marcion did not have the Epistle to the Hebrews in his collection of the epistles of Paul: the author of the canon attributed to Muratori omits it in his list. Irenæus was acquainted with the writing in question, but he did not consider it as belonging to Paul. Clement of Alexandria believed it was Paul's; but he felt a difficulty in attributing it to him, and, to get out of the embarrassment, had recourse to a not very acceptible hypothesis: he assumes that Paul wrote the epistle in Hebrew, and that Luke translated it into Greek. Origen admits also, in a sense, the Epistle to the Hebrews as belonging to Paul, but he recognised that many people denied that it had been written by the latter. Nowhere in it could he discover the style of Paul, and supposes, almost as Clement of Alexandria did, that the origin of the ideas belonged only to the Apostle. "The character of the style of the epistle," says he, "has not the ruggedness of that of the Apostle." This letter is, as regards the arrangement of the words, much more Hellenic, as everybody must avow who is capable of judging of the difference of styles. . . . As for me, if I had to express an opinion, I should say that the thoughts are the Apostle's, but that the style and the arrangement of the words belong to some one who has revoked from memory the words of the Apostle, and who has reduced to writing the discourse of his master. If, then, any church maintains that this epistle belongs to Paul, it has only to prove it; for the ancients must have had some reason to go on handing it down as the work of Paul. As to the question--Who wrote this epistle? God alone knows the truth. Amongst the opinions which have been transmitted to us by history, one appears to have been written by Clement of Alexandria, who was Bishop of the Romans; another by Luke, who wrote the Gospels and the Acts. Tertullian does not observe the same discretion: he unhesitatingly puts forward the Epistle to the Hebrews as the work of Paul. Gaius, a priest of Rome, St Hippolytus, and St Cyprian did not place it among the epistles of Paul. During the novatianistic quarrel, in which, for many reasons, this epistle might have been employed, it is not even mentioned.

Alexandria was the centre where the opinion was formed that the Epistle to the Hebrews should be intercalated in the series of the letters of Paul. Towards the middle of the third century Dionysius of Alexandria appeared to entertain no doubt as to Paul being its author. From that time this became the opinion most generally accepted in the East; nevertheless, protestations did not cease to make themselves heard. The Latins especially protested vigorously; particularly the Roman Church, who maintained that the epistle did not belong to Paul. Eusebius hesitated much, and had recourse to the hypothesis of Clement of Alexandria and of Origen; he was inclined to believe that the epistle had been composed in Hebrew by Paul, and translated by Clement of Rome. St Jerome and St Augustine have been at pains to conceal their doubts, and rarely cite that part of the canon without a reservation. Divers documents insist always in giving as the author of the work either Luke, Barnabas, or Clement. The ancient manuscripts of Latin production sufficed, as we have seen, to attest the repugnance which the West experienced when this epistle was put forward as a work of Paul's. It is clear that when we have made, if we may so speak, the editio princeps of the letters of Paul, the number of letters must be fixed at thirteen. People were no doubt accustomed very early to place after the thirteen epistles the Epistle to the Hebrews--an anonymous apostolic writing, whose ideas approached in some respects those contained in the writings of Paul. Hence, one had only a step to take to arrive at the conclusion that the Epistle to the Hebrew's belonged to the Apostle. Everything induces the belief that this induction was made at Alexandria, that is to say, in a Church relatively modern as compared with the Churches of Syria, Asia, Greece, and Rome. Such an induction is of no value in criticism, if the clear, intrinsic proofs are perverted by another party in attributing the epistle in question to the Apostle Paul.

Now, this is in reality what has taken place. Clement of Alexandria and Origen, very good judges indeed of the Greek style, could not find in our epistle any semblance of the style of Paul. St Jerome is of the same opinion; the fathers of the Latin Church who refused to credit that the epistle was Paul's,-- all gave the some reason for their doubts; *propter styli sermonis que distantiam.* This is an excellent reason. The style of the Epistle to the Hebrews is, in a word, different from that of Paul; it is more oratorical, more periodic; the diction contains a number of idiomatic expressions. The fundamental basis of the thoughts is not far removed from the opinions of Paul, especially Paul as a captive; but the exposition and the exegesis are quite distinct. There is no nominal superscription, which was contrary to the usage of the Apostle; characteristics which one always expects to find in an epistle of Paul's are wanting in the former. The exegesis is particularly allegorical, and resembles much more that of Philo than that of Paul. The author has imbibed the Alexandrian culture. He only makes use of the version called the Septuagint; from the text of this he adduces reasons which exhibit a complete ignorance of Hebrew; his method of citing and of analysing Biblical texts is not in conformity with the method of Paul. The author, moreover, is a Jew; he fancies himself to be extolling Christ when he compares him to a great Hebrew priest; Christianity is to him none other than perfected Judaism; he is far from regarding the Law as abolished. The passage ii. 3, where the author is placed among those who have only indirectly heard of the mysteries of the life of Christ from the mouth of the disciples of Jesus, does not accord at all with one of the most fixed pretensions of Paul. Let us remark, finally, that, in writing of the Christian Hebrews, Paul must have deviated from one of his most fixed rules, which was, never to perform a pastoral not upon the soil of churches Judæo-Christian, so that the apostles of circumcision might not, on their side, encroach upon the churches of uncircumcision.

The Epistle to the Hebrews was not, therefore, written by St Paul. By whom and where was it written? and to whom was it addressed? We shall examine all these points in our fourth volume. For the present, the simple date of a writing so important interests us. Now, this date has been determined with sufficient decision. The Epistle to the Hebrews was, according to all probability, anterior to the year 70, inasmuch as the Levitical service of the Temple is represented in it as being regularly, and without interruption, continued. On the other hand, at xiii. 7, and even at v. 12, there would appear an allusion to the death of the apostles,--of James, the brother of the Lord, for example; at xiii. 13, there seems to be recorded a deliverance to Timothy posterior to the death of Paul; at x. 32, and suivi, and probably at xiii. 7 there is, I think, a distinct mention of the persecutions of Nero in the year 64. It is probable that the passage xiii. 7, and following, contains an allusion to the commencements of the revolt of Judea (year 66), and a foreboding of the misfortunes which are to follow; this passage implies, moreover, that the year 40, after the death of Christ, had not passed, and that this term was drawing near. Everything, therefore, combines to support the hypothesis that the compiling of the Epistle to the Hebrews took place between the years 65 and 70, probably in the year 66.

After having discussed the authenticity, it remains now for us to discuss the integrity of the epistles of Paul. The authentic epistles have never been interpolated. The style of the Apostle was so individual, and so original, that every addition would drop off from the body of the text by reason of its own inertness. In the labour of publication which took place when the epistles were collected, there were, nevertheless, some operations, the import of which must be taken into account. The principle upon which the compilers proceeded appears to have been; 1st, to add nothing to the text; 2d, to reject nothing which they believed to have been dictated or written by the Apostle; 3d, to avoid repetitions which could not fail, especially in the circular letters, but contain identical statements. In like manner, the compilers would appear to have followed a system of patching up, or of intercalating, the aim of which seems to have been to save some portions which would otherwise have been lost. Thus the passage (2 Cor. vi. 14; viii. 1) forms a small paragraph which breaks so singularly the sequence of the epistle, and which disposes one to believe that it has been clumsily pieced in there. The last chapters of the Epistle to the Romans presents facts much more striking, and which will require to be discussed with minuteness; for many portions of the biography of Paul depend upon the system which is adopted in regard to these chapters.

In reading the Epistle to the Romans, after quitting chap. xii., we experience some astonishment. Paul appears to have departed from his habitual maxim, "Mind your own business." It is strange that he gives imperative counsels to a Church he has not founded, and which resembles so closely the impertinence of those who seek to build upon foundations established by others. At to the close of chap. xiv., some peculiarities still more capricious make their appearance. Several manuscripts--que suit Gresbach--according to St John Chrysostom, Theodoretus, Theophylactus, OEcumenius, fix on that place as the finale of chap. xvi. (verses 25-27). The Codex Alexandrinus, and some others, repeat twice this finale--once at the end of chap. xiv., and once more at the end of chap. xvi. Verses 1-13 of chap. xv. excite anew our surprise. These verses repeat and take up tacitly again what has preceded. It is hardly to be supposed that they would be found in the same letter as the one which precedes. Paul repeats himself frequently in the course of the same disquisition; but he never returns to a disquisition in order to repeat and to enfeeble it. It must also be added that verses 1-13 appear to be addressed to Judæo-Christians. St Paul therein makes concessions to the Jews. How singular it is that, in verse 8, Christ is called δάχουος Περιτογης? We might say that we have here a resumé of chapters xii., xiii., xiv., for the use of Judæo-Christian readers, which Paul has seized on, to prove by texts that the adoption of the Gentiles did not exclude the privilege of Israel, and that Christ had fulfilled the ancient promises.

The portion, xv. 14-33, is evidently addressed to the Church of Rome, and to this Church only. Paul expressed himself there without reserve, was proper in writing to a Church which he had not seen, and the majority of which, being Judæo-Christians, was not directly under his jurisdiction. In chapters xii., xiii., xiv., the tone of the letter is firmer; the Apostle speaks there with mild authority; he makes use of the verb Παραχαλῶ, a verb, no doubt, of a very mitigated nature, but which is always the word he employs when he speaks to his disciples.

Verse 33 makes a perfect termination to the Epistle to the Romans, according to Paul's method of making terminations. Verses 1 and 2 of chapter xvi. might also be admitted as a postscript to the Epistle to the Romans; but what follows verse 3 creates veritable difficulties. Paul, as though he had not closed his letter with the word Amen, undertakes to salute twenty-six persons, not to speak of five churches or groups. In the first place, he never thus puts salutations after the benediction and the Amen as the finale. Besides, the salutations here are not the common salutations that one would employ in addressing people one has not seen. Paul had evidently had the most intimate relations with the persons he salutes. Each of these persons has his or her special characteristics; these have laboured with him; those have been imprisoned with him; another has been a mother to him (doubtless in caring for him when he was sick); he knows at what date each has been converted; all are his friends, his fellow-workers, his dearly beloved. It is not natural that he should have so many ties with a Church in which he had never been, one that does not belong to his school, with a Church Judæo-Christian which his principles forbade him labouring for. Not only does he know by their names all the Christians in the Church to which he is addressing himself, but he knows also the masters of those who are slaves, Aristobulus, Narcissus. Why does he designate with so much assurance these two houses, if they are at Rome, a place he has never seen? Writing to the Churches which he has founded, Paul salutes two or three persons. Why does he salute so considerable a number of brothers and sisters of a Church which he has never visited?

If we study in detail the persons he salutes, we shall discover still more evidence that this page of salutations was never addressed to the Church at Rome. Amongst them we find no persons that we know who formed part of the Church at Rome, and we find amongst them many persons who assuredly never belonged to it. In the first line we encounter Aquila and Priscilla. It is universally admitted that only a few months elapsed between the compilation of the first chapter of the Corinthians and the compilation of the Epistle to the Romans. Now, when Paul wrote the first chapter to the Corinthians, Aquila and Priscilla were at Ephesus. In the interval, that apostolic couple were able, it is said, to set out for Rome. This is very singular. Aquila and Priscilla were of the party which was at first driven from Rome by an edict; we find them afterwards at Corinth, then at Ephesus; they return to Rome without their sentence of expulsion having been revoked, on the morrow of the day when Paul had just said adieu to them at Ephesus. This is to attribute to them a life much too nomadic; it is the accumulation of improbabilities. Let as add, that the author of the second apocryphal epistle of Paul to Timothy supposes Aquila and Priscilla to be at Ephesus, which proves that tradition has located them there. The little Roman martyrology (the source of posterior compilations) has a memorandum, of date the 8th July--"in Asia Minori, Aquilæ et Priscillæ uxoris ejus." This is not all. At v. 5, Paul salutes Epenetus, "the first-born of Asia in Christ." What! the whole Church of Ephesus has gone to Rome to take up its abode! The list of names which follows, applies equally as well to Ephesus as to Rome. Doubtless the first Church at Rome was principally Greek by language. Amongst the world of slaves and freedmen from which Christianity was recruited, the Greek names even at Rome were ordinary ones. Nevertheless, in examining the Jewish inscriptions at Rome, P. Garrucci has found that the number of proper Latin names doubled that of Greek names. Now here, of twenty-four names, there were sixteen Greek, seven Latin, one Hebrew, so that the number of Greek names is more than double that of Latin names. The names of the chiefs of the houses of Aristobulus and Narcissus are Greek also.

The verses, Romans xiv. 3-16, were therefore not addressed to the Church at Rome; they were addressed to the Church at Ephesus. The verses 17-20 could not have been addressed to the Romans either. St Paul there makes use of the word, which is habitual to him, when he gives an order to his disciples (Παραχαλῶ); he expresses himself with extreme acerbity in regard to the divisions sown by his adversaries; we see that he is there en famille; he knows the condition of the Church to which he addresses himself; he is delighted with the good reputation of this Church; he rejoices over her as a master would over his pupils (ἐφ᾽ὑμῖν καἰρω). These verses have no meaning, if we suppose them addressed by the Apostle to a church which must have been strange to him. Each sentence proves that he had preached to those to whom he wrote, and that they were solicited by his enemies. These verses could only have been addressed to the Corinthians or to the Ephesians. The epistle, at the end of which they were found, was written from Corinth; these verses, which constitute the close of a letter, had, therefore, been addressed to Ephesus. Seeing that we have shown that the verses 3-16 were likewise addressed to the faithful at Ephesus, we obtain than a long fragment (xvi. 3-20), which most have formed part of a letter to the Ephesians. Hence it becomes more natural to connect with these verses, 3-20, verses 1, 2 of the same chapter--verses which might be considered as a postscript after the Amen, except that it is better to attach them to that which follows. The journey of Phoebe becomes thus more probable. Finally, the somewhat imperative commands of xvi. 2, and the motive with which Paul applied them, are better understood when addressed to the Ephesians, who were under so many obligations to the Apostle, than to the Romans, who were not indebted to him for anything.

The verses 21-24 of chapter xiv. could not, any more than that which precedes, have made a part of the Epistle to the Romana. Why should all these people, who had never been to Rome, who had never known the faithful at Rome, salute the latter? What could these unknown person say to the Church of Rome? It is important to remark that all the names are those of Macedonians or people who could have become acquainted with the Churches of Macedonia. Verse 24 is the close of a letter. The verses (xvi.) 21-24 can then be made the close of a letter addressed to the Thessalonians.

The verses 25-27 give on a new finale, which contains nothing topical, and which, as we have already said, is found in several manuscripts at the end of chapter xiv. In other manuscripts, particularly in the Boernerianus and the Augiensis (the Greek part), this termination is wanting. Assuredly that portion did not constitute a part of the Epistle to the Romans, which terminates with verse (xv.) 33, nor of the Epistle to the Ephesians, which terminates with verse (xvi.) 20, nor of the Epistle to the Churches of Macedonia, which finishes with the verse (xvi.) 24. We arrive, then, at the curious result that the epistle closes four times, and in the Codex Alexandrinus five times. This is absolutely contrary to the practice of Paul, and even to good sense. Here, then, is a difficulty proceeding from some peculiar accident. Must we, with Marcion and with Baur, declare the two last chapters of the Epistle to the Romans to be apocryphal? We are surprised that a critic so acute as Baur should be contented with a solution so crude. Why should a forger invent such insignificant details? Why should he add to a sacred work a list of proper names? In the first and second centuries the authors of apocrypha had almost all some dogmatic motive; apostolic writings were interpolated either with a view to some doctrine, or to establish some form of discipline. We believe we are able to propose a theory more satisfactory than that of Baur. In our view, the epistle addrexsed to the Romans was (1) not addressed entirely to the Romans, and (2) was not addressed to the Romans only.

St Paul, advancing in his career, had acquired a taste for encyclical epistles, designed to be read in several churches. We presume that the intention of the Epistle to the Romans was an encyclical of this kind. St Paul, when he had reached his full maturity, addressed it to the most important churches, at least to three of them, and, as an exception, addressed it also to the Church of Rome. The four endings falling at verses, xv. 33, xvi. 40, xvi. 24, xvi. 27, are the endings of different copies despatched. When the epistles came to be published, the copy addressed to the Church of Rome was taken as a basis; but in order not to lose anything, there was annexed to the text thus constituted the various parts, and notably the different endings of the copies which were set aside. In this way many of the peculiarities are explained:--(1) The double use made of the passage xv. 1-13, with the chapters xii., xiii., xiv., chapters which, being appropriate only to the Churches founded by the Apostle, are not to be found in the copy sent to the Romans, whilst the passage xv. 1-13, not being appropriate to the disciples of Paul, but, on the other hand, perfectly adapted to the Romans; (2) Certain features of the epistle which were only partially adapted to the faithful of Rome, and which went even the length of indiscretion, if they had been addressed only to the latter; (3) The hesitation of the best critics on the question in distinguishing whether the epistle was addressed to the Pagan converts or to the Judæo-Christiana, a hesitation quite simple by our hypothesis, since the principal parts of the epistle had been composed for the simultaneous use of several churches; (4) What surprises is, that Paul should compose a letter so singularly important for a Church with which he was not acquainted, and in respect of which his title could be contested; (5) In a word, the capricious peculiarities of the chapters xv. and xvi., these nonsensical salutations, these four endings, three of which are certainly not to be found in the copy sent to Rome. We shall see, in the course of the present volume, how far this hypothesis is in accord with all the other necessities of the life of St Paul.

We must not omit the testimony of an important manuscript. The Codex Boernerianus omits the name of Rome in the verses 7 and 15 of the first chapter. We must not say that the omission is there made in view of its being read in the churches; the Boernerian manuscript, the work of the philologers of St Gall, about the year 900, proposed to itself a purely exegetic aim, and was copied in a very old manuscript.

I regret that I have not been able to find room in the present book to give an account of the last days of the life of St Paul: to have done that, it would have been necessary to largely increase the size of this volume. Moreover, the Third Book would have thus lost somewhat of the historical solidity which characterises it. After the arrival of Paul at Rome, in fact, we cease to tread on the ground of incontestable data; we begin to grope in the obscurity of legends and of apocryphal documents. The next volume (fourth volume of the beginnings of Christianity) will contain the end of the life of Paul, the occurrences in Judea, the arrival of Peter at Rome, the persecutions of Nero, the death of the apostles, the apocalypse, the taking of Jerusalem, the compilation of synoptic gospels. Then, a fifth and last volume will comprise the compilation of writings more ancient than the New Testament, the interior movements of the Church of Asia Minor, the progress of the hierarchy and of discipline, the birth of the gnostic sects, the definitive constitution of a dogmatic orthodoxy and of the episcopate. When once the last book of the New Testament has been reduced to writing, when once the authority of the Church constituted and armed with a sort of touchstone to discern truth from error, when once the small democratic confraternities of the early apostolic age have abdicated their power into the hands of the bishop, then is Christianity complete. The infant will grow still, but he will have all his members; he will no longer be an embryo: he will acquire no more essential organs. At the same time, however, the last bonds which attached the Christian Church to its mother, the Jewish synagogue, has been snapped; the Church exists as an independent being; she has nothing left for her mother but aversion. The History of the Origins of Christianity ends at this moment. I trust that I shall be spared for five years to finish this work, to which I have wished to devote the most mature years of my life. It will cost me many sacrifices, especially in excluding me from the instruction of the College of France, a second aim I had proposed to myself. But one must not be too exacting; perhaps he to whom, of two designs, it has been given to realise one, ought not to rail against fate, the rather if he has understood these designs as DUTIES.

Footnotes:

1. In a note, the author defines "superscription" to mean the first phrase of the texts, and "title "as the heading of each chapter.--Translator.

CHAPTER I

FIRST JOURNEY OF PAUL--THE CYPRUS MISSION

Journeying from Antioch, Paul and Barnabas, accompanied by John-Mark, reached Seleucia. The distance from Antioch to the latter city is a short day's journey. The route follows at a distance the right bank of the Orontes, winding its way over the outermost slopes of the mountains of Pieria, and crossing by fords the numerous streams which descend from the heights. On all sides there are copses of myrtles, arbutus, laurels, green oaks; while prosperous villages are perched upon the sharply-cut ridges of the mountains. To the left, the plain of Orontes unfolds to view its splendid cultivation. On the south, the wooded summits of the mountains of Daphne bound the horizon. We are now beyond the borders of Syria. We stand on soil classical, smiling, fertile, and civilised. Each name recalls the powerful Greek colony which gave to these regions so high a historical importance, and which established there a centre of opposition that sometimes assumed a violent form against the Semitic genius.

Seleucia was the port of Antioch, and the chief northern outlet of Syria towards the west. The city was situated partly in the plain and partly on the abrupt heights, facing the angle made by the deposits of the Orontes at the foot of the Coryphas, about a league and a half to the north of the mouth of the river. It was here that the hordes of depraved beings, creatures of a rotten secularism, embarked every year to invade Rome and to infect it. The dominant religion was that of Mount Casius--a beautiful, regularly-formed summit, situated on the other side of the Orontes, and with which was associated various legends. The coast is inhospitable and tempestuous. The wind descending from the mountain tops, gives the waves a back stroke, and produces almost always a deep ground swell. An artificial basin, communicating with the sea by a narrow channel, shelters ships from the recurring shocks of the waves. The quays, the mole formed of enormous blocks are still standing and waiting in silence the not far distant day when Seleucia shall again become what she was formerly--one of the grandest termini in the globe. Paul, in saluting for the last time with his band the brethren assembled on the dark sands of the beach, had in front of him the beautiful section of the circle formed by the coast at the mouth of the Orontes; to the right, the symmetrical cone of the Casius, from which was to ascend three hundred years later the smoke of the last Pagan sacrifice; to the left, the rugged steeps of Mount Coryphas; behind him, in the clouds, the snows of Taurus, and the coast of Cilicia, which forms the Gulf of Issus. The hour was a solemn one. Although Christianity had for several years extended beyond the country which was its cradle, it had not yet reached the confines of Syria. The Jews, however, considered the whole of Syria, as far as Amanus, as forming part of the Holy Land, and sharing its prerogatives, its rights and duties. This, then, was the moment when Christianity really quitted its native soil, and launched forth into the vast world.

Paul had already travelled much in order to spread the name of Jesus. He had been for seven years a Christian, and not for a single day had his ardent conviction been lulled to rest. His departure from Antioch with Barnabas marked, however, a decisive change in his career. He began then that Apostolic life, in which he displayed unexampled activity, and an unheard-of degree of ardour and of passion. Travelling was then very difficult, when it was not done by sea; for carriage roads and vehicles hardly existed. This is why the propagation of Christianity made its way along the banks of the large rivers. Pozzuoli and Lyons were Christianised when a multitude of towns in the vicinity of the cradle of Christianity had not heard tell of Jesus.

Paul, it seems, journeyed almost always on foot existing doubtless on bread, vegetables, and milk. What a life of privations and of trials is that of a wandering devotee! The police were negligent or brutal. Seven times was Paul put in chains. Hence, he preferred, when practicable, to travel by water. Certainly, when it is calm, these seas are delightful; but they have also suddenly their foolish caprices; the ship may run aground in the sand, and all that one can do is to seize on a plank. There were perils everywhere. "In labours more abundant, in stripes above measure, in prisons more frequent, in death oft. Of the Jews five times received I forty stripes save one. Thrice was I beaten with rods, once was I stoned, thrice I suffered shipwreck, a night and a day I have been in the deep. In journeyings often, in perils of waters, in perils of robbers, in perils by mine own countrymen, in perils by the heathen, in perils in the city, in perils in the wilderness, in perils on the sea, in perils among false brethren. In weariness and painfulness, in watchings often, in hunger and thirst, in fastings often, in cold and

18

nakedness: I have known all" (2 Cor. xi. 23-27). The Apostle wrote that in the year 56, when his trials were far from being at an end. For nearly ten years longer he must lead that existence, which death alone could worthily crown.

In almost all his journeys Paul had companions; but he systematically refused the assistance from which the other Apostles, Peter, in particular, drew much consolation and succour--I mean, a companion in his Apostolic ministry, and in his labours. His aversion to marriage proceeded from a feeling of delicacy. He did not wish to burden the Church with the support of two persons. Barnabas followed the same rule. Paul reverted often to that fact--he cost the Churches nothing. He deemed it perfectly just that the Apostle should live upon the community,--that the catechist should share everything in common with the catechumen; but he was sensitive on the point; he had no desire to make capital out of that which was legitimate. His constant practice, with one single exception, was to earn his subsistence by his own labour. With Paul this was a question of morals and of good example; for one of his maxims was: "That if any one would not work, neither should he eat" (2 Thess. iii. 10-12). He added to it likewise a naïve sentiment of personal economy, fearing that people might reproach him with what he cost, and exaggerated his scruples, in order to anticipate murmurs; for people had come to be very circumspect in regard to questions of money, because of having to live among those who thought much of it. In every place where Paul took up his abode, he settled down and returned to his trade of tent-making. His exterior life resembled that of an artisan who makes a tour of Europe, and scatters about him the ideas with which he is permeated.

Such a mode of life, which has become impossible in our modern society for any but a working man, was easy in societies in which either religious confraternities or commercial aristocracies constituted a species of freemasonry. The life of Arab travellers--d'Ibn-Batoutah, for example--greatly resembled that which must have been led by St Paul. They wandered from one end of the Mahometan world to the other, halting in every large town, engaging there in the avocation of judge or physician, getting married, finding everywhere a hearty welcome, and the chance of employment. Benjamin de Tudela, and the other Jewish travellers of the Middle Ages, led a similar life, going from Jewry to Jewry, and entering at once upon terms of intimacy with their hosts. These Jewries were distinct quarters, enclosed often by a gate, having a religious chief, who had an extended jurisdiction. In the centre there was a common court, and a place ordinarily used for meetings and for prayers. The relations which exist amongst the Jews in our own day, present still something of the same character. In every place where Jewish life is established and well-organised, the journeys of Israelites, who bear with them letters of recommendation, are made from ghetto to ghetto. That which takes place at Trieste, at Constantinople, at Smyrna, is, in this respect, the exact picture of that which took place in the time of St Paul at Ephesus, at Thessalonica, and Rome. The new-comer who presents himself on Sabbath at the synagogue, is remarked, surrounded, and questioned. He is asked where he hails from, who his father is, and what news he brings. In almost all Asia, and in a part of Africa, the Jews have thus exceptional facilities for travelling,--thanks to the species of secret society which they form, and to the neutrality they observe in the intestine quarrels of the different countries. Benjamin de Tudela travelled over the whole world without having seen any other thing save Jews; Ibn-Batoutah without having seen any one except Mahometans.

These little coteries constituted excellent mediums for the propagation of doctrines. Each knew his neighbour well, each closely watched the other; nothing could be further removed from the vulgar freedom of our modern societies, in which men come in contact with each other so little. The divisions of parties in a city were always made according to religion, when politics was not the paramount consideration. A religious question falling into one of these faithful Israelitish communities, set everything on fire, and settled schisms and strifes. Most frequently a religious question was but a firebrand which was eagerly laid hold of by reason of previous hatreds--a pretext which was seized upon for reckoning up and denouncing one another.

The establishment of Christianity was not discussed outside the synagogues, with which latter the coasts of the Mediterranean were already covered, when Paul and the other Apostles set out upon their missions. These synagogues had ordinarily little to distinguish them; they were like the other houses, forming with the quarter of which they were the centre and link a small vicus (village) or aingiport (small alley). One thing distinguished these quarters; this was the absence of ornaments of sculpture vivant, which necessitated recourse for decoration to expedients, crude, pronounced, and false. But that which more than anything else designated the Jewish quarter to new-comers disembarking at the port of Seleucia or Cæsarea, was the type of race--young women decked in gaudy colours, white, red and green, without medium tints; matrons with pleasing figures, rosy cheeks, slightly embonpoint, with kindly, maternal eyes. Having landed, and received a warm welcome, the Apostles awaited the Sabbath. They then betook themselves to the synagogue. It was a custom, when a stranger appeared intelligent or eager to make himself know, to invite him to address to the people a few words of edification. The Apostle took advantage of this custom, and expounded the Christian thesis. Jesus had proceeded precisely in the same manner. Astonishment was at first the general feeling. Opposition did not manifest itself until a little later, not until some conversions had taken place. Then the elders of the synagogues resorted to violence; forthwith they ordered to be applied to the Apostle the cruel and shameful chastisements which were inflicted on heretics; on other occasions they made an appeal to the authorities to have the innovator either expelled or beaten. The Apostle did not preach to the Gentiles until after he had preached to the Jews. The converts from Paganism were in general the least numerous, and yet they almost all were recruited from the classes of the population which were already in contact with Judaism, and had been brought to embrace it.

This proselytism, as we see,. was confined to the towns. The first apostles of Christianity did not preach in country places. The countryman (paganus) was the last to embrace Christianity. The local patois, which the Greek had not been able to root out in the country districts, was in part the cause of this. To tell the truth, the peasant living outside the towns, was quite a rare thing in the country, at the time when Christianity first began to spread. The organisation of that Apostolic religion, consisting of assemblies (ecclesia), was essentially urban. Islamism, in like manner, is also par excellence a religion of the town. It is not complete without its grand mosques, its schools, its ulemas (doctors), its muezzins (the callers to prayers).

The gaiety, the sprightliness of heart, which these evangelical odysseys breathed, were something new, original, and charming. The Acts of the Apostles, the expression of that first transport of the Christian conscience, is a book of gladness, of serene fervency. Since the Homeric poems, no work so full of such genuine sensation had appeared. A morning breeze, an odour of the sea--if I may be permitted to say so--inspiring a sort of cheerfulness and force, permeates the whole book, and made it an excellent compagnon de voyage, an exquisite breviary for him who followed the ancient landmarks along the Southern seas. It was the second poem of Christianity. The lake of Tiberias and its fishing barques had furnished the first. Now, a current more powerful, aspirations towards lands more distant, allure us on to the high seas.

The first point at which the three missionaries touched, was the island of Cyprus, an ancient, mixed settlement where the Grecian race and the Phoenician race, planted at first side by side, had ended by nearly exterminating one another. It was the native country of Barnabas, and that circumstance doubtless had much to do in determining the direction in which the mission should make its first advance. Cyprus had already received the seeds of the Christian faith; in any case, the new religion embraced several Cypriotes in its fold. The number of Jewries there was considerable. It should, however, be remembered that the whole circle of Seleucia, Tarsus, and Cyprus was by no means extensive; and the small group of Jews scattered over those points, represented nearly what would be the parent families established at St Brieuc, Saint-Malo, and Jersey. Paul and Barnabas, then, set out for the countries with which they were already more or less familiar.

The Apostolic band disembarked at the ancient port of Salamis. They traversed the whole island from east to west, inclining towards the south, and probably following the sea coast. It was the most Phoenician portion of the island, containing the towns of Citium, Amathontus, and Paphos, old Semitic centres whose original customs had not yet been effaced. Paul and Barnabas preached in the synagogues of the Jews. Only a single incident of the journey has been left on record. It occurred at Neo Paphos, a modern town, which had been built at some distance from the ancient town, so celebrated for the worship of Venue (Palæpaphos). Neo Paphos was at that time, as it would seem, the residence of the Roman pro-consul who governed the island of Cyprus. This pro-consul was Sergius Paulus, a man of illustrious birth, who, it appears (although it occurred often with the Romans), permitted himself to be amused with enchantments, and the superstitious beliefs of the country in which chance had placed him. He had near him a Jew named Bar-jesus, who passed himself off for a magician, and gave himself a title which is translated as elim, or "sage." He produced there, it is said, scenes analogous to those which took place at Sebaste between the Apostles and Simon the magician. Bar-jesus raised a bitter opposition against Paul and Barnabas. Later tradition asserts that the occasion of this feud was the conversion of the pro-consul. It is related that in a public discussion, Paul, in order to silence his adversary, was obliged to strike him with temporary blindness, and that the pro-consul, moved by that great wonder, was converted.

The conversion of a Roman of that order at this epoch is a thing absolutely inadmissible. Paul, doubtless, took for faith the manifestations of interest which Sergius evinced towards him; mayhap even he mistook irony for favour. The Orientals do not understand irony. Their maxim, moreover, is that he who is not for them is against them. The curiosity exhibited by Sergius Paulus was in the eyes of the missionaries regarded as a favourable disposition. Like many other Romans, Paulus might be very credulous. Probably the sorceries to which Paul and Barnabas had more than once recourse, but which we are unfortunately precluded from believing, appeared to him very striking and more wonderful than those of Bar-jesus. But, from a feeling of astonishment to conversion, is a long step. The legend appears to attribute to Paulus Sergius the reasonings of a Jew or of a Syrian. The Jew and the Syrian regard the miracle as the proof of a doctrine preached by the Thaumaturgus. The Roman, if he was enlightened, regarded the miracle as a trick by which he could amuse himself, and, if he was credulous and ignorant, as one of those things which happened now and then. But the miracle to him was no proof of doctrine. Absolutely destitute of theological sentiment, the Romans could not imagine that a dogma could be the aim that a god proposed to himself in working a miracle. The miracle was to them either a fantastical, although natural, thing (the idea of the laws of nature was foreign to them, unless they had studied the Grecian philosophy), or an act revealing to them the immediate presence of divinity. If Sergius Paulus had actually believed in the miracles of Paul, the reasoning that he would have employed would have been: "This man is very powerful: he is perhaps a god;" and not, "The doctrine which this man preaches is the truth." In any case, if the conversion of Sergius Paulus rested upon motives so flimsy, we believe we are doing an honour to Christianity in not calling it a conversion, and in striking off Sergius Paulus from the number of the Christians.

What is probable is that he had for the mission a benevolent regard; hence the mission retained for him the remembrance of a wise and good man. The supposition of Saint Jerome, according to whom Saul should have taken from Sergius Paulus his name of Paul, is but mere conjecture: we must not say, however, that that conjecture is improbable. It was from this moment that the author of the Acts constantly substituted the name of Paul for that of Saul. Perhaps the Apostle adopted Sergius Paulus as his patron, and took his name in token of clientship. It is possible, too, that Paul, following the example of a great many Jews, had two names--the one Hebrew, the other obtained by vulgarly Grecianising or Latinising the first (in like manner as the Josephs called themselves Hegesippus, etc.)--and that it was only at the moment when he entered into more intimate and more direct relations with the Pagan world, that he began to bear the single name of Paul.

We do not know how long this Cyprus mission lasted. The mission possessed, evidently, no great importance, inasmuch as Paul never speaks of it in his epistles; and as he never dreamt of seeing again the churches that he had founded in the island, probably he regarded the latter as belonging to Barnabas more than to himself. The first essay of apostolic journeying, in any case, was decisive in the career of Paul. From that time he assumed the tone of master: till then he had been as a subordinate of Barnabas. The latter had been longer in the Church: he had been his introducer and his guarantor; people were more certain of Barnabas. In the course of this mission the rôles were exchanged. The talent of Paul for preaching necessitated that the office of speaking should devolve almost entirely on him. Henceforward, Barnabas was no more than a companion of Paul,--one of his suite. With admirable self-abnegation, that truly holy man lent himself to everything, and left everything to his intrepid friend, whose superiority he recognised. Not so with John-Mark. Disagreements, which soon ended in a rupture, broke out between him and Paul. We do not know the cause of them. Probably the teachings of Paul as to the relations of the Jews and the Gentiles shocked the Jerusalemitish prejudices of John, and appeared to him in contradiction with the ideas of Peter, his master. Perhaps, also, that ever-increasing self-sufficiency of Paul was insupportable to those who each day saw it become more pervading and more imperious.

Nevertheless, it is not probable that Paul, from this time, either took, or allowed himself to be given, the title of Apostle. Up till now, that title had only been borne by the Twelve of Jerusalem; it was not considered as transferable; it was believed that Jesus alone had the power to bestow it. Perhaps Paul had already often said to himself that he also had received it directly from Jesus, in his vision on the road to Damascus; but he had not yet openly arrogated to himself so lofty a pretension. It required the grossest provocations of his enemies to constrain him to an act which at first he would have regarded as one of temerity.

CHAPTER II

CONTINUATION OF THE FIRST JOURNEY OF PAUL--THE GALATIAN MISSION

The mission, satisfied with what it had accomplished at Cyprus, resolved to attack the neighbouring coast of Asia Minor. Alone amongst the provinces of that country, Cilicia had heard the new gospel, and possessed churches. The geographical region that we call Asia Minor was by no means united. It was composed of peoples greatly diverse both as regards race and social status. The western part and the entire coast were embraced, from a remote antiquity, in the great vortex of that common civilisation of which the Mediterranean was the centre. Since the decadence of Greece, and of the Ptolemaic Egypt, these countries were held to be the countries the most lettered that then existed, or, at least, countries which produced the greatest number of men distinguished in literature. The province of Asia, notably the ancient kingdom of Pergamus, was, as is said to-day, at the head of progress. But the centre of the peninsula had been partly civilised. Local life had continued there as in the times of antiquity. Many of the indigenous languages had not yet disappeared. The state of public opinion was very backward. To speak the truth, the whole of these provinces had but one common characteristic, and that was boundless credulity and an extreme penchant for superstition. The ancient religions, under their Hellenic and Roman transformation, retained many of the features of their primitive form. Several of those religions still enjoyed great popularity, and possessed a certain superiority over the Greco-Roman worships. No other country has produced so many theurgists and theosophists. Apollonius of Tyana was preparing there, at the period at which we are now arrived, his strange fate. Alexander of Aboniticus and Peregrinus Proteus began soon to seduce the provinces; the one by his miracles, his prophecies, and his great demonstrations of piety, the other by his legerdemain. Artemidorus of Ephesus and Ælius Aristides presented the strange spectacle of men combining sincere and truly religious sentiments with ridiculous superstitions and the ideas of charlatans. In no part of the empire was the pious reaction which was brought about at the end of the first century in favour of the ancient religions, and opposed to positive philosophy, more pronounced. Asia Minor was, next to Palestine, the most religious country in the world. Entire regions, such as Phrygia, cities such as Tyana, Venasium, Comana, Cæsarea in Cappadocia, Nazianzus, were equally wedded to mysticisms. In many places the priests were still all but sovereigns.

As for the life politic, there was not even a trace of it. All the towns, as if in emulation, were striving to outdo each other in their immoderate adulation of the Cæsars, and of the Roman functionaries. The appellation of "friend of Cæsar" was prized. The cities were disputing with childish vanity the pompous titles of "metropole," of "very-illustrious," conferred by imperial rescripts. The country had submitted to the Romans without a violent conquest, at least without national resistance. History does not mention a single serious political rising. Brigandage and anarchy, which for a long time had erected in Taurus, Isauria, Pisidia impregnable strongholds, had come to an end by yielding to the power of the Romans and their allies. Civilisation had spread with surprising rapidity. The traces of the beneficent actions of Claudius, and of the gratitude of the population towards him, despite certain tumultuous agitations, were encountered at every turn. It was not as in Palestine, where the ancient institutions and manners offered a furious resistance. If we except Isauria, Pisidia, the parts of Cilicia which still retained a shade of independence, and up to a certain point in Galatia, the country had lost all national sentiment. It had never had a dynasty proper. The old provincial individualism of Phrygia, Lydia, and Caria had been dead for a long time as political units. The artificial kingdoms of Perigamus, of Bithynia and of Pontus were likewise dead. The whole peninsula had gladly accepted the Roman domination.

We might add with thankfulness; for never, in fact, had domination been legitimatised by so many benefits. "Providence Augustus" was, in good truth, the tutelary genius of the country. The cult of the Emperor, that of Augustus in particular, and of Livia, were the dominant religions of Asia Minor. The temples to those terrestrial gods, always associated with the divinity of Rome, were multiplied everywhere. The priests of Augustus, grouped by provinces, under archbishops (ἀρχιερεῖς, a sort of metropolitans or primates), succeeded later in forming a clergy analogous to that which became, beginning with Constantine, the Christian clergy. The political Testament of Augustus had become a kind of sacred text, a public teaching as of beautiful monuments, which were entrusted with making offerings on behalf of all, and of perpetuating them. The cities and the tribes were rivals for the epithets which attested the recollection that they preserved of the great Emperor. Ancient Ninoe di Caria argued with his old Assyrian religion of Mylitta, in order to establish his connection with Cæsar, son of Venus. In all this there was servility and baseness; but over and above, there was the sentiment of a new era--a happiness which they had not up till now enjoyed, and which, in fact, endured unchanged for centuries afterwards. A man who probably assisted at the conquest of his country, Denis of Halicarnassus, wrote a Roman history, to demonstrate to his countrymen the excellencies of the Roman people, to prove to them that that people was of the same race as themselves, and that its glory formed a part of theirs.

After Egypt and Cyrenica, Asia Minor was the country in which there were most Jews. There they formed powerful communities, jealous of their rights, easily alarmed by persecution, having the vexatious habit of always complaining of the Roman authority, and of fleeing for protection outside the city They had succeeded in making themselves important toll-gatherers, and were in reality privileged, as compared with other classes of the population. Not only, in fact, was their religion free, but many of the ordinary imposts, which they pretended they could not pay conscientiously, were not exacted from them. The Romans were very favourable to them in these provinces, and almost always took their part in the conflicts which they had with the inhabitants of the country.

Embarking at Neo Paphos, the three missionaries sailed towards the mouth of the Cestrus in Pamphylia, and, ascending the river for a distance of from two to three leagues, arrived at the eminence of Perga, a great and flourishing town, the centre of an ancient worship of Diana, almost as much renowned as that of Ephesus. This religion had a great resemblance to that of Paphos, and it is not impossible that the relations of the two towns, establishing between them a line of ordinary navigation, may have determined the sojourn of the Apostles. In general, the two parallel coasts of Cyprus and Asia Minor seemed to correspond the one to the other. These were the two divisions of the Semitic populations, mixed with divers elements, and which had lost much of their primitive character.

It was at Perga that the rupture between Paul and John-Mark was consummated. John-Mark left the mission and returned to Jerusalem. This incident was doubtless painful to Barnabas, for John-Mark was his relative. But Barnabas, accustomed to submit to everything on the part of his imperious companion, did not abandon the grand design of penetrating into the heart of Asia Minor. The two Apostles plunged into the interior, and travelling always to the north, between the basins of Cestrus and of Eurymedon, traversed Pamphylia, Pisidia, and pressed on as far as mountainous Phrygia. It must have been a difficult and perilous journey. That labyrinth of rugged mountains was guarded by a barbarous population, habituated to brigandage, and whom the Romans had with difficulty subdued. Paul, accustomed to the aspect of Syria, must have been surprised at the romantic and picturesque Alpestrine regions, with their lakes, their deep valleys, which may be compared to the environs of Lake Maggiore and of Tessin. At first one is astonished at the singular route of the Apostles--a route which shunned the large centres of population and the routes the most frequented. There is, moreover, little doubt that they followed in the tracks of the Jewish emigration. Pisidia and Lycaonia had towns, such as Antioch in Pisidia, and Iconium, in which great colonies of Jews had established themselves. There the Jews made many conversions; far away from Jerusalem, and freed from the influence of Palestine fanaticism, they lived on good terms with the Pagans. The latter came to the synagogue; and mixed marriages were not infrequent. Paul had been able to learn from Tarsus what advantageous conditions the new faith would find here, in order to establish itself and to fructify. Derbe and Lystra are not very far from Tarsus. The family of Paul might have had some relations, or, at all events, have been well known in these scattered cantons.

Departing from Perga, the two Apostles, after a journey of about forty leagues, arrived at Antioch in Pisidia or Antioch-Cæsarea, in the very heart of the high plateaux of the peninsula. This Antioch had continued to be a town of mediocre importance until it was raised by Augustus to the rank of a Roman colony, with Italian jurisdiction. It then became very important, and changed in part its character. Till now it had been a town of priests, similar, it would seem, to Comana. The temple which had rendered it famous, with its legions of temple slaves and its rich domains, was suppressed by the Romans (twenty-five years before Christ). But this grand religious establishment, as is always the case, left deep traces on the manners of the population. It was doubtless in the train of the Roman colony that the Jews had been drawn to Antioch in Pisidia.

According to their custom, the two Apostles presented themselves at the synagogue on the Sabbath. After the reading of the Law and the prophets, the presidents, seeing two strangers who had the appearance of being pious, sent to them inquiring whether they had a few words of exhortation to address to the people. Paul spoke, and expounded the mystery of Jesus, his death and his resurrection. The impression made was marked, and they besought him to come the following Sabbath and continue his discourse to them. A great multitude of Jews and of proselytes followed them out of the synagogue, and during the whole week Paul and Barnabas did not cease to exercise an active ministry. The Pagan population were informed of this incident, and their curiosity was excited.

The following Sabbath the whole city assembled at the synagogue; but the sentiments of the orthodox party had much changed. They repented of the tolerance they had shown the previous Sabbath; the eager multitude irritated the notables; a dispute accompanied with violence began. Paul and Barnabas bravely withstood the tempest; they were not permitted, however, to speak in the synagogue. They retired protesting. "It was necessary that the word of God should first have been spoken to you," said he to the Jews; "but seeing ye put it from you, and judge yourselves unworthy of everlasting life, lo, we turn to the Gentiles" (Acts xiii. 46). From that moment, in fact, Paul became more and more confirmed in the idea that his future was not for the Jews but for the Gentiles; that his ministry on new soil bore much better fruit; that God had specially singled him out to be the Apostle to the nations, and to spread the glad tidings to the ends of the earth. His great soul had the special characteristic of enlarging and expanding itself incessantly. The soul of Alexander is the only one I know that had that gift of perennial buoyancy, that indefinable capacity of wishing and of embracing.

The disposition of the Pagan population was found to be excellent. Many were converted and were found at the first attempt to be perfect Christians. We shall see the same thing take place at Philippi, at Alexandria Troas, and in the Roman colonies in general. The attraction that a refined worship had for these good and religious peoples--an attraction which up till then had been manifested through conversions to Judaism--was evinced now through conversions to Christianity. Despite its foreign religion, and perhaps on account of a reaction against that religion, the population of Antioch, like that of Phrygia in general, had a sort of penchant in the direction of monotheism. The new religion, not exacting circumcision and not insisting upon certain paltry observances, was much better calculated than Judaism to attract the pious Pagans; thus, favour was quickly brought over to its side. These scattered provinces, lost amongst the mountains, little accustomed to authority, without historical celebrity and without any importance whatever, were excellent soils for the faith. A Church, somewhat numerous, was established. Antioch in Pisidia became a centre of propagandism whence the doctrine irradiated all around.

The success of the new Gospel amongst the Pagans culminated in putting the Jews into a fury. A pious intrigue was formed against the missionaries. Several of the women of the highest class in the city had embraced Judaism; the orthodox Jews prevailed upon them to speak to their husbands, so as to obtain the expulsion of Paul and Barnabas. The two Apostles, in short, were banished from the city, and from the territory of Antioch in Pisidia, by a municipal decree.

Following the apostolic usage, they shook the dust off their feet against the city. They then directed their steps towards Lycaonia, and reached, after a march of about five days across a fertile country, the city of Iconium. Lycaonia was, like Pisidia, an illiterate country, little known, and which had conserved its ancient customs. Patriotism had by no means died out there; manners were pure, and the minds of men, serious and honest. Iconium was a city of ancient religions and of old traditions-- traditions which, in many points, approached even those of the Jews. The city, still very small, had just received, or was about to receive, from Claudius, when Paul arrived there, the title of Colony. A high Roman functionary, Lucius Pupius Præsens, procurator of Galatia, had been called the second founder of it, and the city hence changed its ancient name for that of Claudia or of Claudiconium.

The Jews, doubtless because of that circumstance, were numerous there, and had gained over many partisans. Paul and Barnabas spoke in the synagogue: a Church was organised. The missionaries made Iconium a second centre of a very active apostleship, and dwelt there a long time. It was there that Paul, according to a very popular romance during the first half of the third century, must have conquered the most beautiful of all his disciples, the faithful and tender Theckla. But the story has no foundation to rest on. One asks oneself why, if it was by an arbitrary choice, the Asiatic priest, the author of the romance, selected for the scene of his narrative the city of Iconium. Even to-day the Greek women of that country are celebrated for their charms, and exhibit the phenomena of endemic hysteria, which the doctors attribute to the climate. Be that as it may, the success of the Apostles was very great. Many Jews were converted; but the Apostles made always more proselytes outside the synagogue, from amongst those sympathetic populations who were no longer satisfied with the old religions. The spotless morality of Paul charmed the good Lycaonians; their credulity, moreover, disposed them to receive with admiration that which they regarded as miracles, and the supernatural gifts of the Spirit.

The tempest which had forced the preachers to quit Antioch in Pisidia, broke out afresh at Iconium. The orthodox Jews sought to stir up the Pagan population against the missionaries. The city became divided into two parties. There was a riot: people spoke of stoning the two Apostles. They took flight, and quitted the capital of Lycaonia.

Iconium is situated near an intermittent lake, at the entrance of the great steppe which forms the centre of Asia Minor, and which has, even up till now, rebelled against all forms of civilisation. The route towards Galatia, properly speaking, and Cappadocia, was closed. Paul and Barnabas essayed to compass the foot of the arid mountains which form a semicircle round the plain on the south side. These mountains are none other than the northern back of the Taurus; but the central plain being raised considerably above the level of the sea, Taurus attains on that side only a moderate elevation. The country is cold and bleak; the soil, now swampy, now sandy, or cracked by the heat, is painfully dismal.

Alone, the mass of the extinct volcano, called now Karadagh, stands like an island in the middle of that boundless sea.

Two small, obscure towns, the position of which is uncertain, became then the theatre of the activity of the Apostles. These two small towns were called Lystra and Derbe. Dropped down in the valleys of the Karadagh, in the middle of poor people devoted to the raising of flocks, in the neighbourhood of the most notorious haunts of brigands that antiquity had known, these two towns stood entirely isolated. A civilised Roman felt himself there to be in the midst of savages. The people spoke Lycaonian. Few Jews were to be found there. Claudius, by the establishment of colonies in the inaccessible regions of Taurus, gave to these outlandish cantons more order and security than they had ever before had.

Lystra was the first to be evangelised. A singular incident happened there. In the first days of the sojourn of the Apostles at that town, the rumour spread that Paul had performed a miraculous cure on a lame person. The credulous inhabitants, and the friends of the person on whom the miracle had been wrought, were thereupon seized with a singular idea. It was believed that the Apostles were two divinities who had taken human form in order to walk about among mortals. The belief in their descent from the gods was widely spread, especially in Asia Minor. The life of Apollonius of Tyana became soon to be regarded as the sojourn of a god upon earth. Tyana was not far from Derbe. As an ancient Phrygian tradition--consecrated by a temple, and annual feast and pretty recitations--made Zeus and Hermes to wander thus about in company, people applied to the Apostles the names of these two divine travellers. Barnabas, who was taller than Paul, was Zeus; Paul, who was the chief speaker, was Hermes. There was just outside the gate of the town a temple of Zeus. The priest, warned that a divine manifestation had taken place, and that his god had appeared in the town, took steps to make a sacrifice. The bulls had already been led out and garlands placed on the front of the temple, when Paul and Barnabas arrived on the scene, rending their clothes and protesting that they were but men. The Pagan races, as we have already said, attached to a miracle a totally different sense than did the Jews. To the latter, the miracle was a doctrinal argument; to the former, it was the immediate revelation of a god. The aim of the Apostles, when they were preaching to people of that kind, was less of preaching Jesus than of preaching God; their preaching thus became again purely Jewish, or rather deistical. The Jews who have become proselytes, have always felt that that which in their religion is adapted to the universality of mankind is at bottom only monotheism; that all the rest, Mosaic institutions, Messianic ideas, etc., form, as it were, a secondary series of beliefs, constituting the peculiar appanage of the children of Israel, a sort of family heritage, which is not transmissible.

As Lystra had only a few or no Jews of Palestine origin, the life of the Apostle there was for a long time very tranquil. One family in that town was the centre and the school of the highest piety. It was composed of a grandmother named Lois, of a mother named Eunice, and of a young son named Timothy. The two women professed, undoubtedly, the Jewish religion as proselytes. Eunice had been married to a Pagan, who probably was dead before the advent of Paul and Barnabas. Timothy, in the society of these two women, advanced in the study of sacred literature, and in the sentiments of the most ardent devotion; but as he frequently visited the houses of the most devout proselytes, his parents had not had him circumcised. Paul converted the two women. Timothy, who might be fifteen years of age, was initiated into the Christian faith by his mother and his grandmother.

The reports of these conversions spread to Iconium and to Antioch in Pisidia, and re-awakened the anger of the Jews of these two cities. They sent emissaries to Lystra, who provoked a disturbance. Paul was seized by the fanatics, dragged outside the city, stoned, and left for dead. The disciples came to his rescue. His wounds were not serious. He re-entered the town, probably by night, and on the morrow set out with Barnabas for Derbe.

They made here a long stay, and won over a great many souls. These two Churches of Lystra and of Derbe were the first Churches which were composed almost entirely of Pagans. We can understand what a difference there must have been between these Churches and those of Palestine, formed in the bosom of pure Judaism, or even that of Antioch, encircled by a Jewish leaven and in a society already Judaised. Here there were subjects completely unprejudiced, honest country folks who were very religious, but of a turn of mind quite different from that of the Syrians. Till now, the preaching of Christianity had prospered only in the large towns, where resided a numerous population, plying their trades. Hence-forward, churches were planted in the villages. Neither Iconium, nor Lystra, nor Derbe was considerable enough in which to found a Church to be compared to that of Corinth or of Ephesus. Paul was in the habit of designating the Christians of Lycaonia by the name of the province in which they dwelt. Now, this province--we mean Galatia--understood the word in the administrative sense in which the Romans had applied it.

The Roman province of Galatia, in fact, by no means embraced simply that country, peopled with Gallic adventurers, of which the town of Ancyra was the centre. It was an artificial agglomeration, corresponding to the transient reunion which was effected at the hands of the Galatian King Amyntas. This personage, after the battle of Philippi, and the death of Dejotarus, received from Antony, Pisidia, then Galatia, together with a part of Lycaonia and of Pamphylia. He was confirmed by Augustus in this possession. At the end of his reign (twenty-five years B.C.) Amyntas possessed, outside of Galatia properly speaking, Lycaonia and Isauria, including even Derbe, the south-east and the east of Phrygia, with the towns of Antioch and Apollonia, Pisidia and Cilicia Trachæa. All these countries at his death formed a single Roman province, with the exception of Cilicia Trachæa and the Pamphylian towns. The province which bore the name of Galatia in the official nomenclature, at least under the first Cæsars, included therefore for certain--(1) Galatia, properly speaking, (2) Lycaonia, (3) Pisidia, (4) Isauria, (5) Mountainous Phrygia, with the towns of Apollonia and Antioch. This state of things lasted for a long time. Ancyra was the capital of this large group, comprising almost the whole of central Asia Minor. The Romans were thus not sorry in order to decompose nationalities, and to efface recollections, to change the ancient geographical acceptations and to create arbitrary administrative groups analogous to our departments.

Paul was accustomed to make use of the administrative name to designate each country. The countries he had evangelised, from Antioch in Pisidia to Derbe, were called by him "Galatia;" and the Christians of these countries were to him "Galatians." That name was to him extremely dear. The Churches of Galatia were embraced amongst those for which the Apostle had the most affection, and which in turn had for him the greatest personal attachment. The recollection of the friendship and the devotion which he had found at the houses of these good people, was one of the deepest impressions of his apostolic life. Several circumstances enhanced the keenness of these recollections. It appears that during his sojourn in Galatia, the Apostle was subject to attacks of weakness, or of the malady which frequently overtook him. The solicitude, the attentions of the faithful proselytes, touched him to the heart. The persecutions that they had to suffer together served to create between them a strong bond. That little Lycaonian centre had in its way great importance: St Paul loved to revert to it, as being his first achievement; it was from there that he drew later on two of his most faithful companions, Timothy and Gaius.

He was for four or five years thus absorbed within a quite limited circle. He thought less then of those great rapid journeys, which towards the end of his life became with him a sort of passion, in order to establish firmly the Churches which might serve him as a base of operations. We do not know whether during that time he had any relations with the Church at Antioch, whose mission he had received. The desire of seeing again that Mother Church was awakened in him. He determined to make a journey thence, and proceeded by the opposite route to the one he had already gone by. The two missionaries visited for the second time Lystra, Iconium, and Antioch in Pisidia. They took up anew their abodes in these towns, confirming the faithful in the faith, exhorting them to perseverance, to patience, and teaching them that it was only through tribulation that they could enter into the Kingdom of God. For the rest, the constitution of these scattered Churches was very simple. The Apostles chose from amongst each of them elders who after their departure were the depositaries of their authority. The ceremony of their departure was touching. There were fastings and prayers, after which the Apostles recommended the faithful to God, and departed.

From Antioch in Pisidia, the missionaries once more attained to Perga. They made there, moreover, it appeared, a mission which was crowned with success. The city processions, pilgrimages, and grand annual panegyrics, were often favourable to the preaching of the Apostles. From Perga, after a day's journey, they reached Attalia, the great port of Pamphylia. There they embarked for Seleucia; then they returned to great Antioch, where they had, by the grace of God, been liberated five years before.

The mission field was by no means a wide one. It embraced the Island of Cyprus in the sense of its length, and in Asia Minor a broken line of about a hundred leagues. It was the first instance of an apostolic journey of that kind: nothing had been pre-arranged. Paul and Barnabas had to wrestle with the greatest external difficulties. We must not compare these journeys with those of a Francis Xavier or of a Livingstone, backed up by rich associations. The Apostles resembled much more the Socialist workmen, spreading their ideas from tavern to tavern, than the missionaries of modern times. Their trade was forced upon them as a necessity; they were compelled to halt in order to pursue it, and to regulate their movements according to the localities in which they could find work. Hence from delays, from dull seasons, there was much time lost. In spite of the enormous obstacles, the general results of that first mission were immense. When Paul had re-embarked for Antioch, there were several churches of Gentiles. The great step had now been made. All steps of that kind which had taken place anteriorly had been more or less undecided. For all that, they were obliged to give an answer, more or less plausible, to the pure Jews at Jerusalem, who maintained that circumcision was the preliminary obligation of the Christian profession. Moreover, the question had assumed a different form. Another tact of the highest importance was again brought to light; that was the excellent disposition which they had been able to discover among certain races, attached to mythological religions, to receive the gospel. The doctrine of Jesus was evidently about to profit by the species of charm which Judaism had until now exercised upon the pious Pagans. Asia Minor, in particular, was destined to become the second

Christian soil. After the disasters which were soon to strike the Churches of Palestine, she was destined to be the principal home of the new faith, the theatre of the most important transformations.

CHAPTER III

FIRST AFFAIR IN REGARD TO CIRCUMCISION

The return of Paul and Barnabas was hailed in the Church of Antioch with a shout of joy. The whole street of Singon was en fête: the Church was assembled. The two missionaries related their adventures and the things which God had done by them. "God Himself," said they, "had opened the door of faith unto the Gentiles" (Acts xiv. 27, 28). They spoke of the Churches of Galatia, which were almost wholly composed of Pagans. The Church of Antioch, which had for a long time on his account recognised the legitimacy of the baptism of the Gentiles, approved their conduct. They remained there several months, resting from their labours, and refreshing themselves at that source with the apostolic spirit. It was then, it appears, that Paul converted and adopted as a disciple, companion, and fellow-worker, a young uncircumcised man named Titus, who had been born of Pagan parents, and whom we find henceforth always with him.

A serious dissension, which nearly destroyed the work of Jesus, broke out at that time, and threw the nascent Church into great disorder. This dissension embraced the very essence of the situation. It was inevitable. It was a crisis that the new religion could not fail but pass through.

Jesus, in raising religion to the highest summit it had ever attained, had not stated very distinctly whether or not he would remain a Jew. He had not indicated what he desired to conserve of Judaism. Sometimes he asserted that he had come to confirm the Law of Moses, at others, to supplant it. To speak the truth, this was, for a great poet like him, an insignificant detail. When one has reached the point of knowing the Heavenly Father, Him whom one adores in spirit and in truth, one no longer belongs to any sect, to any particular religion, or to any school; one has the true religion: all practices become of no account; one does not despise them, for they are the symbols of what has been or is still respectable; but one ceases to impute to them an intrinsic virtue. Circumcision, baptism, the Passover, unleavened bread, sacrifices, all these become equally secondary matters: one thinks no more about them. None of the uncircumcised, moreover, had identified themselves with Jesus, or his life; the question did not hence call for solution. Like all men of genius, Jesus concerned himself with mind alone. Practical questions of the highest importance, questions which appeared paramount to inferior minds, questions which caused the acutest pain to men of application, had no existence for him.

At his death the confusion was general. Abandoned to themselves, deprived of him who had been for them all a living theology, they returned to the practices of Jewish piety. There were men who were in the highest degree devout; but the devotion of the times was Jewish devotion. They preserved their customs, and fell again into those petty observances that ordinary persons looked upon as the essence of Judaism. The world esteemed them as holy men; and by a singular change of front, the Pharisees, who had served as a butt for the keenest satires of Jesus, became almost reconciled to his disciples. It was the Sadducees who showed themselves to be the irreconcilable enemies of the new movement. The minute observance of the Law appeared to them the first condition of being a Christian.

Very soon people encountered, in looking at things from this point of view, the greatest difficulties. For, as soon as the family of Christians increased in numbers, it was exclusively amongst the people of non-Israelitish origin, amongst the sympathetic adherents of Judaism who were uncircumcised, that the new faith found the readiest access. To oblige these to become circumcised was out of the question. Peter, with admirable practical good sense, recognised this clearly. On the other hand, timorous persons, such as James, the brother of the Lord, looked upon it as supreme impiety to admit Pagans into the Church, and to eat with them. Peter put off as far as he was able all solution of the question.

For the rest, the Jews, on their part, found themselves in the same situation, and had taken up a similar position. When proselytes or partisans came to them from all parts, the question presented itself to them. Some advanced minds, honest laymen ignorant of science, and removed from the influence of the doctors, did not insist upon circumcision. Sometimes even they dissuaded the new converts from the practice. These simple-minded and good souls desired only the salvation of the world, and sacrificed all the rest to this. The orthodox, on the contrary, with the disciples of Schammai at their head, declared circumcision to be indispensable. Opposed to the proselytising of the Gentiles, they did nothing to facilitate the cause of religion; on the contrary, they exhibited towards the converts a certain coldness;

Schammai drove them out of his house we are told, with a bâton. This division was clearly manifested in respect of the royal family of Adiabene. The Jew named Ananias who converted her, and who was by no means a savant, strongly dissuaded Izate against circumcision. "One can live as perfectly," said he, "as a Jew can, without circumcision; to adore God was the really important thing." The pious Helene was of the same opinion. A rigorist, named Eleazar, declared, on the contrary, that if the king did not undergo circumcision he was an impious person; that the reading of the Law was of no avail if one did not observe it, and that the highest precept was circumcision. The king, at the risk of losing his crown, followed this advice. The petty kings who embraced Judaism, in view of the rich marriages that the family of Herod offered, submitted to the same rite. But true piety was of a less facile composition than politics and avariciousness. Many of the pious converts led the Jewish life without being subjected to the rite which was reputed by the vulgar as the opening of the door to excesses. It was indeed for them a source of perpetual embarrassment. Society bigots, in whom prejudices are strong, are accustomed to represent their religious practices as matters of good taste, of superior education. Whilst in France the devout man, in order to avow his piety, is compelled to conquer a sort of shame, and of human respect, with the Mussulmans, on the other hand, the man who practices his religion is the gentleman; he who is not a good Mussulman is not the person that he ought to be; his position is analogous to that of a boorish, ill-mannered country man with us. Similarly, in England and in the United States, he who does not observe the Sunday, is put to the ban in good society. Amongst the Jews, the position of the uncircumcised was still worse. Contact with such a being was in their eyes something insupportable; circumcision appeared to them as obligatory on every one who wished to live amongst them. He who would not submit to it, was a creature of low quality; a sort of impure animal that people avoided; a wretch with whom a man of good standing could hold no relations.

The grand duality which is the essence of Judaism, was revealed in this. The Law, which was essentially restrictive, and made for the purpose of isolating, was totally different in spirit from the Prophets who dreamt of the conversion of the world, and embraced the widest fields. Two words borrowed from the Talmudic language well defines the difference that we have indicated. The agada, the opposite of the halaka, designates popular preaching, proposes to itself the conversion of the heathen, in opposition to the learned casuistry which only thinks of the strict execution of the Law, without aiming at converting any one. To use the phraseology of the Talmud, the gospels are the agadas; the Talmud, on the contrary, is the highest expression of the halaka. It is the agada which has conquered the world and made Christianity; the halaka is the foundation of orthodox Judaism, which still endures without seeking to extend itself. The agada is represented as a thing principally Galilæan; the halaka as a thing peculiarly Jerusalemitish. Jesus, Hillel, the authors of apocalypses and apochryphas, are agadists, pupils of the Prophets, inheritors of their infinite aspirations; Schammai, the Talmudists, the Jews posterior to the destruction of Jerusalem, are the halakistes, the adherents of the Law, with its strict observances. We shall see, up to the time of the supreme crisis of the year 70, the fanaticism of the Law increasing each day, and, on the eve of the great national disaster, terminating in a sort of reaction against the doctrines of St Paul; in those "eighteen measures" which afterwards rendered impossible all intercourse between the Jews and the non-Jews, and opened the sad history of exclusive Judaism, hateful and hated, which was the Judaism of the Middle Ages, and is still the Judaism of the East.

It is clear that, for nascent Christianity, here was the point upon which its future depended. Judaism--did it or did it not impose particular rites upon the multitudes which professed it? Did it establish a distinction between the monotheistic basis which constituted its essence, and the observances with which it was surcharged? If the former party had triumphed, as the Schammaites wished it should, the Jewish propaganda would have been wiped out. It is quite certain that the world would not have become Jewish, in the narrow sense of the word. That which constituted the attraction of Judaism, was not its rites, which did not differ in principle from those of other religions: it was its theological simplicity. We accept it as a sort of deism, or religious philosophy; and, in fact--in the mind of a Philo, for example--Judaism was itself very closely associated with philosophical speculations. With the Essenians it had reassumed the form of a social Utopia; with the author of the poem attributed to Phocylides, it had become a simple catechism of good sense and of honesty; with the author of the treatise of "The Empire of Reason," a sort of Stoicism. Judaism, like all religions founded primarily upon caste and tribalism, was encumbered by practices destined to separate the believer from the rest of the world. These practices were no longer an obstacle on the day when Judaism justly aspired to become the universal religion, without either exclusion or separation. It was as Deism and not as Mosaicism that it was to become the universal religion of humanity. "Love all men," said Hillel, "and draw them together with the Law; act not otherwise than you would not wish that others should act to you. Here is the whole Law, the rest is the commentary of it." When we read the treatises of Philo, entitled, "Of the Contemplative Life," or, "That Every Honest Man is Free;" when we read even the Sibylline verses written by the Jews, we are transported into an order of ideas which contain nothing specially Jewish, into a world of general mysticism which is not more Jewish than Buddhist or Pythagorean. The Pseudo-Phocylides goes the length of abolishing the Sabbath. We perceive that all these men, ardent for the amelioration of humanity, seek to reduce Judaism to a general morale, to strip it of all that it possesses of individuality, and of everything that would make of it a restricted religion.

Three capital reasons, in fact, rendered Judaism a thing very exclusive. These were, circumcision, the prohibition of mixed marriages, and the distinction between meats permissible or forbidden. Circumcision was for adults a painful ceremony; a ceremony, moreover, not free from danger, and disagreeable to the last degree. That was one of the reasons which interdicted the Jews from leading a life in common with other races, and made of them a separate caste. At the baths and at the gymnasiums, most important places in ancient cities, circumcision exposed the Jews to all manner of affronts. Every time that the attention of the Greeks or the Romans was drawn to the subject, it was the signal for outbursts of pleasantry. The Jews were very sensitive on the point, and avenged themselves by cruel reprisals. Many, in order to escape the ridicule, and wishing to pass themselves off for Greeks, attempted to dissimulate their original mark by a surgical operation, the details of which have been preserved to us by Celsus. As for the converts who submitted to that initiatory ceremony, there was only one course they could take--that was, to conceal themselves to escape the sarcasms. No man of the world could resign himself to such a situation, and this was doubtless the reason that the conversions to Judaism were much more numerous among the women than among the men, the former not being subjected at first to an experience, shocking and repulsive in every respect. We find many instances of Jewish women being married to Pagans, but there is not a single instance of a Jew being married to a Pagan woman. Hence the origin of much of the jeering. The necessity made itself felt by a broad casuistry which brought peace into troubled households.

Mixed marriages were the origin of difficulties of a similar kind. The Jews regarded these marriages as pure fornication. It was the crime that the kanaim punished with the dagger, simply because the Law in not prescribing any particular punishment for it, left its repression in the hands of zealots. Although united by faith and love to Christ, two Christians could thus be prevented from contracting marriage. The Israelite converted to Jesus who wished to espouse a sister of the Grecian race, expected that union, holy in his eyes, to be called by the most outrageous names.

The prescriptions as to meats being pure or impure were not of the least consequence. We can judge of this by that which still takes place in our own time. Nudity being no longer a part of modern manners, circumcision no longer subjects Israelites to these inconveniences. But the necessity of slaughtering for themselves continues to be very embarrassing for them. It requires of those who are strict not to eat with Christians, and, consequently, to be sequestered from general society. That precept is the principal cause which still places Judaism, in many countries, in the position of an exclusive sect. In countries where Israelites are not separated from the rest of the nation, it is a rock of offence; for, to understand it, it is sufficient on this point to have seen Puritan Jews arrive from Germany or Poland, who are shocked at the licences their co-religionists permit on this side of the Rhine. In cities like Salonica, in which the majority of the population is Jewish, and where the wealth is in the hands of the Jews, the actual trade of the community is on this account rendered impossible. Even in ancient times these restrictions were irksome. A Jewish law, the relic of innumerable centuries during which the responsibilities of property were an essential part of religious legislation, stamped the pig with a brand of infamy, which had no raison d'être in Europe. That old antipathy, having its origin in the East, appeared puerile to the Greeks and the Romans. A multitude of other prohibitions had descended from a time when one of the pre-occupations of the leaders of civilisation was to constrain their subordinates from eating things unclean, or from touching carrion. The hygiene of marriage, in fine, had given room for the enacting of a code of legal impurities for women sufficiently complicated. The peculiarity of these kind of prohibitions is their survival from times when they had a raison d'être, and of their becoming at length so vexatious that they might have had their origin in what was proper and salutary.

One particular circumstance gave to the prohibitions in regard to meat much importance. The flesh provided for the sacrifices made to the gods was considered as impure. Now these meats, after the sacrifices, were often carried to the market, where it became very difficult to distinguish them; hence the inextricable scruples. The strict Jews did not regard as lawful the indiscriminate provisioning of them-selves in the market. They held that the seller should be questioned as to the origin of the meat, and that before accepting the dish the host should be questioned as to how it had been supplied. The imposing of that load of casuistry upon converts had evidently been carried to excess. Christianity would not have been Christianity if, like the Judaism of our day, it had been compulsory to have slaughtering done separately, or if the Christian could not, without violating his conscience, eat with other men. When one has discovered in that network of difficulties religions surcharged with prohibitions pertaining to life; when one has seen the Jew in the East; the Mussulmans separated by their ritualistic laws, as if by a wall, from the European world, where they might take their place, one can comprehend the immense importance of the questions which were to be decided at the time at which we are now arrived. The question to be decided was, whether Christianity should be a religion of formulas and rituals, a religion of ablutions, of purifications, of distinctions between things pure and things impure, or, on the other hand, the religion of mind, the idealistic cult, which has killed or shall kill by degrees religious materialism, all formularies, all ceremonies. Or, better still, the question to be decided was whether Christianity was to be a petty sect or a universal religion; whether the idea of Jesus should be overshadowed by reason of the incapacity of his disciples; or whether that idea, by virtue of its original force, should triumph over the scruples of backward and narrow minds, which were ready to have it replaced and obliterated.

The mission of Paul and Barnabas had presented the question with such a force that there was no way of avoiding a solution. Paul, who in the first period of his ministry had, it appears, preached circumcision, now declared it useless. He had surreptitiously admitted Pagans into the Church; he had constituted Churches composed of Gentiles; Titus, his intimate friend, had not been circumcised. The Church at Jerusalem could not longer close its eyes to facts so notorious. Broadly speaking, this Church was, on the point with which we are now engaged, hesitating, or favourable to the party the most backward. The conservative senate was there. In close proximity to the Temple, in perpetual contact with the Pharisees, the old Apostles, timid and narrow-minded, could not lend themselves to the profoundly revolutionary theories of Paul. Many of the Pharisees, however, had embraced Christianity without renouncing the essential principles of their sect. To such persons, the supposition that one could be saved without circumcision was blasphemy. To them the Law seemed to remain in its entirety. They had been told that Jesus had come to fulfil the Law, not to abrogate it. The privileges of the children of Abraham appeared to them intact: the Gentiles could not enter into the kingdom of God without being previously affiliated with the family of Abraham; in a word, before becoming a Christian, it was necessary to be made a Jew. Never, we can see, had Christianity had to resolve a more fundamental doubt. If one might credit the Jewish party, the love feast even, the common repast, would have been impossible; the two sections of the Church of Jesus would not have been able to commune the one with the other. From the theological point of view, the matter was still more serious; the question was to know whether one could be saved through the works of the Law or by the grace of Jesus Christ.

Some members of the Church of Judæa having arrived at Antioch without, as it would appear, any mission from the apostolic body, provoked discussion. They proclaimed loudly that one could not be saved without circumcision. It is necessary to recall that the Christians, who had at Antioch a name and a distinct individuality, had nothing of the kind at Jerusalem; that which did not oppose whoever came from Jerusalem had not in the whole Church much force, for the centre of authority was there. People were greatly excited. Paul and Barnabas resisted in the most energetic manner. There were long disputes. To bring it to an end, it was decided that Paul and Barnabas should go to Jerusalem to consult with the Apostles and the Elders on the subject.

The question had for Paul a personal importance. His action until now had been almost entirely independent. He had only spent a fortnight at Jerusalem since his conversion, and for eleven years he had not put a foot in it. In the eyes of many he was a sort of heretic, teaching on his own account, and scarcely in communion with the rest of the faithful. He declared proudly that he had had his revelation, his apostleship. To go to Jerusalem was, in appearance at least, to forfeit his liberty, to subject his apostleship to that of the Mother Church, to learn from others what he knew through his own and personal revelation. He did not deny the authority of the Mother Church; but he defied it, because he was acquainted with the obstinacy of some of its members. He therefore took precautions so as not to compromise himself too much. He declared that in going to Jerusalem he would not submit to any dictation; he even feigned, indulging a pretension that was habitual to him, that in this he was obeying a command of Heaven, and of having had a revelation on the subject. He took with him his disciple Titus, who shared all his opinions, and who, as we have said above, was not circumcised.

Paul, Barnabas, and Titus set out on their journey. The Church at Antioch accompanied them on their route as far as Laodicæa-on-the-sea. They followed the coast of Phoenicia, then traversed Samaria, finding at every step brethren, to whom they recounted the marvels of the conversion of the Gentiles. There was great joy everywhere. In this way they reached Jerusalem. This was one of the most solemn hours in the history of Christianity. The grand doubt was now to be solved. The men upon whom rested the whole future of the new religion were going to be ranged face to face. Upon their grandeur of soul, upon their uprightness of heart depended the future of humanity.

Eighteen years had rolled on since the death of Jesus. The Apostles had grown old. One of them had suffered martyrdom. Others probably were dead. We know that the deceased members of the apostolic college were not replaced; that the college became extinct when they had disappeared. On the part of the Apostles, they formed themselves into a college of elders, in which authority was divided. The "Church," the reputed depository of the Holy Spirit, was composed of the Apostles, of the elders, and of all the brotherhood. Amongst the simple-minded brethren themselves there were degrees. Inequality was perfectly admissible; but that inequality was altogether moral; it was neither a question of external prerogative nor of material advantage. The three principal "pillars," as we have said, of the community were still Peter, James, the brother of the Lord, and John, the son of Zebedee. Many Galileans had disappeared. They had been replaced by a certain number of persons belonging to the party of the Pharisees. "Pharisee" was synonymous with "devotee"; but all the best saints of Jerusalem were also strong devotees. Lacking the mind, the finesse, the grandeur of Jesus, they had, after his death, fallen into a kind of stupid bigotry, a state similar to that which their master so strongly combated. They were incapable of irony; they had almost forgotten the eloquent invectives of Jesus against the hypocrites. Some had developed into a sort of Jewish Indian priests, after the manner of John the Baptist and of Banou, monks totally addicted to formulas, and at whom Jesus certainly, if he had been still alive, could not have aimed sarcasms enough.

James, in particular, surnamed the Just, or "the brother of the Lord," was one of the most exact observers of the Law that there was. According to certain traditions--very doubtful, it is true--he was even an ascetic, practising all the Nazarene abstinences, observing celibacy, drinking no intoxicating liquors, eschewing flesh, never cutting his hair, forbidding himself anointings and baths, wearing neither sandals nor garments of wool, clothed in plain linen. Nothing, we see, was more contrary to the idea of Jesus, who, at least from the death of John the Baptist, declared affectations of that kind perfectly vain. Abstinence--already in favour with certain branches of Judaism--became the fashion, and formed the dominant trait of the fraction of the Church which, later on, was to be connected with a pretended Ebion. The pure Jews were opposed to those abstinences; but the proselytes, particularly the women, inclined much to them. James did not stir from the Temple; he remained there alone, it is said, for long hours in prayer, until the callus of his knees had contracted, like those of the chamois. It is believed that he passed his time there after the manner of Jeremiah, a penitent for the people, weeping for the sins of the nation, and turning aside the chastisements that threatened them. He had only to raise his hands to heaven to perform miracles. He had been surnamed the Just, and also Obliam, that is to say, "Rampart of the people," because it was supposed that it was his prayers which prevented the Divine wrath from sweeping everything away. The Jews, as we are assured, held him in the same veneration as the Christians. If that singular man was really the brother of Jesus, he must have been at least one of those inimical brothers who abjured him and wished him arrested; and it is probable to such recollections that Paul, irritated by a mind so narrow, made allusion when he wrote concerning these pillars of the Church at Jerusalem:--"Whatsoever they were, it maketh no matter to me; God accepteth no man's person" (Gal. ii. 6). Jude, the brother of James, was, it seems, in entire agreement with his ideas.

To sum up, the Church at Jerusalem had been more and more broadened by the spirit of Jesus. The dead weight of Judaism had borne it down. Jerusalem was for the new faith an unwholesome centre, and would have ended by destroying it. In that capital of Judaism, it was very difficult to cease being a Jew. Moreover, new men, like St Paul, all but systematically avoided residing there. Forced now, under pain of being separated from the primitive Church, to come to confer with their elders, they found themselves in a position full of hardship; and the work, which could not live except by the power of concord and of abnegation, ran an immense risk.

The interview, in fact, was singularly protracted and embarrassing. People listened favourably at first to the account that Paul and Barnabas gave of their missions; for every one, even the most Judaised, was of opinion that the conversion of the Gentiles was the harbinger of the Messiah. The curiosity to see the man of whom so much was being said, and who had led the sect into so new a path, was at first very lively. They glorified God for having made an Apostle out of a persecutor. But when they came to circumcision, and the obligation of practising the Law, dissension broke out in all its force. The Pharisean party set forth its pretensions in the most uncompromising manner. The party in favour of emancipation responded with triumphant force. They cited the cases of several uncircumcised persons who had received the Holy Ghost. If God made no distinction between Pagans and Jews, how could they have the temerity to do it for Him? How could that be held for unclean which God had purified? Why impose a yoke on the converts that the race of Israel had not been able to bear? It was through Jesus that one was saved, and not through the Law. Paul and Barnabas advanced in support of that thesis the miracles which God had wrought for the conversion of the Gentiles. But the Pharisees objected with no less force that the Law was not abolished; that one never ceased to be a Jew; that the obligations of a Jew remained ever the same. They refused to hold relations with Titus, who was uncircumcised; they openly accused Paul of infidelity, and of being an enemy of the Law.

The most admirable characteristic in the histories of the origins of Christianity is that that radical and serious division, embracing a question of the first importance, did not occasion in the Church a complete schism, which would have been its ruin. The eager and impulsive mind of Paul had here a splendid opportunity of displaying itself; his sound practical sense, his sagacity, and his judgment, remedied everything. The two parties were eager, excited, almost harsh to one another; nobody rejected his advice; the question was not yet shaped; people remained united in the common work. A superior bond, the love that every one had for Jesus, the remembrance which all entertained for him, were stronger than the divisions. The most fundamental dissension that was ever produced in the bosom of the Church, did not lead to reprobation. This is a great lesson that succeeding centuries have seldom been able to imitate.

Paul understood that in large and heated assemblies he could never succeed, because that there narrow minds would always have the sway, and because Judaism was too long at Jerusalem for one to hope to be able to extort from it a concession of principles. He went and saw separately all personages of consideration, in particular, Peter, James, and John. Peter, like all men who exist for the most part on elevated sentiment, was indifferent to questions of party. These disputes grieved him; he wished for union, concord, and peace. His timid and rather contracted mind detached itself with difficulty from Judaism; he would have preferred that the new converts had accepted circumcision, but he saw the impossibility of such a solution. Deep and tender natures are always undecided; they sometimes even have to resort to a little dissimulation. They desire to please everybody--no question of principle seems with them to outweigh the value of peace. They let themselves be carried away by different parties, and to making contradictory promises and engagements. Peter sometimes committed this by no means heinous fault. To Paul, he was for uncircumcision; to the strict Jews, he sided with the partisans of circumcision. The soul of Paul was so grand, so sincere, so full of the new zeal which Jesus had brought into the world, that Peter could not fail to sympathise with him. They loved each other, and when they were together, it was as sovereigns of the entire world of the future, which they divided between them.

It was doubtless at the close of one of their conversations that Paul, with the exaggeration of language and the verve that were habitual to him, said to Peter, "We quite understand one another; yours is the gospel of circumcision; mine is the gospel of uncircumcision." Paul laid hold of these words later on as a sort of regular treaty, which ought to be accepted by all the Apostles. It is difficult to believe that Peter and Paul should dare to repeat outside their private conversations words which would have injured to the highest degree the pretensions of James, and probably even those of John. But the words were uttered. These large schemes, which were hardly those of Jerusalem, struck greatly the enthusiastic soul of Peter. Paul made upon him the greatest impression, and won him over completely. Up to this time Peter had travelled little; his pastoral visits had not, it seems, been extended beyond Palestine. He must have been about fifty years of age. Paul's eagerness for travelling, the recitals of the apostolic journeys, the projects that had been communicated to him in regard to the future, fired his zeal. It was from this time that Peter was seen to absent himself from Jerusalem, and to lead in his turn the wandering life of apostleship.

James, with the sanctity of a life so equivocal, was the chief of the Judaistic party. It was through him that almost all the conversions of Pharisees had been made: the exigencies of that party were imposed on him. Everything tends to the belief that he did not make any concession upon the dogmatic principle; nevertheless, a moderate and conciliatory opinion soon began to make itself manifest. The legitimacy of the conversion of the Gentiles was admitted; it was declared that it was useless to be disquieted in regard to what concerned circumcision; it was only necessary to maintain a few interesting prescriptions, the morale or the suppression of which would shock too keenly the Jews. In order to reassure the Pharisean party, it was remarked that the existence of the Law was not for the sake of compromise, seeing that Moses had from time immemorial, and would always be, for the people to be read in the synagogues. The converted Jews thus remained submissive to the entire Law, and the exemptions only concerned the converted Pagans. In practice, however, people were to avoid shocking those who had more contracted ideas. It was probably these moderate persons, the authors of that harmless contradiction, who counselled Paul to induce Titus to let himself be circumcised. Titus, in fact, had become one of the principal difficulties of the situation. The converted Pharisees of Jerusalem willingly supported the idea that, far removed from them, at Antioch, or in the depths of Asia Minor, there were Christians uncircumcised. But in their midst at Jerusalem, to be obliged to associate with them, and thus to commit a flagrant violation of that Law to which they were attached to the bottom of their hearts, this was what they could not consent to.

Paul took the most infinite precautions in acceding to this demand. It was indeed owned that it was not as a matter of necessity that the circumcision of Titus was demanded, as Titus would remain a Christian even if he did not submit to that rite; but it was asked of him as a mark of condescension for the brethren whose consciences were pledged, and who otherwise could not hold relations with him. Paul consented, but not without uttering some severe words against the authors of such an exaction, against those false brethren who only had entered the Church to diminish the extent of the liberties created by Jesus. He protested that he would in nothing submit his opinions to theirs; that the concession he had made was for once only, for the sake of the general good, and of peace. With such reservations he gave his consent, and Titus was circumcised.

That concession cost Paul much, and the sentence in which he spoke of it is one of the most original that he ever wrote. The language that it cost him seemed not to be able to run off his pen. The sentence, at first sight, appeared to mean that Titus was not circumcised, whilst it implied that he was. The remembrance of that painful moment often returned to him; that semblance of returning to Judaism appeared to him sometimes as a denying of Jesus; he re-assured himself by saying,--"And unto the Jews I became as a Jew, that I might gain the Jews." Like all men who possess a multiplicity of ideas, Paul set little store by forms. He perceived the vanity of everything which was not a thing of the soul, and when the supreme interests of conscience were at play, he, usually so stubborn, abandoned all else.

The capital concession which involved the circumcision of Titus, appeased much of the ill-feeling. It was admitted that in distant countries in which the new converts had no daily intercourse with the Jews, it would be sufficient if they abstained from blood, together with meats offered in sacrifice to the gods, or suffocated, and that they observed the same laws as the Jews in regard to marriage, and the relations between the sexes. The use of pork meat, the interdiction of which was everywhere the symbol of Judaism, was left free. It was almost the embodiment of the Noachic precepts; that is to say, which it was supposed had been revealed to Noah, and which were imposed on all proselytes. The idea that the blood was the life, that the blood was life itself, inspired in the Jews an extreme horror for meats from which the blood had not been let. To abstain from these was for them a precept of natural religion. Demons were supposed to be particularly greedy of blood, so in eating meat not bled people ran the risk of having for companion of the food they partook of a demon. A man who about that period wrote under the usurped name of the celebrated Greek moralist Phocylides a short course of Jewish natural morals, simplified the usages of the non-Jews, by seizing upon similar solutions. That bold impostor did not essay to convert his reader to Judaism; he sought merely to inculcate on him the "Noachical precepts," with some greatly modified Jewish rules in regard to meat and to marriage. The first of these rules was altered by him to accord with hygienic requirements and alimentary convenience, to the abstaining from things forbidden or unclean; the second had reference to the regulating and the purifying of sexual relations. All the rest of the Jewish ritual went for nothing.

For the rest, that which issued from the assembly at Jerusalem was only agreed to by word of mouth, and was not even stated in very strict terms, for we shall see them frequently set aside. The idea of dogmatic canons emanating from a council was not yet heard of. By reason of profound good sense, these simple people attained to the loftiest pinnacle of policy. They saw that the only way of escaping great questions was to leave them unresolved, to take a middle course which would please no one, and to leave problems to wear themselves out, and to die from lack of a raison d'être.

People were content to be divided. Paul explained to Peter, James, and John the gospel that he preached to the Gentiles; the former entirely approved of it, finding nothing in it to reprimand, and not attempting to add anything thereto. Paul and Barnabas were heartily given the right hand of fellowship; their immediate right divine to the apostleship of the Pagan world was admitted; people recognised in them a sort of peculiar grace for what was the special object of their vocation. The title of Apostle of the Gentiles, which Paul had already assumed, was, as he assures us, officially conferred on him; and without doubt people accorded to him, at least by tacit assent, the fact which he prized the most, to wit, that he had had his special revelation as direct as those who had seen Jesus; in other words, that his vision on the way to Damascus was of as much importance as the other appearances of Christ risen from the dead. All that was required of the three representatives of the Church of Antioch in return, was not to forget the poor at Jerusalem. The Church of that city, in fact, by reason of its communistic organisation, its peculiar responsibilities, and the misery which reigned in Judea, appeared to be nearing its last gasp. Paul and his party accepted gladly that idea. They hoped by a kind of contribution to shut the mouth of the intolerant Jerusalemitish party, and to reconcile it with the thought that he existed for the Church of the Gentiles. By means of a trifling tribute they purchased liberty of thought, and remained in communication with the central Church, outside of which one did not dare hope for salvation.

In order that no doubt should remain as to the reconciliation, it was decided that Paul, Barnabas, and Titus, in returning to Antioch, were to be accompanied by two of the principal members of the Church at Jerusalem, Judas Bar-Saba and Silvanus or Silas, who were charged with disavowing the brethren from Judæa who had created the trouble in the Church at Antioch, and to render witness to Paul and Barnabas, whose services and devotion were recognised. The joy at Antioch was very great. Judas and Silas held the rank of prophets: their inspired speech was appreciated extremely by the Church at Antioch. Silas was so much charmed with that atmosphere of life and of liberty, that he had no desire to return to Jerusalem. Judas alone returned to the Apostles, and Silas attached himself to Paul by bonds of brotherhood, which every day became more intimate.

CHAPTER IV

SLOW PROPAGATION OF CHRISTIANITY: ITS INTRODUCTION AT ROME

An idea which, above all things, it is necessary to get rid of, when the question at issue is the propagation of Christianity, is that that propagation had to be made by succeeding missionaries, and by preachers similar to those of modern times, who have to go from city to city. Paul and Barnabas and their companions were the only ones who sometimes proceeded in this manner. The rest was done by workmen whose names remain unknown. Alongside the Apostles who attained celebrity, there was thus an obscure apostleship, whose agents were not dogmatists by profession, but who were none the less most efficacious. The Jews of the period were nomads par excellence. Merchants, servants, small tradesmen, they visited all the large towns of the coast, and pursued their calling. Active, industrious, polite, they brought with them their ideas, their good example, their exaltation, and dominated these populations, degraded in point of religion, with all the superiority that the enthusiastic man possesses over those that are indifferent. Those affiliated to the Christian sect travelled like the other Jews, and carried the glad tidings with them. It was a sort of familiar preaching, and much more persuasive than any other. The gentleness, the gaiety, the good humour, the patience of the new believers, caused them to be received gladly everywhere, and conciliated their minds.

Rome was one of the first points attacked in this manner. The capital of the Empire had heard the name of Jesus long before all the intermediate countries could have been evangelised, just as a high summit is illuminated when the valleys lying between it and the sun are still in darkness. Rome was, in fact, the rendezvous of all the Oriental religious, the point of the Mediterranean with which the Syrians had the most intercourse. They arrived there in enormous bands. Like all poor populations going up to attack the large cities in quest of fortune, they were obedient and humble. With them disembarked troops of Greeks, Asiatics, and Egyptians, all speaking Greek. Rome was literally a bilingual city. The language of the Jewish world and of the Christian world of Rome was for three centuries Greek. Greek was at Rome the language of all that was most wicked and most honest, of all that was the best and the most base. Rhetoricians, grammarians, philosophers, noble pedagogues, preceptors, servants, intriguers, artists, singers, dancers, brokers, artisans, preachers of new sects, religious heroes--they all spoke Greek. The old Roman burgess class lost ground each day, swamped as it was by this flood of strangers.

It is in the highest degree probable that about the year 50 several Jews from Syria, already Christians, entered the capital of the Empire, and disseminated their ideas there. In fact, among the good administrative measures of Claudius, Suetonius placed the following: "He expelled the Jews from Rome, who, at the instigation of Chrestus, indulged frequently in riots." Certainly, it is possible that there might have been at Rome a Jew named Chrestus who fomented troubles amongst his co-religionists, and which led to their expulsion. But it is much more probable that the name of Chrestus was none other than that of Christ himself. The introduction of the new faith provoked, doubtless, in the Jewish quarter at Rome, altercations, quarrels, scenes analogous, in a word, to those which had already taken place at Damascus, at Antioch in Pisidia, and at Lystra. Wishing to put an end to these disorders, the police were compelled to take measures for the expulsion of the perturbators. The chiefs of police may have inquired superficially into the nature of the quarrel, which interested them so little; a report addressed to the Government may have proved that the agitators called themselves Christiani, that is to say, partisans of a certain Christus; that name being unknown, it may have been changed into Chrestus, in consequence of the custom of unlettered persons giving to the names of strangers a form appropriate to their habits. Hence, in order to come to a conclusion that there existed a man of that name, who had been the provoker and the leader of the riots, was but a short step to take; the inspectors of police might have overlooked the fact, and, without further inquiry, pronounced sentence of banishment against the two parties.

The principal Jewish quarter in Rome was situated on the other side of the Tiber; that is to say, in the part of the city the poorest and the most filthy, probably in the neighbourhood of the actual Porta Portese. Here was situated formerly, as in our own times, the port of Rome, the place where merchandise was unloaded which had been brought in flat boats from Ostia. It was the quarter of the Jews and of the Syrians, "nations born to servitude" as is remarked by Cicero. The first nucleus of the Jewish population at Rome had, in fact, been formed of freedmen, descendants, for the most part, of those who had been carried prisoners to Rome by Pompey. They had undergone slavery without changing any of their religious habits. That which is admirable about Judaism, is that simplicity of faith which makes the Jew, though transported a thousand leagues from his country, at the end of many generations a Jew still of the purest type. The intercourse between the synagogues of Rome and those of Jerusalem was continual. The first colony had been reinforced by numerous emigrants. These poor people disembarked by hundreds at Ripa, and lived there by themselves in the quarter adjacent to Transtevere, serving as street porters, engaging in small commerce, exchanging matches for broken glasses, and presenting to the haughty Italian population a type which, later, should become to them too familiar --that of a mendicant skilled in his art. A Roman who respected himself never put his foot into these debased quarters. It was treated as a suburb given over to contemned classes, and to disreputable avocations; tanneries, sausage factories, steeping troughs, were relegated there. So the unfortunates lived quite tranquilly in that despised corner, in the midst of bales of merchandise, infamous taverns, and of litter porters (Syrians), who had here their general quarters. The police did not enter it except when the quarrels were bloody, or when they were too often repeated. Few of the quarters of Rome were so free; politics had nothing to do with it. Not only was religion practised in ordinary times without opposition, but every facility was afforded for active propagandism.

Protected by the contempt which they inspired, little sensitive, moreover, to the railleries of the people of the world, the Jews of Transtevere led thus a very active, religious, and social life. They possessed a few kakamin (schools); nowhere was the ritual and ceremonial of the Law more scrupulously observed; the synagogues had the most perfect organisation that ever was known. The titles of "father" and of "mother of the synagogue" were much prized. Some rich converts took biblical names; they converted their slaves along with themselves; the Scroll was explained by the doctors; they built places of prayer, and showed themselves to be proud of the consideration they enjoyed in that little world. The poor Jew, when begging, found the opportunity, in a trembling voice, to whisper into the ear of the grand Roman dame a few sentences of the Law, and often gained over the matron, who had given him a handful of small change. To observe the Sabbath and the Jewish feasts was, according to Horace, the characteristic which classes a man amongst the weak-minded, that is to say, with the multitude, unus multorum. Universal benevolence, the felicity of reposing with the just, assisting the poor, purity of manners, the sweetness of family life, the mild perception of death, which was considered as a sleep, are the sentiments which are found on the Jewish inscriptions, together with that special note of touching unction of humility, certain hope, which characterises Christian inscriptions. There were many Jews, men of the world, rich and powerful, such as Tiberius Alexander, who attained to the highest honours of the Empire, and who twice or thrice exercised an influence of the first order in public affairs, and had even, to the great chagrin of the Romans, his statue in the Forum; but the latter were no longer good Jews. The Herods, although ostentatiously practising their religion at Rome, were also far from (it was only through their relations with the Pagans) being true Israelites. The poor remained faithful, esteeming these worldlings as renegades; in like manner, we see in our day the Polish or Hungarian Jews treat with severity the aristocratic French Israelites who have deserted the synagogue, and have had their children educated in Protestantism, so as to make their circle more exclusive.

A world of ideas were thus propounded on the common wharf where was unloaded the merchandise of the whole world; but all this is lost in the tumult of a large city like London or Paris. Certainly the proud patricians, who, in their promenades upon the Aventine cast their eyes to the other side of the Tiber, could not suspect that the future was being prepared in the pile of poor houses erected at the foot of Janiculum. The day when, under the reign of Claudius, a certain Jew, initiated in the new beliefs, placed foot on the ground opposite the Emporium, that same day no one knew in Rome that the founder of a second Empire, another Romulus, lodged at the gate on a bed of straw. Near the gate was a kind of lodging-house, well known to the people and the soldiers, which went under the name of Taberna meritoria. There was shown here, in order to attract the credulous, a pretended fountain of oil, issuing from the rocks. Very soon that fountain of oil was regarded by the Christians as symbolical. It was pretended that its appearance had coincided with the birth of Jesus. It appears that later on the Taberna was made into a church. Who knows whether the oldest souvenirs of Christianity were not connected with that resort! Under Alexander Severus we see the Christians and the tavern-keepers contending for a certain spot which had formerly been public, and which that good Emperor adjudged to the Christians. One feels that one is here upon the natal soil of an old popular Christianity. Claudius, about that time, struck with the "progress of foreign superstitions," believed that he was performing an act of good conservative policy in re-establishing the soothsayers. In a report made to the Senate, complaint was made of the indifference of the times for the ancient usages of Italy, and for good discipline. The Senate had invited the Pontiffs to see whether it was possible to re-establish the old customs. Everything went well, in consequence, and it was believed that these respectable impostures were saved for all eternity.

The great question of the moment was the attainment of Agrippa to power, the adoption of Nero by Claudius, and his ever-increasing fortune. No one thought of the poor Jew who uttered for the first time the name of Christus in the Syrian colony, and expounded the faith which brought happiness to those amongst whom he was living. Others soon arrived. The letters from Syria, brought by the newcomers, spoke of the movement which was increasing more and more. A small circle was formed. Everybody "smelled the garlick." These ancestors of the Roman prelates were poor proletariats, filthy, undistinguished, ill-mannered, clothed in dirty smock-frocks, and had the bad breath of people who are ill-fed. Their hovels had that odour of misery which exhales from persons poorly nourished and clothed, and huddled up in a small room. They soon became numerous enough to make a noise. They preached in the ghetto, and the orthodox Jews resisted them. What with the tumultuous scenes which were taking place; what with the scenes recurring night by night; what with the Roman police being interviewed; what (little caring to know what was the cause of the trouble) with addressing a report to the superior authority, and laying the troubles to the account of a certain Chrestus, whom it was impossible to get hold of; what with the expulsion of the agitators having been decided on--there was nothing in that which was not plausible. The passage in Suetonius, and, better still, that of the Acts, would seem to imply that all the Jews were driven out on that occasion; but such a thing is not to be supposed. The likelihood is that the Christians, the partisans of the seditious Chrestus, were alone expelled. Claudius, in general, was favourable to the Jews, and it is even not impossible that the expulsion of the Christians, of which we have just been speaking, took place at the instigation of the Jews--the Herods, for example. These expulsions, however, were always only temporary and conditional. The tide, arrested for the moment, always returned. The edict of Claudius was, in any case, of little consequence, since Josephus does not mention it, and in the year 58 Rome had already a new Christian Church.

The founders of this first Church at Rome, destroyed by the decree of Claudius, are unknown. But we know the names of two Jews who were exiled in consequence of the emeutes of the Porta Portese. They were an old pious couple, the one Aquila, originally a Jew from Pontus, following the same calling as St Paul, that of an upholsterer, the other Priscilla, his wife. They sought refuge at Corinth, where we soon see them en rapport with St Paul, whose intimate friends and zealous fellow-workers they became. Aquila and Priscilla are hence the two oldest known members of the Church at Rome. But they are hardly remembered. Legend, which is always unjust, because it is always swayed by political motives, has expelled from the Christian Pantheon these two obscure workers, in order to attribute the honour of the foundation of the Church of Rome to a name more illustrious, corresponding better to the proud pretensions of universal dominion which the capital of the Empire, now become Christian, could not abdicate. For us, it is not at the theatrical basilica which has been consecrated to St Peter, it is at the Porta Portese, that ancient ghetto, where we really find the starting-point of Western Christianity. It is the traces of those pier wandering Jews, who carried with them the religion of the world,--those men who hardly dreamt, in their misery, of the kingdom of God--we must search out and embrace. We do not contest with Rome its essential title; Rome was probably the first spot of the Western world, and even of Europe, where Christianity was established But in place of these proud and magnificent churches, in place of these insulting devices, Christus vincit, Christus regit, Christus imperat--Christ conquers, Christ reigns, Christ governs--it would be much better to erect a little chapel to the two good Jews of Pontus who were expelled by the police of Claudius for belonging to the party of Chrestus.

After the Church of Rome (if it was not even anterior) the most ancient Western Church was that of Pozzuoli. St Paul found Christians there about the year 61. Pozzuoli was in a certain sense the port of Rome; it was at least the place where the Jews and the Syrians who came to Rome disembarked. This strange soil undermined by fire; these Phlegreens fields; that sulphur bed; these caverns full of burning vapours, which seemed the breath of hell; these sulphurous waters; these myths of giants, and of demons buried in the burning valleys, a sort of Gehennas; these baths, which appeared to the austere Jews and the enemies of total nudity the acme of abomination--greatly impressed the imaginations of the new emigrants, and have left a deep trace on the apocalyptic compositions of the times. The follies of Caligula, of which we still see traces, left also in these places terrible recollections.

In any case, one capital feature, as we have already had occasion to remark, is, that the Church at Rome was not, like the Churches of Asia Minor, of Macedonia and of Greece, a foundation of the school of Paul. It was a Judæo-Christian creation, connected directly with the Church at Jerusalem. Paul was never here on his own ground; he found in that great Church many shortcomings, which he treated with indulgence, but which offended his exalted idealism. Attached to circumcision, and to exterior practices; ebionite by its taste for abstinences, and by its doctrine, more Jew than Christian, in regard to the person and the death of Jesus; strongly attached to millenarianism, the Roman Church presented in its early days the essential features which have distinguished it during its long and marvellous history. The direct daughter of Jerusalem, the Roman Church has always had an ascetic, sacerdotal character, and been opposed to the Protestant tendency of St Paul. Peter was its veritable chief; then, being penetrated by the political and hierarchical spirit of old Pagan Rome, it became, in truth, the new Jerusalem, the city of the pontificate, of religion, hierarchical and solemn, of material sacraments, which are their own justification, the city of ascetics, after the manner of Jacques Obliam, with its callosities on the knees and its plates of gold on the forehead. She was to be the church of authority. If it can be believed, the special sign of the apostolic mission was the showing of a letter signed by the Apostles, the producing of a certificate of orthodoxy. The good and the evil that the Church at Jerusalem did for infant Christianity, the Church of Rome did for the Church universal. It was in vain that Paul addressed to them his beautiful epistle, in order to explain to them the mystery of the cross of Jesus and of salvation by faith alone. This epistle the Church at Rome but vaguely comprehended. But Luther, fourteen and a half centuries later, comprehended it, and opened a new era in the secular series of the alternative triumphs of Peter and Paul.

CHAPTER V

SECOND JOURNEY OF PAUL—ANOTHER SOJOURN AT GALATIA

Hardly had Paul returned to Antioch, when he began forming new projects. His ardent soul could not brook repose. On the one hand, he proposed to enlarge the rather limited field of his first mission: on the other, the desire to see again his dear Churches of Galatia, to confirm them in the faith, pursued him incessantly. The tenderness which that strange nature appeared in some respects to lack, had been transformed into a powerful faculty of loving the communities which he had founded. He had for his Churches the sentiments that other men have for that which they love the most. This was indeed a special gift of the Jews. The feeling of association with which they were imbued caused them to give to the esprit de famille applications altogether novel. The synagogue and the church were thus what the monastery was to the Middle Ages, the beloved home, the hearth of the warmest affections, the roof under which people sheltered that which they held most dear.

Paul communicated his design to Barnabas. But the friendship of the two Apostles, which had been proof against the severest tests, which no susceptibility of amour propre, no freak of character had been able to lessen, received now a cruel blow. Barnabas proposed to Paul to take John, surnamed Mark, with them: Paul flew into a passion. He could not pardon John-Mark for having abandoned the first mission at Perga, at the moment when it had entered upon the most perilous stage of the journey. The man who had once refused to go on with the work, appeared to him as unworthy of being enrolled anew. Barnabas defended his coὗσιν, whose motives, in fact, it is probable Paul judged with too much severity. The quarrel waxed very hot: it was impossible to come to an understanding. That old friendship which had been the condition of the evangelic preaching, gave place for a time to a miserable question of individuals. To speak truly, it is allowable to suppose that the rupture was based on deeper reasons. It is a miracle that the always increasing pretensions of Paul, his pride, his eagerness to be absolute chief, had not already twenty times rendered relations impossible between two men whose reciprocal positions had entirely changed. Barnabas had not the genius of Paul; but who can tell whether in the true hierarchy of souls, which is regulated by the order of goodness, he did not occupy a still higher rank? When we recall what Barnabas had been to Paul; when we think that it was he who at Jerusalem had silenced the not altogether groundless defiances of which the new convert was the object;--who went to seek at Tarsus the future Apostle, as yet isolated and uncertain as to his path;--who introduced him into the young and active life of Antioch;--who, in a word, made him an Apostle,--one cannot help seeing in that open rupture a motive of secondary importance, a gross act of ingratitude on the part of Paul. But the exigencies of the work were too powerful for him. What man of action is there that has not once in his life committed a great crime of the heart?

The two Apostles then separated from each other. Barnabas and John-Mark embarked at Seleucia for Cyprus. History from this point loses sight of his wanderings. While Paul marches on to glory, his companion, falling into obscurity the moment he quitted him who illuminated him with his rays, wears himself out with the labours of an unrecorded apostleship. The enormous injustice which often regulates the things of this world, presides over history like as over everything else. Those who undertake the rôle of self-devotion and unostentation, are ordinarily forgotten. The author of the Acts, with his ingenuous conciliatory policy, has, without wishing it, sacrificed Barnabas to the desire that he entertained of reconciling Peter to Paul. By a sort of instinctive lack of the principle of compensation, on the one hand diminishing and subordinating the importance of Paul, on the other, the author has enhanced the importance of Paul at the expense of a modest fellow-worker, who had not a part cut out for him, and who was not weighted in history with the unequal weights which result from the arrangements of parties. Hence arises the ignorance in which we are placed as to what belongs to the apostleship of Barnabas. We only know that that apostleship continued to be very active. Barnabas remained faithful to the grand rules which Paul and he had established during their first mission. He did not take with him in his peregrinations female companions; he lived always by his work, never accepting anything from the Church. He again encountered Paul at Antioch. The imperious temper of Paul provoked a fresh discord between them; but the nature or sentiment of the holy work carried all before it; the communion between the two Apostles remained intact. Labouring each in his own way, they remained in communication the one with the other, mutually informing one another of their labours. In spite of the greatest dissensions, Paul continued always to treat Barnabas as a fellow-worker, and to consider him as dividing with himself the work of the apostleship of the Gentiles. Ardent, hot-headed, and susceptible, Paul soon forgot, when the great principles to which he had devoted his life were not in question.

In place of Barnabas, Paul selected for his companion Silas, the prophet of the Church at Jerusalem, who had remained at Antioch. He was probably not sorry at the defection of John-Mark, who, it seems, wished to be near Peter. Silas possessed, it is said, the title of a Roman citizen, which, joined with his name of Silvanus, induces the belief that he was not of Judea, or that he had already had occasion to familiarise himself with the world of the Gentiles. Both departed, recommended by the brethren to the grace of God. These forms were not at that time vain. People believed that the finger of God was everywhere; that each step of the Apostles of the new kingdom was directed by the immediate inspiration of Heaven.

Paul and Silas journeyed by land. Taking to the north, across the plain of Antioch, they traversed the defile of Amanus, the Assyrian passes; then rounding the end of the Gulf of Issus they crossed the northern ridge of Amanus by the Amanida pass; they then traversed Cilicia, passing probably through Tarsus, emerging from Taurus doubtless by the celebrated Cilician passes--one of them the most frightful mountain pass in the world; penetrating thence into Lycaonia; finally reaching Derbe, Lystra, and Iconium.

Paul found his dear Churches in the same state in which he had left them. The faithful had persevered, and their numbers had increased. Timothy, who was but an infant at the time of his first journey, had become an excellent subject. His youth, his piety, and his intelligence, delighted Paul. All the faithful of Lycaonia testified highly of him. Paul attached him to himself, loved him tenderly, and always found in him a zealous collaborateur, or, rather, a son (it is Paul himself who uses this expression). Timothy was a man of great candour, modesty, and reserve. He had not assurance enough to undertake the chief rôles; he lacked authority, especially in Greek countries, where the minds of the people were frivolous and fickle; but his self-denial made of him an unequalled deacon and secretary to Paul. Paul moreover declared that he had not another disciple who was so completely according to his heart. Impartial history is compelled to withhold, to the advantage of Timothy and of Barnabas, a portion of the glory monopolised by the all-absorbing personality of Paul.

Paul, in attaching Timothy to himself, foresaw grave embarrassments. He feared that, in his communications with the Jews, Timothy, uncircumcised as he was, could only be a source of repulsion and of trouble. It was, in fact, known everywhere that his father was a Pagan. A multitude of timorous people would decline to hold intercourse with him: the quarrels, which had hardly been laid to rest by the interview at Jerusalem, would be revived. Paul recalled the difficulties he had experienced in regard to Titus. He resolved to anticipate these; and, in order to avoid being brought later to make a concession to the principles he had recoiled from, he circumcised Timothy himself. This was altogether in conformity with the principles which had guided him in the affair of Titus, and which he always practised. But he had never been induced to say that circumcision was necessary to salvation; for, in his eyes, that would have been an error of faith. Yet circumcision being in itself not a wicked thing, he thought that it might be practised, in order to avoid scandal and schism. His great rule was that an apostle ought to be all things to all men, and to yield to the prejudices of those whom he wished to gain over, when these prejudices in themselves were merely frivolous, and did not contain anything absolutely reprehensible. But, at the same time, as if he had a presentiment of the tests that the faith of the Galatians was about to be put to, he made them promise never to listen to another teacher than himself, and to anathematise all other teaching save his own.

From Iconium Paul probably went to Antioch in Pisidia, and completed thus the visit of the principal Churches in Galatia, founded during his first journey. He resolved then to enter upon new territory; but grave doubts restrained him. The thought of attacking the West of Asia Minor, that is to say, the province of Asia, came into his mind. It was the part of Asia the most populated. Ephesus was the capital of it; it contained the beautiful and flourishing cities of Smyrna, Pergamos, Magnesia, Thyatira, Sardis, Philadelphia, Colossus, Laodicæa, Hierapolis, Tralles, Miletus, in which the centre of Christianity was soon to be established. It is not known what turned St Paul away from carrying his efforts in that direction. "The Holy Spirit," says the writer of the Acts, "forbade him going to preach in Asia." The Apostles, it must be borne in mind, were reputed to obey, in choosing the direction of their courses, inspirations from on high. Sometimes there were real motives, reflections, or positive indications which they dissimulated under this language. Sometimes there was also the absence of motives. The opinion that God made known to man his volitions by means of dreams, was widespread, just as it is still in our day in the East. A dream, a sudden impulse, an unpremeditated movement, an inexplicable noise (bath kôl), appeared to them as the manifestations of the Spirit, and decided the route of the mission.

What is certain is that, from Antioch in Pisidia, instead of going in the direction of the brilliant provinces of the south-east of Asia Minor, Paul and his companions plunged more and more into the heart of the peninsula, which contained provinces much less celebrated and less civilised. They traversed Phrygia Epictetus, passed probably through the towns of Synnada and Æzana, and reached the confines of Mysia. There, their indecision returned. Should they turn to the north towards Bithynia, or continue west and enter Mysia? They essayed first to enter Bithynia, but untoward events supervened, which they took for the indications of the will of Heaven. They imagined that the spirit of Jesus did not wish that they should tarry in that country. They then traversed Mysia from one end to the other, and arrived at Alexandria-Troas, a considerable port almost opposite Tenedos, and not far from the site of ancient Troy. The apostolic band made thus, in almost a single journey, a distance of more than a hundred leagues, across a country little known, and which, destitute of Roman colonies and Jewish synagogues, did not offer them any of the facilities they had found elsewhere.

These long journeys in Asia Minor, full of sweet ennuis and mystical dreams, are a singular mixture of sadness and of charm. Often the route is hard; certain cantons are peculiarly rugged and barren. Other parts, on the contrary, are full of freshness, and do not correspond at all to the ideas that we are accustomed to embrace in that vague phrase, the East. The mouth of the Orontes marks, both in relation to nature and in relation to races, a well-defined line of demarcation. Asia Minor, both for aspect and for the style of landscape, recalls Italy or our South, at the eminence of Valence and of Avignon. The European is not out of his native climate there, as he is in Syria or in Egypt. It is, if I may say so, an Aryan, not a Semitic country, and it is not to be doubted that one day it will be occupied anew by the Indo-European race (Greeks and Armenians). Water there is abundant: the towns are as if inundated by it. Certain points, such as Nymphi, Magnesia in Siplyus, are veritable paradises. The smooth mountain slopes which bound almost everywhere the horizon, present such varieties of infinite forms, and sometimes of fantastic shapes, that they would be regarded as idle fancies if an artist dare to imitate them. There are summits indented like the teeth of a saw, sides torn and slashed, strange cones, and perpendicular walls, in which are finely exposed to view all the beauties of the stone. Thanks to the numerous chains of mountains, the waters are living and sparkling. Long rows of poplars, small plane-trees, in the wide surface of the winter torrents, superb stumps of trees, where the feet plunge into pools, and which jut out in dark tufts from the foot of each mountain, these are the solace of the traveller. At the source of each stream the caravans stop to water. The journey continues for days and days upon the narrow lines of antique pavement which for centuries have borne travellers so diverse, and oftentimes fatigued; but the halts are delicious. A repose of an hour, a piece of bread eaten upon the banks of these limpid streams, running in beds of pebbles, sustains one for a long time.

At Troas, Paul, who in certain parts of that journey seems not to have followed any well-defined plan, became once more irresolute as to which route he should choose. Macedonia appeared to him to offer a fine harvest. It appears that he was confirmed in that idea by a Macedonian whom he encountered at Troas. He was a doctor, an uncircumcised proselyte, by the name of Lucanus or Lucas. This Latin name would lead one to believe that the new disciple belonged to the Roman colony of Philippi; his rare knowledge, in fact, of nautical geography and of navigation would, however, rather incline to the idea that he was a Neapolitan: the ports and all the coast of the Mediterranean appear to have been remarkably familiar to him.

This man, to whom was reserved so important a part in the history of Christianity, seeing he was to be the historian of the Christian origins, and seeing his judgment, self-deceptive as to the future, was to regulate the ideas that were formed in the early times of the Church, had received a sufficiently careful Jewish and Hellenic education. He had a gentle and conciliatory mind, a tender and sympathetic soul, a modest temperament, inclining to self-effacement. Paul loved him much, and Luke, on his part, was always faithful to his master. Like Timothy, Luke appeared to have been born expressly to be the companion of Paul. Submission and blind confidence, unbounded admiration, a desire to be submissive, unlimited devotion, were his habitual sentiments. It might be said that it was this absolute abnegation of self that made le moine hibernais in the hands of his abbot. The ideal of "the disciple" was never so perfectly realised. Luke was literally fascinated by the superiority of Paul. His affability as a man of the people proclaimed itself incessantly; his idle fancy showed him always to be a model of perfection and of happiness; an honest man, a good master in his family, of which he was the spiritual head; a Jew at heart, who was converted with all his house. He esteemed the Roman officers, and unhesitatingly believed them to be virtuous. One of the objects he admired the most was a good centurion, pious, benevolent towards the Jews, well served, well obeyed. He had probably studied the Roman army at Philippi, and had been much struck with it. He naturally supposed that discipline and the hierarchy were things of a moral order. His esteem for the Roman functionaries was also great. His title of doctor implies that he possessed medical knowledge, which is proved besides by his writings, but does not imply a scientific and rational culture, which few doctors possessed then. What Luke was par excellence was "the man of firm will"--the true Israelite at heart, he to whom Jesus brought peace. It is he who has transmitted to us, and who probably composed, those delicious canticles of the birth and of the infancy of Jesus, those hymns of the angels, of Mary, of Zachariah, of old Simeon, in which shone out in tones so clear and so joyous the happiness of the new alliance, the Hosanna of the pious proselyte, the accord re-established between the fathers and the sons in the enlarged family of Israel.

Everything tends to the belief that Luke was touched by grace at Troas; that he was attached from that time to Paul, and persuaded him that he would find in Macedonia an excellent field. His words made a great impression upon the Apostle. The latter believed he saw in a vision a Macedonian, standing up, who invited him, saying unto him, "Come over and help us." This was received by the apostolic group as a command of God that they should go to Macedonia, and they waited only a favourable opportunity to depart thence

CHAPTER VI

CONTINUATION OF TI9E SECOND JOURNEY OF PAUL--THE MACEDONIAN MISSION

The mission at this point entered upon entirely new ground. It was what was called the province of Macedonia; but these regions had not formed a portion of the Macedonian kingdom since the time of Philip. They were, in reality, portions of Thracia, anciently colonised by the Greeks, then absorbed by the powerful monarchy the centre of which was at Pella, and which was included for two hundred years in the great Roman unity. Few countries in the world were, in fact, purer in race than the countries situated between Hæmus and the Mediterranean. That they were composed of diverse branches is true, but each genuinely belonged to the Indo-European family, which were superimposed on it. If we except some Phoenician influences coming from Thasos and from Samothracia, almost nothing foreign had penetrated into the interior. Thracia, which was in great part Celtic, had remained faithful to the Aryan life: she preserved the ancient religions, under a form which appeared barbarous to the Greeks and Romans, but which, in reality, was only primitive. As for Macedonia, it was probably the region the most honest, the most serious, the most pious of the ancient world. It was originally a country of feudal boroughs, not of large independent towns; now, the latter is, of all administrations, that which has best conserved human morality, and placed the most forces in reserve for the future. Monarchical through steadfastness of mind and through abnegation, filled with antipathy for charlatanism, and for the frequent barren agitations of small republics, the Macedonians presented to Greece the type of a society analogous to that of the Middle Ages, founded upon loyalism, upon faith in legitimacy and heredity, and upon a conservative spirit, equally removed from the grovelling despotism of the East, and from that democratic fever which, inflaming the blood of the people, wears out quickly those who abandon themselves to it. Thus disencumbered from the causes of social corruption that democracy almost always brings in its train, and yet free from the iron chains which Sparta had invented to fortify herself against revolution, the Macedonians were the people of antiquity who most resembled the Romans. They recall in some other respects the German barons, brave, dissipated, rude, proud, faithful. If they realised but for a moment what the Romans knew how to establish in a durable manner, they would have had less honour in having survived their attempt. The little kingdom of Macedonia, without factions or seditions, with its good interior administration, was the most solid nationality that the Romans had to combat in the East. A strong patriotic and legitimist spirit reigned there to such a degree that after their defeats we see the inhabitants take fire with a singular facility against the impostors who pretended to continue their old dynasty.

Under the Romans, Macedonia remained a land worthy and pure. It furnished to Brutus two excellent legions. We do not see the Macedonians, like the Syrians, the Egyptians, the Asiatics, rushing to Rome in order to enrich themselves with the fruits of their evil practices. Despite the terrible substitution of races which followed, it may be said that Macedonia has always preserved the same character. It is a country placed under the normal conditions of European life,--wooded, fertile, watered by splendid rivers, possessing interior sources of wealth; whilst that Greece, meagre, poor, singular in everything, has nothing left it but glory and beauty. A land of miracles, like Judæa and Sinai, Greece flourished once, but can never flourish again. She has created something unique, which cannot be reproduced. It seems that when God has once manifested Himself in a country, He blasts it for ever. A laud of klephtes and of artists, Greece cannot again take an original part on the day when the world enters into the channels of wealth, of industry, of abundant consumption: she can only produce genius. In passing through it one is astonished that a powerful race was able to live upon that pile of arid mountains, in the middle of which is a somewhat humid and deep valley, a little plain, a kilometre in extent--all this compels our wonder. Never has there been so plainly seen the opposition which exists between opulence and high art. Macedonia, on the contrary, will one day resemble Switzerland or the south of Germany. Its villages are like clumps of gigantic trees. She has everything that is required for becoming a country of great culture, and of great industry--vast plains, rich mountains, verdant prairies, extended prospects, very different from those charming little mazes of the site of Greece. Solemn and grave, the Macedonian peasant has no longer anything of the assurance and the vivacity of the Hellenic peasant. The women, beautiful and chaste, work in the fields like the men. We might say, a country of Protestant peasants: it is a beautiful and strong race, laborious, steady, loving its country, and full of the future.

Embarking at Troas, Paul and his companions (Silas, Timothy, and probably Luke) set sail with a fair wind, touched the first evening at Samothracia, and the morrow approached Neapolis, a town situated upon a small promontory opposite the Isle of Thasos. Neapolis was the port of the great city of Philippi, situated about three leagues thence in the interior. It was the point where the great Egnatine road, which traversed Macedonia and Thracia from west to east, touched the sea. Taking this road, which they did not need to quit until reaching Thessalonica, the Apostles ascended the stony slope cut in the rocks which overlooked Neapolis, emerged from the little chain of mountains which forms the coast, and entered the beautiful plain in the centre of which stands, detached upon a projecting promontory of the mountain, the city of Philippi.

This rich plain, the lowest portion of which is composed of a lake and of marshes, communicates with the basin of Strymon from behind Pangea. The gold mines which at the Hellenic and Macedonian epoch had made the country celebrated, were now almost abandoned. But the military importance of the position of Philippi, squeezed in between the mountain and the morass, had given to it a new life. The battle which ninety-four years before the arrival of the Christian missionaries had opened its gates, brought to it an unexpected splendour. Augustus had established there one of the most considerable Roman colonies, under the jus italicum. The city was much more Latin than Greek; Latin was there the common tongue; the religions of Latium seemed to have been transported thither intact. The surrounding plain, dotted with towns, was equally, at the epoch at which we have now arrived, a kind of Roman canton, thrown into the heart of Thracia. The colony was inscribed in the Voltinian tribune. It had been formed principally of the wrecks of the Antonine party, which Augustus had cantoned on these coasts; it was there mixed with portions of the old Thracian stock. In any case, it was a hard-working population, living orderly and peaceably; besides, it was very religious. The confraternities flourished there, particularly those under the patronage of the god Sylvain, who was considered as a sort of tutelary genius of the Latin domination. The mysteries of the Bacchus of Thracia embraced exalted ideas in regard to immortality, and made the population familiar with the views of a future life, and of an idyllic paradise very similar to that which Christianity had spread. Polytheism was in these countries less complicated than elsewhere. The religion of Sabazius, common to Thracia and to Phrygia, in close rapport with the ancient Orpheism, and yet detached by the syncretism of the times from the Dionysian mysteries, included the germs of monotheism. A certain infantile simplicity of taste prepared the way for the Gospel. Everything indicated habits honest, serious, and amiable. One felt oneself to be in a centre analogous to that in which the agronomic and sentimental poetry of Virgil was created. The ever green plain was favourable for the varied culture of vegetables and flowers. Splendid fountains, gushing from the base of the mountain of shining marble which crowned the city, diffused, when properly applied, wealth, shade and freshness. The thickets of poplars and willows, of fig trees and cherry trees and of wild vines, exhaled the sweetest odours, and scented the brooks, which abounded on all sides. Moreover, the prairies, which were overrun or covered with monster roses, exhibited herds of dull-eyed buffaloes, with enormous horns, with their heads just above the water; whilst the bees and the swarms of black and blue butterflies gyrated from flower to flower. Pangaea, with its majestic summits, which were covered with snow till the middle of June, stretched out as if to unite the city across the morass. Beautiful ranges of mountains bounded the horizon on all the other sides, leaving only an aperture through which the sky vanished, and showing in the clear distance the basin of Strymon.

Philippi offered to the mission a most appropriate field. We have already seen that in Galatia the Roman colonies of Antioch in Pisidia and of Iconium had very favourably received the new doctrine. We shall observe the same thing at Corinth and at Alexandria-Troas. The population, which had been for a long time settled there, and possessing ancient local traditions, gave few signs of innovations. The Jewry of Philippi, if there was one, was little important; at most, it was limited probably to the women celebrating the Sabbath. Even in the towns in which there were no Jews, the Sabbath was usually celebrated by some of the people. In any case, it seems clear that there was no synagogue there. When the apostolic band entered the city, it was on the first day of the week. Paul, Silas, Timothy, and Luke remained some days within doors, awaiting, according to custom, the Sabbath day. Luke, who knew the country, remembered that the people who had adopted Jewish customs were wont to assemble on that day without in the suburbs, upon the banks of a small secluded rivulet, which issued from the ground a league and a half from the city, from an enormous boiling spring, and which was called Gangas or Gangites. Perhaps it went then by the antique Aryan name of the sacred rivers (Ganga). What is certain is that the peaceful scenes recounted in the Acts, and which marked the first establishment of Christianity in Macedonia, took place at the same spot where a century before the fate of the world had been decided. Gangites marked the spot in the great battle of the year 42 before Jesus Christ, where were placed the foremost ensigns of Brutus and of Cassius.

In towns where there was no synagogue, the meetings of those who were affiliated to Judaism were held in small hypethral erections, or frequently simply in the open air in enclosed spaces, which were called proseuchæ. People delighted in establishing these oratories near the sea or rivers, so as to have facilities for ablutions. The Apostles repaired to the place indicated. Many women, in fact, resorted there for devotion. The Apostles spoke to them, and proclaimed to them the mystery of Jesus. They were listened to attentively. One woman, in particular, was touched. "The Lord," says the writer of the Acts, "opened her heart." She was called Lydia or Lydian, because she was from Thyatira. She traded in one of the principal products of Lydian industry--purple. She was a pious person, of the order of those who were called "believing in God," that is to say, a Pagan by birth, but observing the precepts denominated "Noachic." She was baptised, with all her house, and did not rest until, through much entreaty, she induced the four missionaries to take up their abode with her. They remained there some weeks, teaching each Sunday at the place of prayer, upon the banks of the Gangites.

A small Church, almost wholly composed of women, was formed. It was very pious, very obedient, and most devoted to Paul. Besides Lydia, this Church embraced within its bosom Evhodia and Syntyche, who with the Apostle fought valiantly for the Gospel, but who sometimes had disputes in regard to the ministry of deaconesses. Epaphroditus, a courageous man, whom Paul treated as a brother, a fellow-worker, a companion in arms; Clement, and others still, whom Paul called "his fellow-workers, and whose names," said he, "are written in the book of life." Timothy was also much beloved of the Philippians, and he had for them great devotion. It was the only Church from which Paul accepted pecuniary succour, because it was rich, and was little burdened by poor Jews. Lydia was undoubtedly the principal author of these gifts. Paul accepted them from her, for he knew her to be strongly attached to him. This woman gave from the heart; one had not to fear reproaches on her part, nor for an interested return. Paul preferred, doubtless, to be indebted to a woman (probably a widow), of whom he was sure, rather than to men, in respect of whom he would have been less independent, if he had had some acquaintance with them.

The absolute purity of Christian manners disarmed all suspicion. Perhaps, moreover, it is not too audacious to suppose that it is Lydia whom Paul, in his Epistle to the Philippians, calls "my dear spouse." That expression can be taken, if one so desires, as a simple metaphor. Is it, nevertheless, absolutely impossible that Paul may have contracted with that sister a union more intimate? The only thing certain is, that Paul did not take this sister with him in his journeys. Notwithstanding this, a whole branch of ecclesiastical tradition has claimed that he was married.

The character of the Christian woman became more and more outlined. To the Jewish woman, sometimes so strong, so devoted; to the Syrian woman, who is indebted to the soft languor of a distempered organisation for flashes of enthusiasm and of love; to Tabitha, Mary Magdalen, succeeded the Greek women, Lydia, Phoebe, Chloe, vivacious, gay, active, amiable, distinguished, open-hearted to all, yet nevertheless circumspect, giving themselves up to their master to whom they were subordinate, capable of the greatest things, because they were contented to be the fellow-labourers of the men and their sisters, and to aid them when they performed worthy actions. These Greek women, sprung from a fine and healthy race, experienced at the turn of life a change which transformed them. They became pale, and their eyes wandered languishingly; they then covered the bands of thick hair which bounded their cheeks with a black veil, and devoted themselves to austere cares, and brought to bear on these an animated and intelligent ardour. The "female servant," or Greek deaconess, surpassed even her of Syria and of Palestine in courage. These women, guardians of the secrets of the Church, ran the greatest dangers, and endured every torment, rather than divulge anything. They created the dignity of their sex, and justly too, because they did not speak of their rights; they did more than the men, in assuming the attitude of limiting themselves to serving the latter.

An incident happened which hastened the departure of the missionaries. The city began to speak of them, and public imagination was engaged already upon the marvellous virtues which were attributed to them. One morning, as they were repairing to the place of prayer, they encountered a young slave-- probably a ventriloquist--who passed for a witch, and predicted the future. Her masters made a great deal of money out of that ignoble performance. The poor girl, either because she possessed indeed a spirit of divination, or because she was tired of her infamous calling, had no sooner perceived the missionaries than she started to follow them, uttering loud cries. The faithful pretended that she was rendering homage to the new faith and to those who preached it. This was repeated several times. At length, one day, Paul exorcised her. The girl, calmed, pretended to be freed from the spirit which tormented her. But the anger of her masters was extreme. Through the healing of the girl they lost their livelihood. They entered a process against Paul, and Silas as his accomplice, and caused them to be taken to the agora, before the duumvirs.

It would have been difficult to found a claim for indemnity upon such peculiar grounds. The plaintiffs laid special stress on the fact of the trouble caused in the city, and of illegal preaching. "They preach customs," said they, "that we are not allowed to follow, inasmuch as we are Romans." The city, in fact, was under the Italian law, and liberty of worship became the more constrained the nearer people were to the Roman city. The superstitious population, excited by the masters of the witch, made, at the same moment, a hostile demonstration against the Apostles. These sorts of petty uprisings were frequent in ancient towns. The newsmongers, the unemployed, the "plunderers of the agora," as Demosthenes had already denominated them, lived on them. The duumvirs, believing that they were dealing with ordinary Jews, condemned--without informing themselves of, or inquiring into, the position of the accused--Paul and Silas to be beaten. The lictors divested the Apostles of their garments, and beat them cruelly in public. They were next cast into prison, put in one of the innermost cells, and had their feet made fast in the stocks.

Whether they had not been allowed to speak in their own defence, or whether they purposely had courted the glory of suffering humiliation for their Master, it does not appear that either Paul or Silas took advantage of their title of citizens before the tribunal. It was during the night in the prison that they declared their rank. The jailor was much troubled. Thus far he had treated the two Jews with harshness; now he found himself in the presence of two Romans, Paulus and Silvanus, unlawfully condemned. He washed their wounds, and gave them to eat. It is probable that the duumvirs were informed at the same time; for early in the morning they sent the lictors to order the jailor to release the captives. The Valerian and the Porcian laws were express. The application of stripes to a Roman citizen constituted a grave offence. Paul, taking advantage of this circumstance, refused thus to leave his confinement. He demanded, it is related, that the duumvirs should themselves come and give him his liberty. The embarrassment of the latter was somewhat great. They came and besought Paul to quit the city.

The two prisoners, once at liberty, repaired to the house of Lydia. They were received as martyrs. They addressed to the brethren a few parting words of exhortation and consolation, and departed. In no city had Paul ever been so beloved, and so much loved. Timothy, who was not implicated in the prosecution, and Luke, who played a secondary part, remained at Philippi. Luke did not see Paul again until five years after.

Paul and Silas, having departed from Philippi, followed the Egnantine road, which led to Amphipolis. This was one of the most beautiful day's journey Paul ever experienced. In leaving the plain of Philippi, the road enters a smiling valley, dominated by the peaks of Panga. The natives cultivated there flax and the plants of the most temperate countries. Large villages were to be seen in every indentation of the mountain. The Roman road was made of marble flagstones. At each step, almost under every plane tree, deep wells filled with water, coming directly from the snowy vicinage, and filtering through the thick layers of permeable earth, presented themselves to the traveller. Through the openings in the white marble rocks issued rivulets of incomparable limpidity. It is in such a locality that one learns to place pure water in the first rank of the gifts of Nature. Amphipolis was a large city, the capital of a province, and about an hour's journey from the mouth of the Strymon. The Apostles do not appear to have stopped there, probably because it was a purely Hellenic city.

From Amphipolis the Apostles, after quitting the estuary of Strymon, proceeded between the sea and the mountain, across the thick woods and the prairies which extend to the sand on the sea shore. The first halt, under the plane trees, near a cooling fountain which issues from the sand, a few steps from the sea, is a delicious place. The Apostles then entered Aulon of Arethusa, a deep rent, a kind of Bosphorus cut perpendicularly, which served as an outlet from the interior lakes to the sea, and passed, probably without any one knowing it, by the side of the tomb of Euripides. The beauty of the trees, the freshness of the air, the rapidity of the waters, the strong growth of the ferns and shrubs of all kinds, recall the prospect of Grand Chartreuse or of Grésivaudan, thrown into the bottom of a furnace. The basin of the lakes of Mygdonia, in fact, is torrid, having, as we might say, surfaces of molten lead; the snakeweeds, raising their heads out of the water and seeking the shade, imprint there only a few wrinkles. The flocks, towards the south, crowded together round the foot of the trees, seem shrivelled up. If it were not for the hum of the insects and the song of the birds, which alone in creation can resist such oppression, it might be regarded as the kingdom of the dead.

Traversing the small town of Apollonia, without halting, Paul skirted the south side of the lakes, and continuing almost as far as the bottom of the plain whose depressed centre they occupy, he arrived at the foot of the small range of heights which form the east side of the gulf of Thessalonica. When one attains the summits of these hills, the outline of Olympus is seen in all its splendour. The base and the middle regions of the mountain are blended with the azure of the sky; the snows of the summit appear as an ethereal dwelling suspended in space. But, alas! the holy mountain had been already disenchanted. Man had ascended it, and had clearly seen that the gods no longer dwelt there. When Cicero, in his exile at Thessalonica, saw their white summits, he knew that there was there only snow and rocks. Paul, doubtless, had no regard for these enchanted places belonging to another race. A great city was before him, and from experience he divined that he would find there an excellent base for establishing something grand.

Since the Roman domination, Thessalonica had become one of the most important commercial ports of the Mediterranean. It was a very wealthy and populous city. It had a grand synagogue, serving as a religious centre to the Judaism of Philippi, of Amphipolis, and of Apollonia, all of which had only oratories. Paul followed here his usual practice. For three consecutive Sabbaths he spoke in the synagogue, repeating his uniform discourse on Jesus, proving that he was the Messiah, that the Scriptures had found in him their fulfilment, that he had to suffer, and that he had risen again. Some

Jews were converted; but the conversions were numerous, especially among the Greeks "fearing God." It was always this class which furnished to the new faith its most zealous adherents.

The women came in crowds. All that was best in the feminine society of Thessalonica had already for a long time observed the Sabbath and the Jewish ceremonies; the élite of these pious dames flocked to the new preachers. The ordinary phenomena of thaumaturgy, of glossology, of the gifts of the Holy Spirit, of mystical effusions, and of ecktases were produced. The Church of Thessalonica soon rivalled that of Philippi in piety and in delicate attentions to the Apostle. Paul nowhere expended more ardour, tenderness, and penetrating grace. This man, naturally vivacious and passionate, exhibited in his mission a surprising gentleness and calmness; he was a father, a mother, a nurse, as he himself said; while his austerity and rudeness served but to enhance his charm. Stubborn and stern natures have, when they wish to be unctuous, unequalled powers of seduction. Severe language, never flattery, has much more chance of being made agreeable, with women in particular, than softness, which is often the indication of feeble and interested views.

Paul and Silas lived at the house of one Jesus, an Israelite by race, who, according to the usage of the Jews, had Grecianised his name to that of Jason; but they would accept nothing but lodgings. Paul laboured at his trade night and day, in order to cost the Church nothing. The rich purple merchants of Philippi and the sisterhood would, moreover, have been grieved if others than they had furnished to the Apostle the things requisite for existence. On two occasions, during his sojourn at Thessalonica, Paul received from Philippi an offering which he accepted. That was altogether contrary to his principles; his rule was to maintain himself, without receiving anything from the Churches; yet he would have made a scruple about refusing this present of the heart: the pain that he would have given to pious women prevented him. Perhaps, moreover, as we have already stated, he preferred to contract obligations from the women, who never restrained his action, except in regard to men like Jason, in respect of whom he desired to preserve his authority.

Nowhere, it seems, had Paul so much as at Thessalonica succeeded in realising his ideal. The population to which he addressed himself was chiefly composed of laborious workmen; Paul entered into their spirit: he preached to them order, industry, and to hold fast to the good in sight of the heathen. A complete new series of precepts were added to his lessons; to wit, economy, application to business, industrial honour founded upon ease and independence. By a contrast, which ought not to surprise us, he expounded to them, at the same time, the most fantastic mysteries of the Apocalypse that had ever been described to them. The Church at Thessalonica was a model that Paul afterwards delighted to cite, and whose good odour, like a perfume of edification, spread everywhere. There were nominated, besides Jason, among the notables of the Church, Gaius, Aristarchus, and Secundus; Aristarchus was circumcised.

That which had happened twenty times before happened again at Thessalonica. The discontented Jews fomented trouble. They employed a band of idlers, of vagabonds, and of those poor creatures of every description who in ancient cities passed the day and night under the columns of the basilicas, ready to make a noise for whoever paid them for it. They went in a body to assail the house of Jason. They called loudly for Paul and Silas. As they did not find them, the rioters seized Jason, together with some of the faithful, and brought them before the politarcs or magistrates. The most confusing cries were raised. "Revolutionaries are in the city," said some, "and Jason has received them." "All these people," said others, "are in revolt against the edicts of the emperor." "They have a king they call Jesus," said a third party. The excitement was great, and the politarcs were somewhat alarmed. They compelled Jason and the faithful who had been arrested with him to give bail, then sent them away. The following night the brethren led Paul and Silas out of the city, and had them conducted to Beræa. The persecutions of the Jews against the little Church continued, but that only served to consolidate it.

The Jews of Beræa were more liberal and better educated than those of Thessalonica. They listened willingly, and allowed Paul, without interruption, to expound his ideas in the synagogue. For several days it was to them a lively source of curiosity. They passed the time in perusing the Scriptures, in order to find there the texts cited by Paul, and to see whether they were correct. Many were converted, among others a certain Jew, named Sopater or Sosipater, son of Pyrrhus. Here, nevertheless, as in all the other Churches of Macedonia, the women were in the majority. The converts belonged all to the Greek race, to that class of devout persons who, without being Jews, practised the Jewish ceremonies. Many Greeks and proselytes were also converted, and the synagogue for once remained peaceable. The storm came from Thessalonica. The Jews of that city, learning that Paul had preached with success at Beræa, came to the latter city, and renewed there their plotting. Paul was again obliged to depart hurriedly, and without taking Silas with him. Many of the brethren of Beræa accompanied him as an escort.

The warning given by the synagogues of Macedonia was such that sojourning in this country seemed to have become impossible to Paul. He saw himself tracked from city to city, and the rioters to spring up, as it were, from under his feet. The Roman police were not very hostile to him; but they acted in the circumstances according to the habitual practice of police. When there was disturbance in the street, they would blame everybody, and without fretting themselves as to that which served as the true pretext for the excitement, they would beg of people to be quiet or to move on. It was in effect an encouragement to disturbance, and to establish in principle that it only needed a few fanatics to deprive a citizen of his liberty. The policeman never piques himself much on philosophy. Paul hence resolved to depart, and to go to some distant country, where the hatred of his adversaries could not follow him. Leaving Silas and Timothy in Macedonia, he, with the Beræans, directed his steps towards the sea.

Thus ended that brilliant Macedonian mission, the most successful of any that Paul had as yet accomplished. Churches composed of entirely new elements had been formed. It was no longer the easy-going Syrian woman, the good-natured Lycaonian woman; it was the subtle, delicate, elegant, spiritual races, who, prepared by Judaism, now embraced the new religion. The coast of Macedonia was completely covered with Greek colonies. The Greek genius had there borne its choicest fruits. These noble Churches of Philippi and of Thessalonica, composed of the most distinguished women of each city, were unquestionably the two greatest conquests that Christianity had yet made. The Jewish woman was outstripped; submissive, retired, and obedient, participating little in religion, the latter was not easily converted. It was the woman "fearing God," the Greek woman, wearied of the goddesses brandishing their spears on the summit of the Acropolis, the virtuous woman turning her back on a worn-out Paganism, and seeking the pure religion, who was attracted heavenwards. These were the second foundresses of our faith. Next to the Galileans who followed Jesus and served him, Lydia, Phoebe, the obscure pious women of Philippi and of Thessalonica are the true saints to whom the new faith owed its most rapid progress.

CHAPTER VII

CONTINUATION OF THE SECOND JOURNEY OF PAUL--PAUL AT ATHENS

Paul, accompanied still by the faithful Beræans, sailed for Athens. From the end of the Gulf of Thermmus to Phalera, or to Piræus, the voyage in a small craft occupies three or four days. The traveller passes the foot of Olympus, of Ossa, and of Pelion; he follows the sinuosities of the interior sea which Euboea separates from the rest of the Ægæan Sea, and touches the singularly narrow strait of Euripus. On either bank one skirts that truly holy ground where perfection is at once discovered, where the ideal has really existed,--that soil which has seen the noblest of races found at once art, science, philosophy, and politics. Paul, no doubt, experienced on landing there that species of filial sentiment which cultivated men experience when touching this venerated soil. It was another world: his holy ground was elsewhere.

Greece had not recovered from the terrible blows she had received during the previous centuries. Like the sons of Earth, these aristocratic tribunes had torn one another to pieces; the Romans had completely exterminated them; the old families had nearly disappeared; the ancient cities of Thebes and of Argos had become poor villages; Olympus and Sparta had been humiliated; Athens and Corinth were the sole survivors. The country was almost a desert: the images of desolation which we gather from the descriptions of Polybius, Cicero, Strabo, and Pausanias are heart-rending. The appearances of liberty which the Romans had left in the towns, and which only disappeared under Vespasian, were little else than irony. The wicked administration of the Romans had ruined everything; the temples were no longer maintained; at each step there were pedestals from which the conquerors had stolen the statues, or which adulation had consecrated to the new rulers. Peloponesus, in particular, had been struck dead. Sparta had killed her; consumed by the proximity of this foolish Utopia, that poor country never sprang into life again. At the Roman epoch, moreover, the administration of the large cities had absorbed and superseded the numerous small ruling centres: Corinth attracted to itself all the life.

The race, if we except Corinth, had, however, remained quite pure; the number of Jews outside of Corinth was inconsiderable. Greece had received but a single Roman colony. The invasions of slaves and of Albanians, which have so completely changed the Hellenic blood, did not take place till later. The old religions were still flourishing. Some women, unknown to their husbands, practised much in secret, at the far corner of the gymnasiums, the foreign superstitions, especially those of the Egyptians. The sages, however, protested. "What a God he must be," said they, "who is pleased with the surreptitious homage of married women! A wife ought not to have other friends besides those of her husband. The gods, are they not our best friends?"

It seems that, either during the voyage or at the moment of his arrival in Athens, Paul regretted having left his companions in Macedonia. Perhaps that new world astonished him, and he found him-self there too much isolated. What is certain is, that in dismissing the faithful Beræans he charged them to request Silas and Timothy to come and join him at the earliest possible moment.

Paul therefore found himself for some days alone at Athens. This had not happened to him for a long time. His life had been as a whirlwind, and he had never journeyed without two or three companions. Athens, to the world, was something unique--at all events, something totally different from anything that Paul had seen before; hence, he was extremely embarrassed. In waiting for his companions, he amused himself by roaming, in the widest sense, over the city. The Acropolis, with the innumerable statues which covered it, and which constituted it a museum such as had never before been seen, must, in particular, have been to him a subject of the deepest reflection.

Athens, although she had suffered much from Sylla, although, like Greece, she had been pillaged by the Roman administrators, and was already in part despoiled by the gross avidity of its masters, had yet the appearance of being ornamented with almost all her master-pieces of art. The monuments of the Acropolis were intact. Some clumsy additions of detail, quite a sufficient number of mediocre works which were already glittering in the sanctuary of high art, some silly substitutions, which consisted in placing Romans on the pedestals of ancient Greeks, had not changed the sanctity of that immaculate temple of the beautiful. Poecile, with its brilliant decoration, was as fresh as it was on the fast day. The exploits of the odious Secundus Carinas, the purveyor of statues for the gilded House, did not commence until some years after, and Athens suffered less from this than did Delphos and Olympus.

The false taste of the Romans for colonnaded cities had not penetrated here; the houses were poor and by no means commodious. That exquisite city was moreover an irregular city, with narrow streets which were the conservators of its old monuments, and archaic souvenirs were preferred to streets scientifically laid out. Many of these marvellous things affected Paul but little; he beheld the only perfect objects which had ever existed, which shall ever exist,--the Propylæum, that chef-d'oeuvre of grandeur; the Parthenon, which absorbed every other grandeur save its own; the Temple of Victory without wings, worthy of the battles which it consecrated; the Erechthæum, a prodigy of elegance and of finish; the Errhephoræ, these divine young women with a bearing so full of grace; he beheld all that, and his faith was not overcome, nor was he disquieted. With the prejudices of the iconoclastic Jew, insensible to the plastic beauties which blinded him, he took these incomparable figures for idols. "His spirit," says his biographer, "was stirred in him when he saw the city wholly given to idolatry." Ah! thou lovely and chaste images, true gods and goddesses, tremble! Behold him who raised against you the hammer! The fatal words had gone forth: "Ye are idols!" The error of that pitiful little Jew was your death-warrant!

Surrounded by so many things which he did not understand, there were two which greatly struck the Apostle: first, the very religious character of the Athenians, which was manifested by a multitude of temples, altars, and sanctuaries of every description, symbols of a tolerant eclecticism which they carried into religion; in the second place, certain anonymous altars which were erected to the "unknown gods." These altars were somewhat numerous at Athens and in the environs. Other cities of Greece possessed them also. Those at the port of Phalera (Paul must have seen them on landing) were celebrated; they belonged to the legends of the Trojan War. They bore this inscription:--"To the unknown gods." Some of them were even thus inscribed:--

ΑΓΗΩΣΤΩΙΘΕΩΙ

"To an unknown God." These altars owed their existence to the extreme scrupulousness of the Athenians for things religious, and to their habit of seeing in everything the manifestation of a mysterious and special power. Fearing, without knowing it, to offend some god of whose name they were ignorant, or of neglecting a powerful god, or even of wishing to obtain a favour which might depend upon a certain divinity with whom they were unacquainted, they either erected anonymous altars, or placed up the afore-mentioned inscriptions. It is possible, too, that these fanciful inscriptions were taken from altars which were originally anonymous, to which, in the work of making a general census, had to be affixed some such an epigraph, for lack of the knowledge of that which properly belonged to them. Paul was greatly surprised at these dedications. Interpreting them with his Jewish mind, he imputed to them a meaning which did not belong to them. He believed that they had reference to a God called par excellence "The Unknown God." He saw in that Unknown God the God of the Jews, the only God, towards whom Paganism itself might have had some mysterious aspirations. This idea was the more natural, because in the eyes of Pagans that which in particular characterised the God of the Jews was, that he was a God without name, a doubtful God. It was further probable that it was in some religious ceremony, or m some philosophical discussion, that Paul heard the hemistiche:--

Τοῦ γὰρ χαὶ γένος ἐσμέν

borrowed from the hymn of Cleanthes to Jupiter, or from the Phenomena of Aratus, and which was frequently used in the religious hymns. He grouped in his mind those features of local colouring, and sought to compose a discourse on them appropriate to his new auditors: for he felt that here it was necessary for him to modify greatly his preaching.

Certain it is Athens was far from being then what she had been for centuries, the centre of human progress, the capital of the republic of mind. Faithful to her ancient character, this divine mother of art was one of the last asylums of liberalism and of the republican spirit. She was what might be called a city of opposition. Athens was always on the side of the lost cause. She energetically declared for the independence of Greece, and for Mithridates against the Romans, for Pompey against Cæsar, for the republicans against the triumvirs, for Antony against Octavius. She raised statues to Brutus and to Cassius by the side of those of Harmodius and of Aristogiton; she honoured Germanicus to the point of compromising herself; she merited the insults of Piso. Sylla plundered her in an atrocious manner, and dealt the final blow to her democratic constitution. Augustus, although merciful to her, did not show her any favour. Her title as a free city was never taken away, but the privileges of free cities were gradually diminished under the Cæsars and the Flavii. Athens was thus in the condition of a city suspected and disgraced, but justly ennobled through her disgrace. At the advent of Nerva, there began for her a second life. The world, having returned to reason and to virtue, recognised its mother. Nerva, Herod Atticus, Hadrian, Antonine, Marcus Aurelius, restored her, endowing her even with monuments and new institutions. Athens became again for four centuries the city of philosophers, of artists, of genius, the holy city of every liberal soul, the pilgrim city of those who loved the beautiful and the true.

But let us not anticipate events. At the sad moment at which we are now arrived, the ancient splendour had disappeared, and the new had not yet dawned. She was no longer "the city of Theseus," and was not yet "the city of Hadrian." In the century before our era, the philosophic school of Athens had been very brilliant; Philo of Larissa, and Antiochus of Ascalon, had continued or modified the academy; Cratippus taught there peripatetics, and understood how to be at once the friend, the master, the consoler, or the protégé of Pompey, of Cæsar, of Cicero, and of Brutus. Romans, the most celebrated and most eminent in business, attracted to the Orient by ambition, halted at Athens to listen to the philosophers in vogue. Atticus, Crassus, Cicero, Varro, Ovid, Horace, Agrippa, Virgil, either studied or resided there as amateurs. Brutus passed there his last winter, dividing his time between the peripatetic Cratippus and the academician Theomnestus. Athens was, on the eve of the battle of Philippi, a centre of opinion of the highest importance. The instruction which was given there was entirely philosophic, and much superior to the insipid eloquence of the school of Rhodes. That which was indeed prejudicial to Athens was the advent of Augustus and the universal pacification. The precepts of philosophy were from that time suspected--the schools lost their importance and their activity. Rome, on the other hand, by reason of the brilliant literary evolution which she had achieved, became for some time semi-independent of Greece in regard to matters of thought. Other centres were formed: as a school of varied instruction, Marseilles was preferred. The original philosophy of the four great sects had come to an end. Eclecticism, a sort of flabby, unsystematic style of philosophising, had commenced. If we except Ammonius of Alexandria, the master of Plutarch, who founded about that time at Athens a species of literary philosophy, which was to become the fashion, beginning with the reign of Hadrian, there was no one illustrious, about the middle of the first century, in the one city of the world which had produced or attracted the most celebrated men. The figures which were now consecrated with deplorable prodigality on the Acropolis were those of consuls, of pro-consuls, of Roman magistrates, and of members of the imperial family. The temples which were erected there were dedicated to the goddess Rome, and to Augustus. Nero had even his statues there. Artists of talent having been attracted to Rome, the Athenian works of the first century were, for the most part, of a mediocre quality that is surprising. Still monuments, such as the clock of Andronicus Cyrrhesta, the portico of Athene Archegetes, the temple of Rome and of Augustus, the mausoleum of Philopappus, were either a little anterior or posterior to the time when Paul saw Athens. Never had the city, during its long history, been more mute and peaceful.

She still preserved, however, a great portion of her nobility. She still occupied the first rank in the regards of the world. Despite the harshness of the times, the respect for Athens was profound, and every one bowed to her. Sylla, though so terrible in consequence of her rebellion, had pity on her. Pompey and Cæsar, before the battle of Pharsalia, caused it to be proclaimed by a herald that all the Athenians were to be spared, as priests of the goddesses Thesmophores. Pompey gave a large sum of money to adorn the city: Cæsar refrained from avenging himself on her, and contributed to the erection of one of the monuments. Brutus and Cassius, who comported themselves as private persons, were received and flattered like heroes. Antony loved Athens, and liked to reside there. After the battle of Actium, Augustus pardoned her for the third time, and his name, like that of Cæsar, was inscribed on an important monument. His family and entourage were looked upon at Athens as benefactors. The Romans were at great pains to prove that they left Athens free and honoured. Spoiled children of fame, the Athenians lived thenceforward on the recollections of their past history. Germanicus, while he resided at Athens, wished to be preceded by only one lictor. Nero, though not superstitious, did not dare to enter the city for fear of the Furies which lived under the Areopagus,--of those terrible "Semnes," which the parricides dreaded. The recollection of Orestes made him tremble. He dare no more affront the mysteries of Eleusis, at the threshold of which the herald proclaimed that the profligate and the impious were to be careful not to approach. Noble foreigners, descendants of dethroned kings, came to spend their fortunes at Athens, and were delighted to find themselves decorated with high-sounding and mock titles. All the small barbarian kings emulated one another in rendering service to the Athenians, and in restoring their monuments.

Religion was one of the principal causes of this exceptional favour. Essentially municipal and political in its origin, having for its basis the myths relating to the foundation of the city and to its divine protectors, the religion of Athens was at first only the religious consecration of patriotism and of the institutions of the city. It was the cult of the Acropolis. "Aglaure" and the oath which the young Athenians took upon the altar had no other meaning; just as if religion with us consisted in drawing the conscription, in drilling, and in honouring the colours. It soon became insipid enough; it possessed nothing infinite, nothing that touched man through his destiny, nothing universal. The railleries of Aristophanes against the gods of the Acropolis proved by themselves alone that these gods could not bring every race under subjection. The women were turned early in the direction of petty foreign devotions like those of Adonis. The mysteries, in particular, were successful; philosophy in the hands of Plato was a kind of delicious mythology, whilst art created for the multitude images really admirable. The Athenian gods became the gods of beauty. The old Athene Poliade was but a mannikin, without apparent arms, swathed in a peplos, like the old virgin of Loretta. Toreutic accomplished an unexampled miracle; she made realistic statues after the model of the Italian and Byzantine Madonnas, adorned with appropriate ornaments, which were at the same time marvellous masterpieces. Athens succeeded in possessing, after a sort, one of the most perfect religions of antiquity. This religion underwent at that time a kind of eclipse, on account of the misfortunes of the city. The Athenians were the first to defile their sanctuary. Lachares stole the gold from the statue of Athene. Demetrius Poliorcetes was installed by the inhabitants themselves in the opisthodome of the Parthenon. He harboured his courtesans near himself, and people were amused by the scandals that such surroundings must have caused to the chaste goddess. Aristion the last defender of the independence of Athens, permitted the immortal lamp of Athene Poliade to be extinguished. Such, however, was the glory of that unique city, that the universe seemed to take to heart the adoption of her goddess, at the moment when she deserted her. The Parthenon, through the action of foreigners, regained her honours. The mysteries of Athens were a religious attraction for the whole Pagan world.

But it was principally as a city of schools that Athens exercised a peculiar prestige. That new destiny which, through the assiduity of Hadrian and Marcus Aurelius, came to possess a character so decided, had been begun two centuries before. The city of Miltiades and Pericles had been transformed into a university city, a sort of Oxford, the resort of all the young noblesse, who scattered gold in handfuls. It contained nothing but professors, philosophers, rhetoricians, pedagogues of every description, sophmores, tutors, gymnasts, pædotribes, hoplomates, masters of fencing and of riding. From the time of Hadrian the cosmetists or prefects of the students assumed to a certain extent the importance and the dignity of the archons. People fixed the date of the years by them: the old Greek education, destined in principle to form the free citizen, became the pedagogic law of the human species. Alas! she produces henceforth little else than rhetoricians; bodily exercises, formerly a real occupation of the heroes upon the banks of the Illissus, became now a mere matter of pose. A circus grandeur, the gestures of Franconi, have replaced solid grandeur. But it is the peculiar attribute of Greece to have ennobled everything. Even the work of the schoolman became with her a moral ministry. The dignity of the professor, in spite of more than one abuse, was one of her creations. The jeunesse dorée could sometimes remember the fine discourses of its masters. She was, like all youths, republican; she flocked to the appeal of Brutus; she was mown down at Philippi. The day was employed in declaiming on tyrannicide and on liberty, in celebrating the noble death of Cato, and in making a eulogy on Brutus.

The population had always been sprightly, spirituelle, curious. Every one lived in the open air, in perpetual contact with the rest of the world, breathing, under smiling skies, a serene atmosphere. The strangers, who were numerous and eager after knowledge, evinced great activity of mind. Publicity, the journalism of the ancient world--if one may be permitted to make use of such an expression--had its centre at Athens. The city not being commercial, everybody had but one care, which was to learn the news, to be made au courant of what was said and of what was being done in the universe. It is very remarkable that the great development of religion did not destroy rational culture. Athens might have been at once the most religious city of the world, the Parthenon of Greece, and the city of philosophers. When we see in the theatre of Dionysius the marble arm-chairs which surround the orchestra bearing each the name of the priesthood the titulary of which came to sit there, we should say that here was a city of priests; and yet it was pre-eminently the city of free-thinkers. The religions in question had neither dogmas nor holy writ. They had not for physics the horror that Christianity has always evinced, and which has led it to condemn positive researches. The priest and the Epicurean atomist, except for a few broils, lived peaceably enough together. The true Greeks were perfectly contented with such accord, founded not upon logic, but upon mutual tolerance and mutual regard.

This was for Paul a species of existence altogether new. The cities in which he had up till now preached were for the most part commercial cities, resembling Leghorn or Trieste, and having large Jewries rather than brilliant centres, cities of the great world and of great culture. Athens was profoundly Pagan; Paganism was bound up with every pleasure, with every interest, with every glory of the city. Paul hesitated a great deal. Timothy at length arrived from Macedonia; Silas, for reasons which we do not know was not able to come.

There was a synagogue at Athens, and Paul disputed in it with the Jews, and with the "devout persons;" but in such a city any successes in the synagogue counted for little. That brilliant agora in which was displayed so much mind, that portico Poecile in which was asked every conceivable question, tempted him. He spoke there not as a preacher addressing himself to the multitude assembled, but as a stranger feeling his way--putting forth his ideas timidly, and seeking to create for himself some point d'appui. "Jesus and the resurrection" (anastasis) appeared foreign words, and destitute of meaning. Several of them, as it would appear, took anastasis for the name of a goddess, and believed that Jesus and Anastasia were some new divine couple that these Oriental dreamers had come to preach. Some Epicurean and Stoic philosophers, it is said, came near and listened.

This first contact of Christianity with Greek philosophy was not very encouraging. We have never seen a better example of how men of mind ought to distrust themselves and to guard against laughing at an idea, however foolish it may seem to them. The bad Greek spoken by Paul, his incorrect and halting phraseology, were not calculated to make him accredited at Athens. The philosophers turned their backs disdainfully at his barbarous speech. "He is a babbler" (spermologos), said some. "He is a preacher of strange gods," said others. No one could have suspected that this babbler would one day supplant them, and that, four hundred and seventy-four years later, their professorships would be suppressed as useless and injurious, in consequence of the preaching of Paul. What a grand lesson! Proud of their superiority, the Athenian philosophers disdained the questions pertaining to popular religion. In their midst superstition flourished. Athens almost equalled in that respect the most religious cities of Asia Minor. The aristocracy of thinkers cared little for the social wants which made themselves felt under the cover of so many unpolished worships. Such a renunciation is always punished. When philosophy declares that she will not occupy herself with religion, religion responds by extinguishing her; and this is just, for philosophy is something only when she shows to humanity the way, when she takes up seriously the infinite problem which is the same for all.

The liberal spirit which reigned at Athens assured Paul of complete security. Neither Jews nor Pagans attempted anything against him; but that tolerance was even worse than hatred. Moreover, the new doctrine produced a lively reaction, at least in the Jewish society; here it could find only curious and blasé auditors. It appears that one day the auditors of Paul, wishing to obtain from him a sort of official exposition of his doctrine, conducted him to the Hill of Mars, and there summoned him to declare what religion he preached. It is indeed possible that there is some legend here, and that the celebrity of the Areopagus may have led the narrator of the Acts, who had not been an eyewitness, to select this illustrious audience to enable him to deliver on his hero a pompous discourse, a philosophic harangue. This hypothesis, nevertheless, is not necessary. The Areopagus had retained, under the Romans, Its ancient organisation. It had even seen its prerogatives increased, as a result of the policy which led the conquerors to suppress in Greece the ancient democratic institutions, and to replace them by the Council of Notables. The Areopagus had always been the aristocratic corporation of Athens: it gained what the democracy had lost. Let us add that people were living in an epoch of literary dilettanteism, and that that tribunal, by its classic celebrity, enjoyed a great prestige. Its moral authority was recognised by the entire world. The Areopagus thus became again, under Roman domination, what it had been at different times in the history of the Athenian Republic, a political body, almost divested of judicial functions, the real senate of Athens, intervening only in certain cases, and constituting a conservative nobility of retired functionaries. Beginning with the first century of our era, the Areopagus figures in the inscriptions as head of the powers of Athens, superior to the Council of Six Hundred, and to the people. The erection of statues, in particular, was made by it, or at least with its authorisation. At the epoch at which we are now arrived, it had just decreed a statue to Queen Berenice, daughter of Agrippa I., with whom we shall soon see Paul en rapport. It seems also that the Areopagus exercised a certain superintendence over instruction. It was a chief council of religious and moral censure, before which was brought all that concerned laws, manners, medicine, luxury, ædileship, the religions of the city; and there is no-thing unlikely in the fact that when a novel doctrine was promulgated, that the preacher should be invited to come and make his declarations before such a tribunal, or at least to the place in which it held its sessions. Paul, it is said, stood up in the middle of the assembly and spoke thus:

"Ye men of Athens, I perceive that in all things ye are too superstitious. For as I passed by, and beheld your devotions, I found an altar with this inscription:--To the Unknown God.' Whom, therefore, ye ignorantly worship, him declare I unto you. God that made the world, and all things therein, seeing that he is lord of earth, dwelleth not in temples made with hands, neither is worshipped with men's hands, as though he needed anything, seeing he giveth to all life and breath, and all things. And hath made of one blood all nations of men for to dwell on all the face of the earth, and hath determined the times before appointed, and the bounds of their habitation. That they should seek the Lord, if haply they might feel after him, and find him, though he be not far from every one of us. For in him we live and move and have our being; as certain also of your own poets have said, For we are all his offspring.' Forasmuch, then, as we are the offspring of God, we ought not to think that the godhead is like unto gold, or silver, or stone, or graven by art of man's device. And the times of this ignorance God winked at; but now commandeth all men everywhere to repent. Because he hath appointed a day in which he will judge the world in righteousness, by that man whom he hath ordained; whereof he hath given assurance unto all men, in that he hath raised him from the dead" (Acts xvii. 22-31).

At these words, according to the narrator, Paul was interrupted. Hearing him speak of the resurrection of the dead, some mocked, and others said:--"We will hear thee again of this matter."

If the discourse which we have just related was really delivered, it must indeed have produced a very singular impression upon the cultivated minds which heard it. That almost barbarous speech, now incorrect and formless, now scrupulously correct; that unequal eloquence, strewn with happy fancies and disagreeable failings; that profound philosophy, embracing beliefs the most singular, and extending, seemingly, to another world. Immensely superior to the popular religion of Greece, such a doctrine was in many things below the level of the current philosophy of the age. If, on the one hand, it extended the hand to that philosophy through the elevated notion of divinity and the beautiful theory which it proclaimed of the moral unity of the human mind, on the other, it embraced in part supernatural beliefs that no informed mind could admit. In any case, it is not surprising that Christianity had no success in Athens. The motives which were to work the success of Christianity, were elsewhere than in the circle of letters. They were lodged in the hearts of pious women, in the secret aspirations of the poor, the slaves, and the afflicted of every description. Before philosophy could approach the new doctrine, it was necessary that philosophy itself should be much debased, and that the new doctrine should be renounced from the grand chimera of the near judgment, that is to say, from the concrete ideas with which from its first formation it had been enveloped.

Whether it was delivered by Paul, or by one of his disciples, this discourse, in any case, shows us an endeavour, almost the only one in the first century, made to reconcile Christianity with philosophy, and even, in one sense, with Paganism. The author, giving proof of a breadth of views most remarkable amongst the Jews, discovers in all races a sort of innate sense of the divine, a sort of secret instinct of monotheism which might lead to the knowledge of the true God. To be believed in, Christianity is nothing more than natural religion, which one arrives at by consulting simply one's own heart, and by interrogating oneself conscientiously--the two-sided idea which was soon to reproach Christianity with deism, and to inspire a pride of which it had been shorn. This is the first example given of the tactics of certain apologists of Christianity, in advance of philosophy, using or feigning to use scientific language; speaking with complaisance or politeness of the reason advanced by the other side of wishing to have it believed, by means of skilfully grouped quotations, that in the main it might be understood by lettered people; but which led to misunderstandings that were inevitable, for they plainly declared their opinions, and spoke of their supernatural dogmas. One can already perceive the effort to translate into the language of Greek philosophy Jewish and Christian ideas; one can foresee Clement of Alexandria and Origen. Biblical ideas, and those of Greek philosophy, aspired to embrace one another; but in order to that many concessions had to be made; for that God in which we live and move is far removed from the Jehovah of the prophets, and from the celestial father of Jesus.

Be that as it may, the times were far from being ripe for such an alliance; at any rate, it was not to take place at Athens. Athens, at the point which it had reached in history, that city of grammarians, of gymnasts, and of fencing-masters, was likewise as ill adapted as it was possible to be, for receiving Christianity. The power over vassals, the hardness of heart of the schoolman, were unpardonable sins in the eyes of grace. The pedagogue is the least convertible of men; for he has a religion of his own, which is routine, faith in old authors, and a taste for literary exercises. This satisfies him, and extinguishes in him all other desires. There has been found at Athens a series of hermes-portraits of cosmetics of the second century. The latter are splendid men, grave, majestic, with a noble mien, and yet Hellenic. From the inscriptions we learn of the honours and pensions which were conferred on them: the really great men of the ancient democracy never had so many of these. Assuredly if Paul had encountered some of the predecessors of these superb pedants, he could not have achieved much more success than, during the Empire, would have had a romancist imbued with neo-Catholicism, attempting to convert to his views a Universitarian attached to the religion of Horace, or than would in our own days a socialist humanitarian declaiming against English prejudices before the fellows of Oxford or Cambridge.

In a society so different from that in which he had till now lived, in the midst of rhetoricians and professors of dialectics, Paul found himself indeed from home. His thoughts constantly reverted to the dear Churches of Macedonia and Galatia, where he had discovered such an exquisite religious sentiment. He thought many times of departing for Thessalonica. A lively desire carried him thence, the more so as he had received news that the faith of the young Church had been subjected to many severe tests, and he feared that the proselytes might succumb to the temptations. Some obstacles, that he attributed to Satan, prevented him from carrying out that project. When he could no longer forbear, as he himself said, he separated once more from Timothy, whom he sent to Thessalonica to confirm, to exhort, and to console the faithful, and remained alone again at Athens.

He laboured there with renewed vigour, but the soil was unpropitious. The sprightly Athenian mind was diametrically opposed to that tender and profound religious disposition which produced conversions, and which was predestined to Christianity. The truly Hellenic ground was little inclined to the doctrine of Jesus. Plutarch, living in an atmosphere purely Greek, had not the least wind of it in the first half of the second century. Patriotism, attachment to old recollections of country, turned the Greeks against exotic worships. "Hellenism" became an organised, almost rational religion, which admitted a great part of philosophy. The "gods of Greece" appeared to wish to be regarded as the universal gods of humanity.

That which characterised the religion of Greece formerly, that which still characterises it in our day, is the want of infinity, of the unconfined, of compassion, of feminine softness. The profoundness of German and Celtic religious sentiment is lacking in the true Hellenic race. The piety of Greek orthodoxy consists in practices and in exterior signs. The orthodox Churches, sometimes very elegant, have none of the terrors which one feels in a Gothic Church. In that Oriental Christianity there are no tears, prayers, or outward compunctions. The funerals there are almost gay. They take place at night, or at the setting of the sun, when the shadows have become lengthened, and are accompanied by songs set in a medium key, and are a display of bright colours. The fanatical gravity of the Latins is distasteful to those brisk, cheerful, and sprightly races. The infirm one is not cast down; he watches death softly approach; all about him is smiles. Herein lies the secret of that divine gaiety of the Homeric poems and of Plato--the narration of the death of Socrates in Phædon shows hardly a taint of sadness. Life produces its flower, then its fruit; what is wanted more? If, as it can be maintained, the pre-occupation of death is the most important characteristic of Christianity and of modern religious sentiment, then the Greek race is the least religious of races. It is a superficial race, treating life as a thing devoid of the supernatural, and having no future. Such simplicity of conception is owing in great measure to the climate, to the purity of the atmosphere, to the astonishing joy that one breathes, but even more so to the instincts of the Hellenic race, finely idealistic. Anything--a tree, a flower, a lizard, a tortoise, calls up the recollection of a thousand metamorphoses which have been sung by the poets; a jet of water, a small crevice in the rock which is called a cave of the nymphs; a well with a drinking-cup at the brink; an arm of the sea so narrow that the butterflies cross it, and nevertheless navigable for the largest ships, like the Bosphorus; orange groves, cypress trees, whose shades are reflected on the sea; a small pine wood in the midst of rocks--suffice in Greece to produce the contentment which is awakened by beauty. People walk in the gardens during the night to listen to the nightingales; sit down in the clear moonlight to play the flute; go to drink the pure mountain water, carrying with them a piece of bread, and a flask of wine, which is drunk while singing. At family feasts, there is suspended above the doors a crown of branches, to match with the headpieces of flowers; on days of public festivals, thyrsi are carried, adorned with leaves; the days are passed in dancing, playing with tame goats; these are the delights of the Greeks, the pleasures of a race, poor, economical, eternally young, inhabiting a charming country, finding its welfare within itself, and in the gifts that the gods have given it. The shepherd's song or pastoral, after the manner of Theocritus, was in the Hellenic countries a reality. Greece al-ways delighted in that unpretentious species of delicate and amiable poetry, the species the. most characteristic of her literature, the mirror of her own life, though almost always silly and artificial. Good humour and the delights of life are Greek traits par excellence. This race is always twenty years old; for she, indulgere genio is not the deep drinking of the English, or the gross diversions of the French; it is simply to think that nature is kind, that one can and one ought to unbend to it. For Greece, in fact, nature is a counsellor of elegance, a mistress of justice and of virtue:--"concupiscence." The idea that nature induces us to do evil is to her a not-sense. The taste for personal adornment which distinguishes the palicare, and which is exhibited with so much innocence in the Greek girl, is not the pompous vanity of the barbarian, the vulgar pretension of the bourgeois, swollen with the ridiculous pride of an upstart; it is the pure and delicate sentiment of unsophisticated youth, which feels itself to be the legitimate heir of the true inventors of beauty.

Such a race, one can understand, would have received Jesus with a smile. It was a subject these exquisite children were incapable of learning from us--serious, profound, really simple devotion without glory, goodness without parade. Socrates is a moralist of the first order, but he has nothing to do with the history of religion. The Greek always appears to us a little cold and heartless; he has wit, action, subtlety, but has nothing of the pensive or the melancholic. On the other hand, with us Celts and Germans, the source of our genius is our heart. Our deepest recesses (au fond de nous) resemble a fairy fountain, a fountain clear, fresh, and deep, in which is reflected the infinite. With the Greek, love of self and vanity is mixed with everything; vague sentiment is unknown to him; reflection upon his own destiny ap-pears to him unprofitable. Pushed to the length of caricature, so incomplete a mode of understanding life as it is conditioned, at the Roman epoch, the græculus esuriens, grammarian, artist, charlatan, acrobat, physician, amuser of the whole world, greatly resembling the Italian of the sixteenth and seventeenth centuries; at the Byzantine epoch, the theological sophist making religion degenerate into subtle disputes; in our day, the modern Greek, sometimes foolishly vain and ungrateful; the orthodox fathers, with their egotistical and materialistic religion. Unfortunate he who arrests that decadence! Shame upon him who, in front of the Parthenon, dreams of holding it up to ridicule! Nevertheless, this has to be acknowledged: Greece was never seriously Christian, nor is she to this day. No race in our Middle Ages was less romantic, more destitute of chivalrous sentiment. Plato built all his theory of the beautiful en se passant without reference to woman. To think of a woman in order to be incited to do great things! a Greek would have been surprised at such language. For him, he thought of men assembled around the agora, he thought of his country. In this respect the Latins were nearer to us. Greek poetry, incomparable in the grander species of it, such as the epic, the tragic, the disinterested lyric poetry, had not, it seems, the sweet elegiac note of Tibullus, of Virgil, of Lucretius, a note so much in harmony with our sentiments, so closely related to that which we love.

The same difference is found between the piety of St Bernard, of St François d'Assisi, and that of the saints of the Greek Church. These splendid schools of Capadocia, of Syria, of Egypt, of the Fathers of the desert, approximate the philosophical schools. The popular holy writings of the Greeks are more mythological than those of the Latins. The majority of the saints represented in the iconostase of a

Greek house, before which a lamp burns, are not great authors, great men like saints of the West: they are often fanciful beings, old gods transfigured, or at least a combination of historic and mythological personages, like St George. And that admirable temple of St Sophia! It is an Aryan temple: the whole human species might have made its prayers there. Not having had either people, inquisition, scholasticism, or Middle Age barbarism, having always preserved a leaven of Arianism, Greece rejected with greater facility than any other country a supernatural Christianity, just as those Athenians of former times were at once (thanks to a sort of vivacity which was a thousand times more profound than the seriousness of our dull races) the most superstitious of peoples, and the nearest approach to Rationalism. The popular Greek songs are still to-day charged with Pagan images and ideas. Differing so widely from the West, the East remained during the Middle Ages, and down to modern times, true "Hellenists;" at bottom more Pagan than Christian, living on a religion of old Greek patriotism, and of old authors. These Hellenists were, in the fifteenth century, the promoters of the Renaissance in the West, to which they affixed Greek texts, the basis of all civilisation. The same spirit has presided, and will continue to preside, over the destinies of new Greece. When we have fully studied that which made of us bears the caul of a cultivated Hellenist, we see that there is in him very little Christianity: he is Christian in form, as a Persian is a Mussulman, but at bottom he is "Hellenist." His religion is the adoration of the ancient Greek genius. He pardons every heresy to philo-Hellenism, to him who admires its past: he is much less a disciple of Jesus and of St Paul, than of Plutarch and of Julian.

Wearied by his little success at Athens, Paul, without awaiting the return of Timothy, departed for Corinth. He had not formed at Athens any considerable Church. There were only a few isolated persons, among others a certain Dionysius, who belonged, it is said, to the Areopagus, and a woman, named Damaris, who had adhered to his doctrines. This was, then, in his apostolic career, his first and almost only check.

Even in the second century the Church at Athens is of little importance. Athens was one of the cities which was the last to be converted. After Constantine, she is the centre of opposition against Christianity, the bulwark of philosophy. By a rare privilege she preserved the temples intact. These prodigious monuments, protected through the ages, thanks to a sort of instinctive respect, were to come down to us as an eternal lesson of good sense and honesty, given by artists of genius. Even to-day we feel that the Christian covering which is spread over the old Pagan foundation is very superficial. It is hardly necessary to modify the actual names of the churches at Athens to find again the names of the ancient temples.

CHAPTER VIII

CONTINUATION OF THE SECOND JOURNEY OF PAUL--FIST SOJOURN AT CORINTH

Departing from Phalera or Piræus, Paul arrived at Cenchrea, which was the port of Corinth on the Ægæan Sea. It is a pretty enough little harbour. It is surrounded by verdant hills and pine woods, and is situated at the extremity of the Gulf of Saronica. A beautiful open valley, nearly two leagues in extent, reaches from that port to the great city built at the foot of the colossal dome from which can be seen the two seas.

Corinth was a field much better adapted than Athens to receive the new seed. It was not like Athens a sort of sanctuary of thought, a city sacred and unique to the world; it was even hardly a Hellenic city. Ancient Corinth had been razed to. its foundations by Mummius. For a hundred years the soil of the Achaian Confederation was desert. In the year 44 B.C. Julius Cæsar rebuilt the city and made it an important Roman colony, which he peopled principally with freedmen. This is equivalent to saying that the population was very heterogeneous. It was composed of a conglomeration of those peoples of every sort and of every origin which loved Cæsar. The new Corinthians remained for a long time strangers to Greece, where they were regarded as intruders. Their entertainments consisted of the brutal games of the Romans, which were repulsive to true Greeks. Corinth became thus a city like so many others on the shores of the Mediterranean, very populous, wealthy, brilliant, frequented by many strangers, a centre of commercial activity, one of those conglomerate cities, in short, which no longer contained patriots. The dominant trait which rendered its name proverbial was the exceeding corruption of manners which was remarked there. In this again it constituted an exception amongst the Hellenic cities. The purely Greek manners were simple and gay, and could on no account be held to be luxurious and debauched. The affluence of the mariners who were attracted thence by the two ports, had made of Corinth the last sanctuary of the worship of Venus Pandemos, a remnant of the ancient Phoenician establishments. The great temple of Venus had more than a thousand consecrated courtesans; the whole city was like a vast pandemonium, where numerous strangers, sailors particularly, resorted to spend their wealth foolishly.

There was at Corinth a colony of Jews, which was probably established at Cenchrea, one of the ports which was used in trading with the East. A short time before the arrival of Paul, a colony of Jews, which had been expelled from Rome by the edict of Claudius, had disembarked, and among the number were Aquila and Priscilla, who, it seems, at that time already professed the faith of Christ. From all this there resulted a concomitance of circumstances most favourable. The isthmus formed between the two masses of the Greek continent has always been the seat of a world-wide commerce. It had always been one of those emporiums, quite irrespective of race or of nationality, designed to be the headquarters, if I might say so, of infant Christianity. New Corinth, on account of its having few Hellenic nobility, was a city already semi-christianised. With Antioch, Ephesus, Thessalonica, and Rome, she became an ecclesiastical metropolis of the first rank. But the immorality which reigned should at the same time have presaged that the first abuses in the history of the Church would be produced there. In a few years Corinth shall present tows the spectacle of incestuous Christians, and of drunken people sitting down to the table of Christ.

Paul quickly divined that a long sojourn at Corinth would be necessary. He resolved hence to take up there a fixed abode, and to prosecute his trade of upholsterer. Now, strictly speaking, Aquila and Priscilla followed the same trade as Paul. He went there to live with them, and the three set up a small shop, which was stocked by them with ready-made articles.

Timothy, whom Paul had sent from Athens to Thessalonica, soon rejoined him. The news from the Church at Thessalonica was excellent. All the faithful continued in the faith and in charity, and in their attachment to their master. The persecutions of their fellow-citizens had not shaken them; brotherly love prevailed throughout Macedonia. Silas, whom Paul had not seen since his flight from Beræa, had probably been joined by Timothy, and returned with the latter. What is certain is, that the three companions found themselves reunited at Corinth, and that they lived there together for a long time.

The attention of Paul was, as usual, first directed to the Jews. Each Sabbath he spoke in the synagogue. He found there dispositions greatly diverse, One family, that of Stephenephorus or Stephanus, was converted, and were all baptised by Paul. The orthodox resisted energetically, even to the extent of injuring and of anathematising them. One day, finally, there was an open rupture. Paul shook the dust off his raiment upon the incredulous of the assembly, made them responsible for the consequences, and declared to them that, seeing they closed their ears to the truth, he would go unto the Gentiles. Having uttered these words, he left the hall. He taught henceforth in the house of one Titus Justus, a man that feared God, and whose house was contiguous to the synagogue. Crispus, the chief of the Jewish community, belonged to the party of Paul; he was converted with his whole house, and Paul baptised him himself, a thing of rare occurrence.

Many others, both Jews and Pagans, and those "fearing God," were baptised. The number of converted Pagans appeared to be here relatively considerable. Paul displayed prodigious zeal. Several divine visions which came to him during the night fortified him. The fame of the conversions he had made at Thessalonica, nevertheless, preceded him, and had favourably disposed the religious society in his behalf. The supernatural phenomena were not wanting: there were some miracles. Innocence was not the same thing here as at Philippi and Thessalonica. The corrupt manners of Corinth crossed sometimes the threshold of the Church; at any rate, all those who entered it were not equally pure. But, in return, few of the Churches were more numerous; the community of Corinth irradiated the whole province of Achaia, and became the home of Christianity in the Hellenic peninsula. Without speaking of Aquila and of Priscilla--almost received in the rank of apostles--and of Titus Justus, of Crispus, of Stephanus--mentioned above--the Church numbered in its bosom Gaius, who was himself also baptised by Paul, and who extended hospitality to the Apostle during the second sojourn of the latter in Corinth; Quartus, Achaicus, Fortunatus, Erastus, rather an important personage, who was treasurer of the city; a woman named Chloe, who had a numerous household. We have only vague and uncertain notions in regard to one Zenas, a doctor of Jewish law. Stephanus and his household constituted the most influential group, the one which had the most authority. All the converts, nevertheless, with the probable exception of Erastus, were simple-minded people, without much instruction, without social distinction, drawn, in a word, from the humblest ranks.

The port of Cenchrea had likewise its Church. Cenchrea was in great part peopled by Orientals. There one could reverence Isis and Eschmoun, while the Phoenician Venus was not neglected. It was like Calamaki in our days, less a city than a mass of shops and inns for seafaring men. In the midst of the corruption of these filthy hovels of seafarers, Christianity produced its miracle. Cenchrea possessed an admirable deaconess, who, one day, as we shall see later on, concealed under the folds of her woman's garments the whole future of Christian theology, the writing which was to regulate the faith of the world. She was named Phoebe. She was an active person, never at rest, always eager to render service, and who was very precious to Paul.

The sojourn of Paul at Corinth lasted for eighteen months. The beautiful rock of Acrocorinth, the snowy summits of Helicon and of Parnassus, remained for a long time in his regards. Paul contracted in that new religious family some deep friendships, although the taste of the Greeks for disputation displeased him; while on more than one occasion his natural timidity may have been increased by the disposition of his auditors to subtlety. He could not detach himself from Thessalonica, from the simplicity he had found there, from the lively affections he had there left behind him. The Church at Thessalonica was the model which he never ceased to proclaim, and to-wards which he always reverted. The Church at Philippi, with its pious women, its rich and good Lydia, was not allowed to be forgotten. That Church, as we have seen, enjoyed a singular privilege; which was, to nourish the Apostle when his labour did not suffice to do so. At Corinth he received from her fresh succour. As if the somewhat sprightly nature of the Corinthians, and of the Greeks in general, had inspired him with distrust, he would not accept anything of this kind from them, although more than once he found himself reduced to want during his sojourn in their midst.

It was with difficulty, nevertheless, that the anger of the orthodox Jews, always so active, was restrained from breaking out. The preachings of the Apostle to the Gentiles, his broad principles in regard to the adoption of all those who believed, and their incorporation into the family of Abraham, irritated to the highest pitch the partisans of the exclusive privilege of the children of Israel. The Apostle, on his part, was not very sparing in hard words. He announced to them that the anger of God was about to break out against them. The Jews had recourse to the Roman authorities. Corinth was the capital of the province of Achaia, comprising the whole of Greece, and which ordinarily was joined to Macedonia. The two provinces had been made senatorials by Claudius, and in virtue of which they had a pro-consul. That position was filled at the time of which we speak by one of the most amiable and best instructed men of the century--Marcus Annæus Novatus, elder brother of Seneca, who had been adopted by the rhetorician L. Junius Gallio, one of the litterateurs of the society of the Senecas: Marcus Annæus Novatus took hence the name of Gallio. He had a great mind and a noble soul, was a friend of the poets and of the celebrated authors. Every one who knew him adored him. Statius called him *dulcis Gallio*, and probably he was the author of some of the tragedies which proceeded from that literary roof. He wrote, it seems, upon natural philosophy. His brother dedicated to him his book on Anger and Happy Life; people attributed to him one of the most intellectual works of the period. It appears that it was his high Hellenic culture which, under the learned Claudius, led to his selection for the administration of a province which all governments, somewhat enlightened, surrounded with delicate attentions. His sanctity obliged him to abandon the post. Like his brother, he had, under Nero, the honour of expiating by his death his distinction and his honesty.

Such a man was little disposed to agree to the demands of fanatics coming to ask the civil power, which they protested against in secret, to rid them of their enemies. One day Sosthenes, the new ruler of the synagogue, who had succeeded Crispus, brought Paul before the judgment seat, and accused him of preaching a religion contrary to the law. Judaism, in fact, which had old authorisations, and all sorts of guarantees, pretended that the dissentient sect, as soon as they had made a schism in the synagogue, enjoyed no longer the charters of a synagogue. The situation was one which would have brought before the French law liberal Protestants on the day they separated themselves from recognised Protestantism. Paul was going to answer, but Gallio restrained him, and, addressing the Jews, said: "If it were a matter of wrong or wicked lewdness, O ye Jews, reason were that I should bear with you; but if it be a question of words and of names, and of your law, look ye to it, for I will be no judge of such matters." This was an admirable response, worthy of being set up as a model to civil governments when they are invited to meddle with religious questions. Gallio, after he had pronounced it, gave orders to drive away both parties. A great tumult ensued. Everybody was seized with the desire to fall upon Sosthenes, and he was beaten before the judgment seat, and no one could tell whence the blows proceeded. Gallio paid little heed, and caused the place to be cleared. The sage politician had avoided entering into a dogmatic quarrel; the well-educated man refused to mix himself up with a quarrel of vulgar people; and when he saw violence break out, he sent every one away.

No doubt it would have been wiser not to appear so disdainful. Gallio was well inspired in declaring himself to be incompetent to judge in a question of schism and of heresy; but yet men of mind have sometimes little prescience! It was discovered later that the quarrel of these abject sectaries was the great affair of the century. If, instead of treating a religious and social question with that unceremoniousness, the government had taken the trouble to make an impartial investigation, to make a searching public investigation, and to discontinue giving an official sanction to a religion become completely absurd; if Gallio had been disposed to take into account what it was that constituted a Jew and a Christian, to read Jewish books, to keep himself au courant of what was passing in the subterranean world; if the Romans had not been so narrow-minded, so little addicted to the study of science, many misfortunes would have been avoided. How very singular! There was, in the case now under consideration, on the one hand, a man who was one of the most intellectual and the most studious; on the other, a soul which was one of the most robust and the most original of his time, and they passed the one before the other without either perceiving the fact; and, surely, if the first blows had fallen upon Paul instead of upon Sosthenes, Gallio would have been equally indifferent. One of the things which causes the most faults to be committed by people of the world, is the superficial disgust which badly educated and unmannerly people inspire in them yet manners are only a matter of form, and those who have them not are found sometimes not to be destitute of good sense. The society man, with his frivolous sneers, passes continually, without knowing it, the man who is going to create the future; they do not belong to the same world; yet the common error of society people is to think that the world which they see is the entire world.

These difficulties, however, were not the only ones that the Apostle had to encounter. The Corinthian mission was thwarted by obstacles which, for the first time, he had met with in his Apostolic career,--obstacles proceeding from the bosom of the Church itself, from intractable men who had been introduced to it, and who opposed him, or from many Jews who had been attracted to Jesus, but more attached than Paul to legal observances. The false spirit of the degenerated Greek who, starting from the fourth century, corrupted Christianity so much, was already making itself felt. The Apostle then called to mind his beloved Churches at Macedonia, that unlimited docility, that purity of morals, that frank cordiality, which had procured for him at Philippi and Thessalonica such happy days. He was seized with an ardent desire to go and see once more the faithful of the Lord, and when be received from them an expression of the same desire, he could hardly restrain himself. In order to comfort himself in this embarrassment, and to protect himself from the importunities of those with whom he was surrounded, it pleased him to write to them. The epistles dated from Corinth bear the imprint of a kind of sadness,-- praises of the most lofty description for those to whom Paul wrote; but these letters were completely silent, or contained some unfavourable allusions to those from whose midst he wrote.

CHAPTER IX

CONTINUATION OF THE SECOND JOURNEY OF PAUL--FIRST EPISTLES--INTERIOR CONDITION OF THE NEW CHURCHES

It was at Corinth that the apostolic life of Paul attained its highest degree of activity. To the cares of the grand Christianity which he was engaged in founding, he had just added the prepossessions of the communities that he had left behind him. A sort of jealousy, as he has told us himself, devoured him. He thought less at that moment of founding new Churches than of caring for those which he had created. Each of his Churches was to him as a bride which he had promised to Christ, and which he wished to preserve pure. The power that he claimed over these little corporations was absolute. A certain number of rules, which he regarded as having been laid down by Jesus himself, was the sole canonical law anterior to himself that he recognised. He was thought to have divine inspiration for adding to those rules all those which the new circumstances called for, and which had to be obeyed. But was not his example a supreme rule to which all his spiritual children might conform themselves?

Timothy, whom he employed to visit the Churches that were far away from him, could not, had he been indefatigable, satisfy the immense ardour of his master. It was then that Paul conceived the idea of supplying by correspondence what he was prevented from saying himself or through his principal disciples. There did not exist in the Roman Empire anything which resembled our postal establishment for private letters; all correspondence had to be forwarded incidentally, or by express. St Paul hence made it a point to take everywhere with him persons of a second order, who could be used as messengers. Correspondence between the synagogues already existed in Judaism. The envoy charged with bearing the letters was himself a dignitary drawn from the synagogues. The epistolary style formed amongst the Jews a species of literature which was continued amongst them down to the heart of the Middle Ages, as a consequence of their dispersion. Without doubt, from the period when Christianity was extended to the whole of Syria, Christian epistles existed; but in the hands of Paul these writings, which up till then had not, for the most part, been preserved, were, equally with his speaking, the instruments of progress in the Christian faith. It was held that the authority of the Epistles equalled that of the Apostle himself; they were all to be read before the Church assembled; some of them had even the character of circular letters, and were communicated successively to various Churches. The reading of the correspondence thus became an essential part of the offices of the Sabbath. And it was not merely at the moment of its reception that a letter served thus for the edification of the brethren; deposited in the Church archives, it was taken from there on days of assembling, and read as a sacred document, and as a perpetual source of instruction. The epistle was thus the form of primitive Christian literature. It was an admirable form, perfectly adapted to the conditions of the times, and to the natural aptitude of Paul.

The condition of the new sect, in fact, did not by any means permit of connected discourse. Infant Christianity was wholly disengaged from texts. The hymns even were composed by each for him-self, and were not written. People believed in watching for the final catastrophe. The sacred books, which we call the "Scriptures," were the books of the ancient Law. Jesus had added no new book. He must return to fulfil the ancient Scriptures, and to open an age in which he himself would be the living book. Letters of consolation and of encouragement were the only means which could produce a similar state of mind. If already, about the time at which we are arrived, there had been more than a small booklet, designed to assist the memory in regard to "the sayings and doings" of Jesus, these booklets were of an entirely private character. They were not authentic, official writings, universally received in the community; they were notes of which persons au courant of events took little account, and were considered as altogether an inferior authority to tradition.

Paul, as regarded himself, had not a mind adapted to the composition of books. He had not the patience that is required for writing; he was incapable of system; the labour of the pen was disagreeable to him, and he preferred to delegate it to others. Correspondence, on the contrary, so obnoxious to those who are accustomed to employ an art in putting forth their ideas, suited well his feverish activity, and the necessity of expressing on the spur of the moment his impressions. Now brisk, crude, polite, snarlish, sarcastic, then suddenly tender, delicate, almost roguish and coaxing; happily expressed and polished to the highest degree; skilful in sprinkling his language with reticences, reserves, infinite precautions, malignant allusions, and ironical dissimulations, he came to excel in a style which required above everything original impulses. The epistolary style of Paul is the most individual that we have ever had. Its language, if I may say so, is ground up (hoyee), without a single consecutive phrase. It would be impossible to violate more audaciously, I do not say the genius of the Greek language, but the logic of human language. It might be described as a rapid conversation, stenographed and reproduced without corrections. Timothy was quickly trained to fulfil for his master the functions of secretary, and as his language came to resemble somewhat that of Paul, he replaced him frequently. It is probable that in the Epistles and perhaps in the Acts we have more than one page of Timothy; but such was the modesty of that singular man, that we have no certain marks by which to single them out.

Even when Paul corresponded directly, he did not write with his own hand; he dictated; sometimes when the letter was finished he re-read it. His impetuous soul carried him away at such moments; he made marginal additions to it, at the risk of injuring the context, and of producing suspended and entangled sentences. He transmitted the letter thus effaced, regardless of the numberless repetitions of words and of ideas which it contained. With his marvellous fervour of soul, Paul has yet a singular poverty of expression. A phrase besets him, he recurs to it in a page at every turn. It was not sterility, it was contentiousness of mind and complete indifference to the requirements of a correct style. In order to avoid the numerous frauds to which the passions of the times gave rise, the authority of the Apostle and the material conditions of antique epistolography, Paul was in the habit of sending to the Churches a specimen of his writing, which was easily recognisable; this done, it was sufficient for him, according to a usage then general, to put at the end of his letters some words in his own hand as a guarantee of their authenticity.

There is no doubt that the correspondence of Paul was considerable, and that what is remaining of it to us constitutes only a small portion. The religion of the primitive Churches was so detached in every way, so purely idealistic, that people did not realise the immense value of such writings. Faith was everything: each one carried it in one's heart, and cared little for stray leaves of papyrus, which, besides, were not holograph. These epistles were for the majority mere occasional pieces; nobody suspected that one day they would become sacred books. It was only towards the end of the life of the Apostle that people bethought themselves of retaining his letters because of their intrinsic merit,--of passing them on and of preserving them. Then each Church guarded preciously its own, consulted them often, had regular lectures on them, allowed copies to be taken of them; still, a multitude of letters of the first period were irrecoverably lost. As for the letters in response to those of the Churches, all have disappeared; and it could not be otherwise; Paul in his wandering existence never had any other archives than his memory and his heart.

Two letters only of the second mission remain with us: they are the two epistles to the Church at Thessalonica. Paul wrote them from Corinth, and joined with his own name in the superscription those of Silas and Timothy. They have the appearance of being composed at a short interval from one another. They are two productions full of unction, tenderness, emotion, and charm. In them the Apostle does not conceal his preference for the Churches of Macedonia: He made use of the latter to give utterance to that love for glowing expressions, for images the most endearing; he represents himself as the kind nurse cherishing her children in her bosom, as a father charging his children. This was indeed what Paul was for the Churches he had established. He was an admirable missionary, and, what was more, an admirable director of consciences. Never did he appear to better advantage than in having the charge of souls; never did any one take up the problem of the education of man in a more enthusiastic and thorough manner. But it must not be thought that he acquired that ascendency through fawning and flattery. No; Paul was blunt, disagreeable, and sometimes ill-tempered. In no respect did he resemble Jesus; he had not his charming indulgence, his habit of excusing everybody, his divine incapacity of seeing evil. He was often imperious, and made his authority to be felt with a haughtiness which shocks us. He commanded, he blamed severely, he spoke of himself with assurance, and unhesitatingly held himself up as a model. But what haughtiness! what purity! what disinterestedness! Upon the last point he is painfully minute. Ten times he reverts with pride to the apparently puerile fact that he had cost no man anything, that he had never eaten gratis the bread of any one, that he had laboured day and night with his hands, although he might well have done like the other Apostles, and lived by religion. The bent of his zeal was, in a manner infinite, a love of souls.

The kindness, the innocence, the fraternal spirit, the unlimited charity of the primitive Churches, are a spectacle which will never again be seen. It was wholly spontaneous, unconstrained, and yet these little associations were as solid as iron. Not only could they resist the perpetual bickerings of the Jews, but their interior organisation possessed surprising force. In order to understand them, it is necessary to think, not of our grand churches open to all, but of religious orders endowed with a most intense individual life,--of confraternities firmly consolidated, in which the members by turns embraced, animated, quarrelled with, loved, hated one another. These Churches had a kind of hierarchy: the oldest members, the most active, those who were en rapport with the Apostle, enjoyed a precedence! But the Apostle himself was the first to repress everything which had the appearance of domineering; he held himself to be only "the promoter of the common joy."

The "elders" were sometimes elected by the common voice,--that is to say, by a show of hands,--sometimes installed by the Apostle, but always considered as chosen by the Holy Spirit, that is to say, by that superior instinct which directed the Church in all its acts. People began already to call them "deacons" (episcopi, a word which in the language of politics had passed into the eranes), and to consider them as "pastors" charged with the conduct of the Church. Certain of them, moreover, were regarded as having a sort of speciality for teaching; these were catechists, going from house to house, and imparting the word of God in private admonitions. Paul made it a rule, at least in particular cases, that the catechumen, during his instruction, was to share all that he possessed in common with his catechist.

Full authority belonged to the Church assembled. This authority was extended to the minutest details of private life. All the brethren watched one another, corrected one another. The Church assembled, or at at least those who were called "the devout," reprimanded those who were in fault, consoled the cast-down, and undertook the office of skilled directors, versed in the knowledge of the heart. Public penitences had not yet been instituted; but they no doubt already existed in embryo. As no exterior force restrained the faithful, nor prevented them from splitting or abandoning the Church, we should have thought that such an organisation, which appears to us insupportable, in which is only to be seen a system of espionage and of accusation, would speedily have come to an end. But nothing of the kind. We do not find, at the period at which we have now arrived, a single example of apostacy. Every one submitted humbly to the sentence of the Church. He whose conduct was irregular, or who had strayed from the traditions of the Apostles, or who was not attentive to his duties, was marked; he was avoided; no one would hold communion with him. He was treated as an enemy, though he was at the same time admonished as a brother. This isolation covered him with shame, and he repented. The gaiety in these little companies of good people living together, always sprightly, occupied, eager, loving and hating much, the gaiety, I say, was very great. Verily the words of Jesus had been fulfilled; the reign of the meek and lowly had come, and had been manifested by the extreme felicity which flowed from every heart.

People had a perfect horror of Paganism, but were very tolerant in their treatment of Pagans. Far from fleeing from them, people sought to attract them and to gain them over. Many of the faithful had been idolaters, or had parents who were; they knew with what good faith one might be in error. They recalled their honest ancestors, who had died without having known saving truth. A touching custom, baptism for the dead, was the consequence of that sentiment. People believed that in being baptised for those of their ancestors who had not received holy water, they conferred on them the merits of the sacrament; thus the hope of not being separated from those that they loved was not frustrated. A profound idea of solidarity dominated every one; the son was saved through his parents, the father through the son, the husband through the wife. People could not be brought to condemn a man of good intentions, or who through any side way whatever clung to the saints.

Manners were severe, though not sad. That virtuous gloom which the rigorists of modern times (Janissaries, Methodists, etc.) preach as a Christian virtue, had no existence then. The relations between men and women, far from being interdicted, were multiplied. One of the scoffs of the Pagans was to represent the Christians as effeminate, deserting common society for the conventicles of young women, old women, and children. Pagan nakednesses were severely condemned. The women, in general, were closely veiled: not a single precaution for protecting timid chastity was omitted; but the bashful woman is also a voluptuous woman, and the ideal dream which is in man is susceptible of a thousand applications. When we read the Acts of St Perpetue, the legend of St Dorothy, we see that they are the heroines of an absolute purity; but how little do they resemble a Port Royal female religionist! Here, one-half of the instincts of humanity is suppressed; there, these instincts, which later on came to be regarded as Satanic suggestions, had received only a new direction. It may be said that primitive Christianity was a sort of moral romanticism, a powerful revulsion of the faculty of loving. Christianity did not diminish that faculty; it took no precautions against it; it did not place it under suspicion--it nourished it with air and with light. The danger of these liberties was not yet manifest. In the Church, the bad was, in some sort, impossible, for the root of evil, which is wicked desire, was taken away.

The position of catechist was often filled by women. Virginity was regarded as a state of sanctity. This preference accorded to the celibate was not a negation of love and of beauty, like that which found place in the barren and unintelligible asceticism of later centuries. It was, in a woman, that just and true sentiment which virtue and beauty prize so much the more the more it is concealed; so that she who has not found that rare peril of strong love, guards, by a sort of pride and of reserve, its beauty and moral perfection for God alone, for God conceived as jealous, as the co-partner of close secrets. Second marriages, though not forbidden, were regarded as a mark against one. The popular sentiment of the century ran in that groove. The beautiful and touching expression of σύμβιος became the ordinary word for "spouse." The words Virginius, Virginia, Παρθενιχός, indicating the husbands who had not formed other alliances, became terms of eulogy and of tenderness. The spirit of the family, the union of husband

and wife, their reciprocal esteem, the recognition by the husband of the cares and the foresight of his wife, permeated in a touching manner the Jewish inscriptions, which in this only reflected the sentiment of the humble classes amongst which the Christian propaganda recruited converts. It is a singular thing that the most elevated ideas on the sanctity of marriage have been spread in the world by a people amongst whom polygamy had never been universally interdicted. But it required, in the fraction of Jewish society in which Christianity was formed, that polygamy should actually be abolished, since the Church did not seem to think that such an enormity needed to be condemned.

Charity, brotherly love, was the supreme law, and common to all the churches and all the schools. Charity and chastity were par excellence Christian virtues,--virtues which made a success of the new gospel, and converted the entire world. One was commanded to do good to all: nevertheless, co-religionists were regarded as being worthy of preference. A taste for work was held to be a virtue. Paul, a good workman, vigorously reproved indolence and idleness, and repeated often that naïf proverb of a man of the people: "He that would not work, neither should he eat." The model that he conceived was a punctual artisan, peaceable, applying himself to his work, eating tranquilly--his mind at ease--the bread that he earned. But how far are we from the primitive ideal of the Church at Jerusalem, wholly communistic and monastical, or even from that of Antioch, wholly preoccupied with prophecies, with supernatural gifts, with apostleship! Here the Church is an association of honest workmen, cheerful, content, not jealous of the rich, for they are more happy than the latter, for they know that God does not judge like the worldly, and prefers the honest soiled hand to the white and intriguing hand. One of his principal virtues was to conduct his affairs orderly; "that ye may walk honestly toward them that are without, and that ye may have lack of nothing." There were some members of the Church, of whom St Paul had heard tell, who worked not at all, but were busy-bodies, and who are severely reprimanded. That combination of practical good sense and of delusion ought not to surprise. Does not the English race in Europe and in America present to us the same contrast, so full of good sense as regards things of this world, so absurd as regards things pertaining to heaven? Quakerism, even, commenced with a tissue of absurdities, and retained them until the day, thanks to the influence of William Penn, it became something practical, great, and fruitful.

The supernatural gifts of the Holy Spirit, such as prophecy, were not neglected. But we can well see that in the Churches of Greece, composed of Jews, these fantastic exercises possessed no longer much meaning, and we can believe that they soon fell into desuetude. Christian discipline turned on a kind of deistic piety, which consisted in serving the true God, in praying and in doing good. A powerful hope gave to these precepts of pure religion the efficacy that of themselves never could possess. The dream that had been the soul of the movement inaugurated by Jesus, continued still to be the fundamental dogma of Christianity; everybody believed in the near future of the kingdom of God, in the unseen manifestation of a great glory, from the midst of which the Son of Man would appear. The idea that people had of that marvellous phenomena was the same as in the times of Jesus. A great storm--that is to say, a terrible catastrophe--was near at hand: that catastrophe would strike all those whom Jesus would not have saved. Jesus was to show himself in the heavens as "king of glory, surrounded by angels." Then the judgment was to take place. The saints, the persecuted, were to go and range themselves about Jesus, in order to enjoy with him eternal rest. The unbelievers who had persecuted them (the Jews especially) were to be the prey of fire; their punishment was to be eternal death. Chased from before the face of Jesus, they were to be hurried away to the abyss of destruction. A destroying fire, in short, was to be lighted and was to consume the world and all those who had rejected the gospel of Jesus. That final catastrophe was to be a kind of great and glorious manifestation of Jesus and his saints, an act of supreme justice, a tardy reparation for the iniquities which had been up to that time the rule of the world.

Objections were naturally raised against this strange doctrine. One of the principal of them arose from the difficulty of conceiving what should be the portion of the dead at the moment of the advent of Jesus. Since the visit of Paul, there had been several deaths in the Church at Thessalonica, and these first deaths had made, on all sides, a very deep impression. Was it necessary to compassionate, and to regard as excluded from the kingdom of God, those who had thus disappeared before the solemn hour? The ideas upon individual immortality and a special judgment were yet too little developed to enable people to sustain auy such objection. Paul responded with remarkable clearness:--

"That ye may walk honestly toward them that are without, and that ye may have lack of nothing. But I would not have you to be ignorant, brethren, concerning them which are asleep, that ye sorrow not, even as others which have no hope. For if we believe that Jesus died and rose again, even so them also which sleep in Jesus will God bring with him. For this we say unto you by the word of the Lord, that we which are alive and remain unto the coming of the Lord shall not prevent them which are asleep. For the Lord himself shall descend from heaven with a shout, with the voice of the archangel, and with the trump of God: and the dead in Christ shall rise first; then we which are alive and remain shall be caught up together with them in the clouds, to meet the Lord in the air: and so shall we ever be with the Lord."

People sought to discover the day of that grand appearance. St Paul condemned these inquisitive speculations, and made use of them in order to show the almost worthlessness of the words themselves which people had attributed to Jesus.

"But of the times and the season, brethren, ye have no need that I write unto you. For yourselves know perfectly that the day of the Lord so cometh as a thief in the night. For when they shall say, Peace and safety; then sudden destruction cometh upon them, as travail upon a woman child; and they shall not escape. But ye, brethren, are not in darkness, that that day should overtake you as a thief. Ye are all the children of light, and the children of the day; we are not of the night, nor of darkness. Therefore let us not sleep, as do others; but let us watch and be sober."

The preoccupation of that near catastrophe was extreme. The enthusiasts believed that they had discovered the date by means of special revelations. There existed already several apocalypses; people went even the length of causing forged letters of the Apostle to be circulated, in which this end of things was announced,--

"Now we beseech you, brethren, by the coming of our Lord Jesus Christ, and by our gathering together unto him, That ye be not soon shaken in mind, or be troubled, neither by spirit, nor by word, nor by letter as from us, as that the day of Christ is at hand. Let no man deceive you by any means; for that day shall not come, except there come a falling away first, and that man of sin be revealed, the son of perdition. Who opposeth and exalteth himself above all that is called God or that is worshipped; so that he as God sitteth in the temple of God, shewing himself that he is God. Remember ye not, that, when I was yet with you, I told you these things! And now ye know what withholdeth that he might be revealed in his time. For the mystery of iniquity doth already work; only he who now letteth will let, until he be taken out of the way. And then shall the Wicked be revealed, whom that Lord shall consume with the spirit of his mouth, and shall destroy with the brightness of his coming; even him, whose coming is after the working of Satan with all power and signs and lying wonders, and with all deceivableness of unrighteousness in them that perish; because they received not the love of the truth that they might be saved. And for this cause God shall send them strong delusion, that they should believe a lie."

We see that in these texts, written twenty years after the death of Jesus, only a single essential element has been added to the description of the day of the Lord such as Jesus had conceived it, namely, the character of an Anti-Christ, or false Christ, which was to spring up before the grand appearance of Jesus himself--a sort of Satanic Messiah, who was to work miracles, and desire to be worshipped. Apropos of Simon the Magician, we have already met with the singular idea that the false prophets worked miracles exactly like the true prophets. The opinion that the judgment of God would be preceded by a terrible catastrophe, by the spread of impiety and abominations, by the passing triumph of idolatry, by the advent of a sacrilegious king, was, however, very ancient, going back as far as the first origins of the apocalyptic doctrines. Gradually that ephemeral reign of evil, the precursor of the final victory of the good, which would happen to the Christians, would be personified in a man who was conceived to be the exact converse of Jesus, a sort of Christ of the infernal regions.

The type of that future misleader was composed in part out of recollections of Antiochus Epiphanes, such as he is presented in the book of Daniel, combined with the reminiscences of Balaam, of Gog and Magog, of Nebuchadnezzar, and partly from ideas borrowed from the circumstances of the times. The ghastly tragedy that was being enacted at Rome at that moment, in face of the world, could not fail but excite greatly the imaginations of men. Caligula, the anti-deity, the first emperor who sought to be worshipped during his life, suggested in all probability the circumstance to Paul, when the aforesaid person exalted himself above all the pretended gods, all the idols, and took his seat in the temple of Jerusalem, desirous of being regarded as God himself. The Anti-Christ was thus conceived in the year 54 as a continuer of the foolish sacrilege of Caligula. Reality affords but too many opportunities to explain away such presages. A few months after Paul wrote that strange passage, Nero came to the throne. It was in him that the Christian conscience should see later on the hideous precursor of the coming of Christ. What was the cause, or rather who was the personage, that alone, in the year 54, still prevented, according to Saint Paul, the appearance of Anti-Christ? This has been left in obscurity. The question's here asked may perhaps have been a mysterious secret, no strange thing in politics, which the faithful discussed among themselves, but which they did not commit to paper, for fear of compromising one another. The mere seizure of a letter would have sufficed to bring about the most atrocious persecutions. Here, as in other points, the habit which the early Christians had of not writing down certain things, has created for us irremediable obscurities. It has been supposed that the personage in question was the Emperor Claudius, and we have seen in the language of Paul a play of words on his name,--Claudius = qui claudit = ὁ χατέχων. At the date when that letter was written, in fact, the death of poor Claudius--circumvented by fatal snares laid by the villainous Agrippa--seemed only to be a question of time; everybody expected it; the Emperor himself spoke of it; dark presentiments showed themselves at every turn; natural prodigies like those which, fourteen years later, struck so forcibly the author of the Apocalypse, tormented the popular imagination. People spoke in terror of the monstrous foetus,--of a son which had the long claws of a sparrow-hawk; all this made people tremble for the future. The Christians, like ordinary people, participated in these terrors; the prognostications, and the superstitious fears of natural calamities, were the essential cause of the Apocalyptic fears.

That which is clear; that which still is revealed for us in these inestimable documents; that which explains the wonderful success of the Christian propaganda, is the spirit of devotion, the high morality which reigned in those little Churches. They might be compared to the reunions of the Moravian brothers, or to pious Protestants addicted to the extremest devotion, or, again, to a sort of third order of a Catholic congregation. Prayer and the name of Jesus were constantly on the lips of the faithful. Before each act, before partaking of food, for example, they pronounced a short benediction or short act of grace. It was looked upon as an injury done to the Church, to bring an action before the civil judges. The belief in the near destruction of the world raised a revolutionary ferment which carried into every mind a great portion of its sourness. The invariable rule of the Apostle was, that it was necessary for one to abide in the state to which one had been called. "Is any person called (being) circumcised, let him not dissimulate circumcision; is any person called uncircumcised, let him not be circumcised; is any one a virgin, let her remain a virgin; is any one married, let such remain married; is any one a slave, seek not to be made free; and even if one can obtain one's freedom, let such a one remain in slavery. The slave who is called, is the free servant of Christ; the free man who is called, is the slave of Christ." A marvellous resignation had taken possession of souls, which rendered everything indifferent, and shed over all the weariness of that world, extinct and forgotten.

The Church was a permanent source of edification and of consolation. It must not be imagined that the Christian gatherings of those times were modelled after the cold assemblies of our days, in which the unforeseen, the individual initiative, had no part. It is rather of the English Quakers, the American Shakers, and the French Spiritualists, that one must think. During the meeting all were seated, and each spoke when he felt inspired. The inspired one would then rise up, and deliver, through the impulse of the Spirit, discourses of various forms, which it is difficult for us to distinguish to-day--psalms, canticles of acts of grace, eulogies, prophecies, revelations, lessons, exhortations, consolations, and treatises on language. These improvisations, considered as divine oracles, were sometimes chanted, sometimes delivered in a speaking tone of voice. Each invited his neighbour to do this; each excited the enthusiasm of others: it was what was called singing to God. The women remained silent. As every one believed oneself to be constantly visited by the Spirit, every image, every throb which crossed the brain of the believers, seemed to contain a deep meaning, and, with the most perfect good faith in the world, they drew a real nourishment of soul from pure illusions. After each eulogy, each prayer thus improvised, the multitude had a collective inspiration through the word Amen. In order to mark the diverse acts of the mystic seance, the president interposed, either by the invitation Oremus; or by a sigh directed towards heaven--Sursum Corda! or in recalling that Jesus, according to his promise, was in the midst of the assembled--Dominus Vobiscum. The cry Kyrie Eleison was also repeated frequently in a suppliant and plaintive tone.

Prophecy was esteemed a high gift: some women were endowed with it. In many cases, especially when the matter in hand had reference to philology, people hesitated; people sometimes even believed themselves to be dupes of a cunning device of the evil spirits. A particular class of the inspired, or, as was said, of the "spiritual," was charged with the interpretation of these fantastic outbursts,--to find sense in them, to discern the minds from which they proceeded. These phenomena had great efficacy in the conversion of Pagans, and were regarded as the most demonstrative miracles. The Pagans, in fact--at least those of them who were supposed benevolent--were drawn into the assemblies. Then there would often follow strange spectacles. One or several of the inspired would address the intruder, address him alternately with rudeness or with gentleness, reveal to him inner secrets which he believed he himself only knew, and unfold to him the sins of his past life. The wicked were astonished, confounded. The shame of that public manifestation, which in that assembly had been exposed in a state of spiritual nudity, created between him and the brethren a strong bond, which was not again to be broken. A sort of confession was sometimes the first act which was done in entering the sect. The intimacy, the affection which such exercises established between the brothers and the sisters, was without reserve: all became indeed as one person. It required nothing less than a perfect spirituality to hinder such relations from springing up, and to check abuse.

We can conceive the immense attraction that a soul-movement so active would exercise amongst a society freed from moral bonds, especially amongst the common classes, who were neglected equally by the state and by religion. Hence the grand lesson which is to be derived from that history for our century; the times resemble each other; the future belonged to the party who took up the masses and educated them. But, in our days, the difficulty is indeed greater than it has ever been. In antiquity, upon the coasts of the Mediterranean, material life could be simple: the wants of the body were secondary, and easily satisfied. With us, these wants are numerous and imperative; popular associations are weighed to the earth as with a weight of lead. It was the sacred feast, "the Lord's Supper" especially, that had an immense moral efficacy; it was considered as a mystic act by which all were incorporated with Christ, and as a consequence united in the same body. There was hence a perpetual lesson of equality, of fraternity. The sacramental words which were connected with the last supper of Jesus were present to all. It was believed that that bread, that wine, that water, were the body and blood of Jesus himself. Those who partook of it were accounted to eat Jesus, were united to him, and bound to him by an ineffable mystery. The prelude to it was the giving of "the holy kiss," or "kiss of love," without any of the scruples which came to trouble the innocence of another golden age. Ordinarily the men gave it to one another, and the women gave it amongst themselves. Some Churches, however, pressed the holy liberty to the point of not making any distinction of sexes in the kiss of love. Profane society, little capable of comprehending such purity, made this the occasion of divers calumnies. The chaste Christian kiss awakened the suspicions of the libertines, and soon the Church was constrained to the point of taking severe precautions; but in the beginning it was an essential rite inseparable from the Eucharist, and completing the high signification of the symbol of peace and love. Some abstained from it in youth, and in the time of mourning and of fasting.

The first monastic Church at Jerusalem broke bread every day. Twenty or thirty years after, people had come to celebrate the holy feast only once a week. This celebration took place in the evening, and, according to the Jewish usage, by the light of numerous lamps. The day chosen for this was the day following the Sabbath, the first day of the week. This day was called "the day of the Lord," in remembrance of the "resurrection," and also because it was believed that on the same day God had created the world. Alms were done, and collections made on this day. The Sabbath, which all Christians probably celebrate still in a manner not equally scrupulous, was distinct from the day of the Lord. But without doubt the day of rest tended more and more to be confounded with the day of the Lord, and it is permissible to suppose that in the Churches of the Gentiles, who had no reason to prefer the Saturday, that change was already made. The ébonim of the East, on the contrary, rested on Saturday.

Little by little the supper tended to become purely symbolical in form. At the first it was a real supper, at which one ate as much as one wanted, only with an elevated mystic intention. The supper was prefaced by a prayer. As at the dinners of the Pagan fraternities, each brought his basket and consumed what he brought: the Church, no doubt, furnishing the accessories, such as hot water, pilchards, that which was called the ministerium. People loved to think of two invisible servants, Irene (Peace) and Agapæ (Love), the one pouring out the wine, the other mixing it with hot water; and, perhaps, at certain moments during the repast, one would be heard to say, with a sweet smile, to the deaconesses (ministræ), that from which they derived their names: Irene, da calda (hot water)--Agape, misce me (pour me out). A spirit of delicate reserve and of discreet sobriety presided at the feast. The table at which people sat was in the form of a hollow semi-circle, or of a crescent, sigma (a symbol); the elder was placed in the centre; the cups or saucers which were used for drinking out of were the objects of particular care. The bread and the wine, which were blessed, were carried to the absent by the minister of the diocese.

In time the supper came to be no more than a ceremony. People ate at home to appease hunger; at the assembly people eat only a few mouthfuls; drank only a few sups, in view of the symbol. People were led by a kind of logic to distinguish the common fraternal repast from the mystical act which consisted solely of a fraction of bread. The fraction of bread became each day more sacramental; the supper, on the contrary, in proportion as the Church increased, became more profane. Sometimes the supper was reduced almost to nothing, and in being thus reduced, lost all the importance of a sacramental act. Sometimes the two things subsisted, but separately; the supper was a prelude or a sequel to the Eucharist; people dined together before or after the communion. Then the two ceremonies were separated entirely; the pious repasts were acts of charity towards the poor, sometimes the remnants of Pagan usages, and had no longer any connection with the Eucharist. As such, they were in general suppressed in the fifth century. The "eulogia" or "consecrated bread" remained, then, the sole souvenir of a golden age in which the Eucharist was invested with the more complex and less purely analytic forms. For a long time, still, however, the custom was preserved of invoking the name of Jesus in drinking, and people continued to consider as a eulogy the act of breaking bread and of drinking together, which were the last traces, and the traces well-nigh effaced, of the admirable institutions of Jesus.

The name which, at the first, the eucharistic feast bore, expressed admirably all that there was in that excellent rite of divine efficacy and of salutary morality. They were called agapæ, that is to say, "loves" or "charities." The Jews--the Essenians especially--had already attached a moral sense to the religious feasts; but in passing into the hands of another race, these Oriental usages took an almost mythological significance. The Mythriatic mysteries which began soon to be developed in the Roman world had as their principal rite the offering of bread and of the cup, over which were pronounced certain words. The resemblance was such, that the Christians explained it as a ruse of the devil, who wished by this means to have the infernal pleasure of counterfeiting their most holy ceremonies. The secret bonds between all these things are very obscure. It was easy to foresee that grave abuses would so quickly be mixed up with such practices, that one day the feast (the agapæ, properly speaking) would fall into desuetude, and that there would only remain the eucharistic wafer, the sign and memorial of the primitive institution. One could no longer be surprised to learn that strange mysteries should be made the pretext for calumnies, and that the sect which pretended to eat, under the form of bread and wine, the body and the blood of its founder, should be accused of renewing the feasts of Thyestes, of eating infants covered with pastry, and of anthropophagistic practices.

The annual feasts were always the Jewish feasts, especially Easter and Pentecost. The Christian Easter was generally celebrated on the same day as the Jewish Passover. Nevertheless, the cause which had transferred the holy-day of each week from the Saturday to the Sunday regulated also Easter, not from usage and Jewish souvenirs, but from the souvenirs of the passion and of the resurrection of Jesus. It is not impossible that, from the time of Paul, in the Churches of Greece and Macedonia, that change had already been effected. In any case, the thought of that fundamental feast was profoundly modified. The passage of the Red Sea became a thing of little account after the resurrection of Jesus; people no longer thought of it, except to find in it a figure of the triumph of Jesus over death. The true Paschal Lamb was henceforth Jesus, who had been offered up for all; the true unleavened breads were truth, justice; the old leaven had lost its power, and ought therefore to be rejected. For the rest, the feast of the Passover had indeed more anciently undergone with the Hebrews an analogous change of signification. It was certainly in its origin a feast of spring time, which was connected by an artificial etymology with the remembrance of the flight from Egypt.

Pentecost was also celebrated on the same day as with the Jews. Like Easter, that feast took a signification altogether new, which put into the shade the old Jewish idea. Right or wrong, people believed that the principal incident of the Holy Spirit upon the assembled Apostles had taken place on the day of Pentecost which followed the resurrection of Jesus; the ancient harvest festival of the Semites became thus in the new religion the feast of the Holy Ghost. About the same time that feast underwent an analogous transformation amongst the Jews; it became with them the anniversary of the promulgation of the law upon Mount Sinai.

No edifice had been built or any building rented expressly for the meetings;--no art, consequently no images. The assemblies took place in the houses of the brethren the best known, or who had a room well adapted for the purpose. People preferred for this the apartments which, in Oriental houses, formed the first floor, and corresponding to our drawing-room floor. These apartments are high, containing numerous windows, very fresh, very airy; it was here that one received one's friends, where one held feasts, where one prayed, where one laid out the dead. The groups thus formed constituted "domestic churches," or pious coteries full of moral activity, and resembling greatly those "domestic colleges," examples of which were to be found about that time in the bosom of Pagan society. All great things are thus founded in inconsiderable centres, where one is tightly squeezed the one against the other, and where souls are warmed by a powerful love.

Up to this time Buddhism alone had elevated man to this degree of heroism and of purity. The triumph of Christianity is inexplicable, if it is studied only in the fourth century. It happened with Christianity as happens almost always in human things: it succeeded when it began to decline morally; it became official when it no longer had anything to rest upon except itself; it came into vogue when its true period of originality and of youth had passed away. But it did none the less merit its high recompense: it had merited this by its three centuries of virtue, or by the incomparable predilection for the good which it had inspired. When we think of that miracle, no hyperbole about the excellence of Jesus appears illegitimate. It was he, always he, who was the inspirer, the master, the principle of life in his Church. His divine mission grew each year, and this was but just. He was no longer only a man of God, a great prophet, a man approved and authorised of God, a man powerful in works and in speech; these expressions which suffice, which were sufficient for the faith and the love of the disciples of early times, passed now for silly fables. Jesus is the Lord, the Christ, a personage entirely superhuman, not yet God, but very near being it. One lives in him, one dies in him, one rises in him; almost everything that one says of God, one says of him. He was in truth already a divine personality, and when it is wished to identify him with God, it is only a question of words, a mere "communication of idioms" as the theologians say. We shall see that Paul himself attained to this: the most advanced formulas that are to be found in the Epistle to the Colossians existed already in germ in the older epistles. "For to us there is but one God, the Father, of whom are all things, and we in him, and one Lord Jesus Christ, by whom are all things, and we by him" (1 Cor. viii. 6). Again, and Jesus shall be the logos, creator; the most exaggerated of the consubstantialists of the ninth century could already be foreshadowed.

The idea of the Christian redemption in the Churches of Paul underwent a similar transformation. People knew little of the parables or the moral teachings of Jesus: the Gospels did not yet exist. Christ, having lived, is not to the Churches something approaching a real personage: he is the image of God, a heavenly minister, having taken upon himself the sins of the world, charged with reconciling the world to God; he is a divine reformer, creating all things new, and abolishing the past. It is death for all; all are dead through him to the world, and ought no longer to live, except for him. He was rich in all the richness of divinity, and he became poor for us. All Christian life ought hence to be a contradiction of the human sense: weakness is the true strength, death is the true life; cardinal wisdom is folly. Happy he who carries in his body the dying of Jesus, he who is continually exposed to death for Jesus' sake. He shall live again with Jesus; he shall see his glory face to face, and shall be transformed unto him, rising uninterruptedly from glory to glory. The Christian thus lives in the hope of death, and in a state of perpetual groaning. In proportion as the exterior man (the body) falls into ruin, the interior man (the soul) is renewed. One moment of tribulation is worth more to him than an eternity of glory. What matters it that his terrestrial house is dissolved? He has in Heaven an eternal house, not made with hands. Terrestrial life is exile; death is return to God, and equivalent to the absorption of all that is mortal in life, only the treasure of hope which the Christian carries in earthen vessels, and until the great day when all shall be made manifest before the judgment seat of Christ, he must tremble.

CHAPTER X

RETURN OF PAUL TO ANTIOCH--QUARREL BETWEEN PETER AND PAUL--
COUNTER-MISSION ORGANISED BY JAMES, BROTHER OF THE LORD

Paul, however, felt the necessity of revisiting the Churches of Syria. It was three years since he had left Antioch; notwithstanding that his stay there had been shorter than formerly, this new mission had become much more important. The new Churches, recruited from lively, energetic populations, brought to the feet of Jesus homage of an infinite value. Paul had just recounted all this to the Apostles, and bid them attach themselves to the Mother Church, the model of all others. In spite of his taste for independence, he felt sure that, outside of the communion of Jerusalem, there was only schism and dissension. The admirable mixture of opposite qualities which could be discerned in him, allowed him to ally, in the most unexpected fashion, docility with pride, revolt with submission, severity with gentleness. Paul chose as a pretext for his departure the celebration of the Passover of the year 54. To give the utmost solemnity to his resolution, and to avoid the possibility of changing his decision, he made a vow to celebrate that Easter at Jerusalem. The mode of performing vows of this kind was to shave the head, and to undertake to say certain prayers, and to abstain from wine during thirty days before the festival. Paul said good-bye to his Church, had his head shaved at Cenchrea, and embarked for Syria. He was accompanied by Aquila and Priscilla, who intended to stop at Ephesus, and perhaps also by Silas. As for Timothy, it is probable that he did not go away from Corinth or from the shores of the Ægæan Sea. We find him again at Ephesus within a year.

The ship stayed for some days at Ephesus. Paul had time to go to the synagogue and to dispute with the Jews. They begged him to stay; but he put forward his vow, and declared that at any cost he would celebrate the festival in Jerusalem; all they could get from him was a promise to return. He took leave then of Aquila and Priscilla, and of those with whom he had already entered into relationships, and took ship again for Cæsarea of Palestine, whence he speedily made his way to Jerusalem.

There he celebrated the festival in the way in which he had vowed to do. Perhaps this Hebrew scruple was a concession, like so many others, that he made to the spirit of the Church at Jerusalem. He hoped by an act of great devotion to obtain pardon for his daring, and to conciliate the Judaisers. The discussions were scarcely pacified, and peace was only kept for the sake of business. It is probable that he profited by the opportunity to remit to the poor people in Jerusalem a considerable amount of money as alms. Paul, as usual, stayed for a very short time in the metropolis: here there were susceptibilities which could not have failed to bring about divisions if he had prolonged his stay. He, accustomed to live in the exquisite atmosphere of his truly Christian Churches, found here, under the name of Brethren of Jesus, only Jews. He thought that they did not give a sufficiently exalted place to Jesus; he grew indignant that, after Jesus, people should be found to attribute any value whatever to those things which had existed before him.

The head of the Church of Jerusalem was now James, the brother of the Lord. It was not that the authority of Peter had diminished, but he was no longer resident in the city. Partly in imitation of Paul, he had embraced the active apostolic life. The idea that Paul was the Apostle of the Gentiles, and Peter the Apostle of the Circumcision, had more and more gained ground. In accordance with this idea, Peter went about preaching the Gospel to the Jews all over Syria. He carried about with him a sister, as spouse and deaconess, thus giving the first example of a married Apostle--an example which the Protestant missionaries more lately followed. John, surnamed Mark, appeared always also as his disciple, his companion, and his interpreter, a circumstance which causes it to be generally believed that the Prince of the Apostles knew no Greek. Peter had in some sort adopted John-Mark, and treated him as a son.

The details of the pilgrimage of Peter are unknown to us. What was told about him in later days is mainly fabulous. We only know that the life of the Apostle of the Circumcision was, like that of the Apostle of the Gentiles, a series of trials. It may be believed also that the itinerary which serves as foundation for the fabulous acts of Peter--a journey which conducts the Apostle from Jerusalem to Cæsarea, from Cæsarea along the coast by Tyre, Sidon, Beyrout, Byblos, Tripoli, Antaradus to Laodicea-upon-the-sea, and from Laodicea to Antioch--is but imaginary. The Apostle certainly visited Antioch; we think even that he used it as his headquarters after a certain date. The lakes and the ponds formed by the Orontes and the Arkeuthas about the town, which furnished to the lower classes of the people fresh water fish of inferior quality, perhaps afforded him the opportunity of again taking up his old trade of fisherman.

Many of the brothers of the Lord, and some members of the Apostolic College, travelled even from the bordering parts of Judæa. As Peter, and in a different manner to that of the missionaries of the school of Paul, they travelled with their wives, and lived at the cost of the Churches. The trade which they had exercised in Galilee was not, like that of Paul, of a nature to enable them to subsist upon it, and they had abandoned it a long time ago. The wives who accompanied them, who were called "sisters," were the origin of those novices, a kind of deaconesses and of nuns, living under the direction of a clergyman, who played an important part in the history of ecclesiastical celibacy.

Peter having thus ceased to be the resident chief of the Church of Jerusalem, several members of the Apostolic Council having in the same way taken up with an itinerant life, the first place in the Mother Church was given up to James. He was thus "the bishop of the Hebrews," that is to say, of that part of the disciples who spoke the Semitic languages. That did not compromise the chief part of the universal Church: no one had been exigent enough to claim the right to such a title, people being divided between Peter and Paul; but his presidency of the Church at Jerusalem, joined to his quality of brother of the Lord, gave James an immense power, since the Church at Jerusalem always remained the centre of concord. James was, moreover, very old; some ambitious movements, too much prejudice, were the consequences of such a position. All the faults which must later make the Court of Rome the flail of the Church, and the principal agent of its corruption, were already germinating in this primitive community of Jerusalem.

James was a worthy man in many respects, but with a narrow mind, that Jesus would have assuredly pierced with his keenest railleries, if he knew him, or even if be knew him as he has been represented to us. Was he really the brother, or only a coῦσιν-german, of Jesus? All the witnesses in this respect agree so well together, that one is forced to believe the latter hypothesis. But, in that case, Nature must have played one of her most fantastic tricks. Perhaps this brother, being converted only after the death of Jesus, possessed less of the true tradition of the Master than those who, without being his relations, had accompanied him in his lifetime. It is less surprising that two children born of the same mother, or of the same family, should have been at first enemies, then reconciled; should remain so profoundly diverse, that the only known brother of Jesus would have been a kind of Pharisee, an ascetic exterior, a devotee tainted with all the absurdities that Jesus attacked without mercy. One thing is certain, namely, that the person who has been called up to this time "James, brother of the Lord," or "James the Just," or the "Rampart of the People," was in the Church of Jerusalem the representative of the most intolerant Jewish party. Whilst the active Apostles travelled all over the world, in order to conquer it for Jesus, the brother of Jesus at Jerusalem did all that was possible to destroy their work, and to contradict Jesus after his death, in a more profound fashion perhaps than he had done in his life-time.

This society of half-converted Pharisees, this world which was in reality more Jewish than Christian, living around the temple, preserving the old practices of the Jewish religion, as if Jesus had not declared them vain, formed unbearable company for Paul. That which particularly annoyed him was the opposition of all this class to his missionary work. Like the Jews of the strict observance, the partisans of James did not wish to make proselytes. The ancient religious parties often had such contradictions. On the one hand, they proclaimed that they alone had possession of the truth; on the other, they only wished to enlarge their sphere: they pretended to preserve the truth for themselves. French Protestantism presents in our days a similar phenomenon. Two opposite parties, the one desiring, before everything else, the preservation of old customs; the other capable of gaining to Protestantism a world of new adherents, being produced in the bosom of the reformed Church. The conservative party has waged, in a second ground, a war to the knife. It has repulsed with scandal all that has resembled an abandonment of the family traditions, and it has preferred to the brilliant destinies that are offered to them, the pleasure of remaining a little club, without importance, shut up, composed of well-thinking men,--that is to say, of men partaking of the same prejudices, and regarding the same things as aristocratic. The feeling of defiance that the members of the old party of Jerusalem experienced before the stern missionary who introduced to them multitudes of new brethren without titles of Jewish nobility, must be something analogous. They looked upon themselves as overruled, and instead of falling at the feet of Paul, and thanking him, they found in him a disturber, an intruder who forced his way with men recruited from every place. More than one hard word, it seems, had been exchanged. It is probable that at this moment James, the brother of the Lord, conceived the unsuccessful project of overthrowing the work of Jesus,--I mean the project of a counter mission charged to follow the Apostle of the Gentiles, to contradict his dogmas, to persuade converts that they must be circumcised, and practise all the Law. Sectarian movements are not produced without schisms of this kind; when one recalls the heads of Saint-Simonianism quarrelling amongst themselves, but yet remaining ardent Saint-Simonians, and as such voluntarily reconciled by the survivors after his death.

Paul avoided these scandals by setting out as soon as possible for Antioch. It was probably then that Silas left him. The latter was the founder of the Church at Jerusalem. He remained there, and henceforth attached himself to Peter. Silas, as the compiler of the "Acts," appears to have been a conciliatory man, oscillating between the two parties, and in turn attached to each of the two chiefs; a thoroughly good Christian, and of the opinion which in triumphing saved the Church. Never, in fact, did the Christian Church bear in its bosom a cause of schism so deep as that which agitated it at this moment. Luther and the most fossilised scholar differed less than Paul and James. Thanks to some gentle and generous spirits--Silas, Luke, Timothy--all the attacks were softened, all the heartburnings concealed. A beautiful tale, calm and dignified, has not allowed it to be seen that the fraternal understanding in these years was traversed by such terrible rents.

At Antioch Paul breathed freely. He there met with his old companion Barnabas, and without doubt they felt great joy at seeing each other; for the motive which had separated them for a short time was not a question of principle. Perhaps Paul also found at Antioch his disciple Titus, who had not shared the second journey, but who henceforth attached himself to him. The recital of miraculous conversions wrought by Paul astonished the young and active Church. Paul, for his part, felt a lively joy at revisiting the town which had been the cradle of his apostleship--the places where, ten years before, he had conceived the Church which had conferred on him the title of Missionary of the Gentiles. An incident of the greatest gravity was soon to interrupt these sweet effusions, and to revive with a degree of gravity those divisions which up to then had been lulled for a moment.

Whilst Paul was at Antioch, Peter arrived there. This at first only redoubled the joy and cordiality. The Apostle of the Jews and the Apostle of the Gentiles loved each other as very good and very ardent natures always love each other, when they found themselves in relation to each other. Peter communicated without reserve with the converted Pagans, and even, in open violation of the Jewish Law, he did not object to eating with them; but soon this good understanding was disturbed. James had executed his fatal project. Some brethren, provided with letters of recommendation signed by him as the chief of the Twelve, and as the only one who had the right to authorise a mission, set out from Jerusalem. Their pretext was that one could not preach the doctrine of Christ if he had not been to Jerusalem to compare his doctrine with that of James, the brother of the Lord, and if he did not carry an attestation from the latter. Jerusalem was, according to them, the source of all faith,--of every apostolic commission: the true Apostles lived there. Whoever preached without a letter of authority from the chief of the Mother Church, and without having sworn obedience to him, ought to be repelled as a false prophet and a false apostle, as an emissary of the devil. Paul, who had no such letters, was an intruder, boasting of personal relations with them without reality, and of a mission the title to which he could not produce. He alleged his visions, contending even that the fact of having seen Jesus in a supernatural fashion was worth much more than the fact of having known him personally. "What can be more chimerical?" said the Jerusalemites. No vision was so valuable as the evidence of the senses: visions are not actualities. The spectre that he saw was perhaps an evil spirit: idolaters had visions as well as saints. When the apparition was questioned, it answered all that was wanted: the spectre shone for an instant, and then disappeared quickly; there was no time to talk to it at leisure. The mind of the dreamer was not his own: in that state volition ceases. To see the Son out of the flesh! but that is impossible: one would die of it. The superhuman brightness of that light would kill. Even an angel, to make himself visible, is obliged to assume a body!"

The emissaries cited on this head a number of visions which had been seen by infidels and heretics, and concluded from them that the chief Apostles, those who had seen Jesus, had an immense superiority. They even declared that they could show texts of Scripture proving that visions came from an offended God, whilst to converse face to face was the privilege of his friends. "How can Paul assert that by an interview of an hour Jesus had rendered him capable of teaching? It needed a whole year of lessons for Jesus to form his Apostles. And if Jesus really appeared to him, how did he know that he did not teach the reverse of the doctrine of Jesus? Let him prove the reality of the interview which he had had with Jesus, by conforming himself to His precepts, by loving His Apostles, by not declaring war with those whom Jesus had chosen. If he wished to serve the truth, let him make himself the disciple of Jesus' disciples, and then he could be a useful auxiliary."

The question of ecclesiastical authority and of individual revelation, of Catholicism and of Protestantism, showed itself with a real grandeur. Jesus had settled nothing clearly in this matter. So long as he lived, and throughout the first years following his death, Jesus was so essentially the soul and body of His little Church, that no idea of government or of constitution offers itself. Now, on the contrary, it was necessary to know if there was a power representing Jesus, or if the Christian conscience remained free; if to preach Jesus, subscription to articles of faith were necessary, or if he had the command received from Jesus sufficed. As Paul did not offer any other proof of his immediate mission than his affirmation, his position was weak in many ways. We shall see with what prodigies of eloquence and of activity the great innovator, attacked in every quarter, will face all assaults and maintain his position without absolutely breaking with the Apostolic College, whose authority he recognised each time that his liberty was not straitened. But the struggle rendered him less amiable to us. A man who disputes, resists, speaks of himself; a man who maintains his opinion and his prerogative, who gives pain to others, who denounces them to their face, such a man is antipathetic to us. Jesus, in such a case, yielded everything, escaped from his difficulty by some charming word.

The emissaries of James arrived at Antioch. James, while admitting that converted Gentiles could be saved without observing the Law of Moses, in no way admitted that a true Jew, a circumcised Jew, could, without sin, violate the law. The scandal of the disciples of James was at its height when they saw the chief of the Churches of the circumcision act like a true Pagan, and destroy those exterior compacts that a respectable Jew looked upon as titles of nobility and marks of his superiority. They spoke keenly to Peter, who was much frightened. This man, profoundly good and just, wanted peace above everything: he scarcely knew how to contradict anybody. This made him changeable: at least he was so to all appearance; he was easily disconcerted, and did not know how to find a quick reply. Already, from the life of Jesus, this kind of timidity, coming from awkwardness rather than from want of heart, had led him into a fault which cost him many tears. Knowing little about argument, incapable of holding up his head against contradiction, in difficult cases he was silent and hesitated. Such a kind of temper made him again commit a great act of feebleness. Placed between two classes of people, one of whom he could not content without annoying the other, he isolated himself completely, and lived apart, refusing all communications with the uncircumcised. This manner of acting keenly wounded the converted Gentiles. What was graver still, was that all the circumcised imitated him; even Barnabas allowed himself to follow this example, and avoided uncircumcised Christians.

Paul's anger was extreme. When we recall the ritual meaning of the meal in common, refusing to eat with a part of the community meant excommunication. Paul broke out into reproaches, treated this kind of thing as hypocrisy, accused Peter and his imitators of falsifying the meaning of the gospel. The Church must soon assemble: the two Apostles would meet there. To his face, and before all the assembly, Paul violently apostrophised Peter, and reproached him for his inconsequence. "If thou," said he to him, "being a Jew, livest after the manner of Gentiles, and not as do the Jews, why compellest thou the Gentiles to live as do the Jews?"

Then he developed his favourite theory of the salvation coming by Jesus, and not by the Law,--of the abrogation of the Law by Jesus. It is probable that Peter did not answer him. Exactly, it was Paul's advice; as all men who seek by innocent artifices to get out of a difficulty, he did not pretend to be right; he only wanted to satisfy one side, and not to alienate others. In this manner one only succeeds, as a general rule, in being in opposition to everybody.

Only the removal of the envoys of James made an end to the disagreement. After their departure, good Peter began again without doubt to eat with the Gentiles as before. These singular alternatives of violence and of fraternity are one of the features of a Jewish character. Modern critics conclude from certain passages in the Epistle to the Galatians that the quarrel between Peter and Paul absolutely made them contradict each other, not only in the "Acts" but in other passages from the Epistle to the Galatians. Ardent men pass their life in disputing with each other, without ever actually quarrelling. It is not necessary to judge these tempers after the manner of things whose actions happen in our time between men well educated and susceptible upon the point of honour. This last word, in particular, has scarcely ever had any meaning to the Jews.

It seems certain, nevertheless, the quarrel of Antioch left deep traces. The great Church on the borders of the Orontes was split in two, if we are permitted to explain thus, that in two parishes there was on the one hand the parish of the circumcised, on the other, that of the uncircumcised. The separation of these two portions of the Church continued for a long time. Antioch, as they tell us later, had two bishops, one appointed by Peter and the other by Paul. Evhode and Ignatius are named as having filled up after the Apostles that office.

As for the animosity of the emissaries of James, it only increased. The quarrel of Antioch left them a feeling, the indignant expression of which, a century after, one still finds in the writings of the Judæo-Christian section. The eloquent adversary who had almost destroyed the Church of Antioch, without any real reason became their enemy. They vowed vengeance, which even in his lifetime raised up for him troubles without number, and after his death bloody anathemas and atrocious calumnies. Passion and religious enthusiasm are far from overcoming human weaknesses. On leaving Antioch, the agents of the Jerusalemite party vowed to overthrow the foundations of Paul, to destroy his Churches, and to throw down what he had built up with so much labour. It seems that on this occasion new letters were sent from Jerusalem in the name of the Apostles. It is possible that a specimen of those hateful letters may have been preserved for us in the Epistle of Jude, brother of James, and like him "brother of the Lord," which forms part of the canon. It is a manifesto of the most violent description against nameless adversaries, who are presented as rebels and impure men. The style of this piece, which comes much nearer to classic Greek than that of the greater portion of the writings of the New Testament, has much analogy with the style of the Epistle of James. James and Jude did not probably know any Greek: the Church of Jerusalem had perhaps Hellenic secretaries for communications of this kind. "Beloved, when I gave all diligence to, write unto you of the common salvation, it was needful for me to write unto you and exhort you, that ye should earnestly contend for the faith which was once delivered unto the saints. For there are certain men crept in unawares, who were before of old ordained to this condemnation, ungodly men, turning the grace of our God into lasciviousness, and denying the only Lord God, and our Lord Jesus Christ. I will therefore put you in remembrance, though ye once knew this, how that the Lord, having saved the people out of the land of Egypt, afterwards destroyed them that believed not. And the angels which kept not their first estate, but left their own habitation, he hath reserved in everlasting chains under darkness unto the judgment of the great day. Even as Sodom and Gomorrah, and the cities about them in like manner, giving themselves over to fornication, are set forth for an example, suffering the vengeance of eternal fire. Likewise also these filthy dreamers defile the flesh, despise dominion, and speak evil of dignities. Yet Michael the archangel, when, contending with the devil, disputed about the body of Moses, durst not bring against him a railing accusation, but said, the Lord rebuke thee. But these speak evil of things which they know not, but what they know naturally, as brute beasts, in those things they corrupt themselves. Woe unto them! for they have gone in the way of Cain, and ran greedily after the error of Balaam for reward, and perished in the gainsaying of Core. These are spots in your feasts of charity, when they feast with you, feeding themselves without fear: clouds they are without water, carried about of winds; trees whose fruit withereth, without fruit, twice dead, plucked up by the roots. Raging waves of the sea, foaming out their own shame; wandering stars, to whom is reserved the blackness of darkness for ever. And Enoch, also, the seventh from Adam, prophesied of these, saying, Behold, the Lord cometh with ten thousand of his saints, to execute judgment upon all, and to convince all that are ungodly among them of all their ungodly deeds which they have committed, and of all their hard speeches which ungodly sinners have spoken against him. These are murmurers, complainers, walking after their own lusts; and their mouth speaketh great swelling words, having men's persons in admiration because of advantage. But, beloved, remember ye the words which were spoken before of the apostles of our Lord Jesus Christ: how that they told you there should be mockers in the last time who should walk after their own ungodly lusts."

Paul from this moment was for a section of the Church one of the most dangerous of heretics, a false Jew, a false Apostle, a false prophet, a new Balaam, a Jezebel, a villain who prophesied (lit. preluded.) the destruction of the temple--in two words, a Simon Magus. Peter was angrier than all, and was always busy in fighting him. They were accustomed to designate the Apostle of the Gentiles by the sobriquet of Nicholas (Conquerer of the People), a name akin to Balaam. This seemed a happy nickname; a Pagan seducer, who had visions although an infidel, a man who persuaded people to sin with Pagan women, appeared the true type of Paul, this false missionary, this partisan of mixed marriages. His disciples for the same reason were called Nicolaitans. Far from forgetting his character of persecutor, they insisted on it in a most odious fashion. His gospel was a false gospel. It was of Paul that the question was raised, when the fanatics of the party talked between themselves in innuendoes of a person whom they called "the apostate," or "the enemy," or "the impostor," the forerunner of Anti-Christ, that the chief of the Apostles follows in his footsteps to repair the evil which he does. Paul was "the frivolous man" of whom the Gentiles, having seen their ignorance, have received the doctrine which is opposed to the Law; his visions, which he calls "depths of God," they qualified as "the depths of Satan," his Churches, they named "the synagogues of Satan;" in spite of Paul, they proclaim boldly that the Twelve only are the foundation of the Church of Christ. A whole legend begins from this time to be formed against Paul. They refuse to believe that a true Jew could have been capable of committing such an atrocity as that of which he had been guilty. They pretended that he had been born a Pagan, and that he had been made a proselyte. And why? Calumny is never without plenty of reasons for it. Paul was circumcised because he wished to marry the daughter of the High Priest. The High Priest, being a wise man, having refused her to him, Paul, out of spite, began to declaim against circumcision, the Sabbath, and the Law. . . . That is the reward which one obtains from fanatics for having served their cause, otherwise than they understand it; let us say rather, for having served the cause which they lost by their narrow spirit and their foolish exclusiveness.

James, on the contrary, became for the Judæo-Christian party the head of all Christianity, the bishop of bishops, the president of all the good Churches, of those that God had truly founded. It was probably after his death that they created for him this apocryphal character; but there is no doubt that legend in this case may be based in several respects upon the real character of the hero. The grave and rather emphatic delivery of James; his manners, which recalled a sage of the old world, a solemn Brahmin or an antique mobed; his pompous and ostentatious sanctity made him conspicuous in the popular eye, an official, holy man, even already a species of Pope. The Judæo-Christians accustomed themselves to believe that he had been clothed with the Jewish priesthood; and as a sign of the High Priest was the pétalon or breastplate of gold, they decorated him with it. "The Rampart of the people," with his golden breastplate, thus became a sort of Jewish bonze, an imitation High Priest, for the use of the Judæo-Christians. They supposed that, as the High Priest, he entered, by virtue of a special permission, once a year into the sanctuary; they even pretended that he belonged to the sacerdotal race. They asserted that he had been ordained by Jesus the bishop of the Holy City; that Jesus had entrusted him with his own episcopal throne. The Judæo-Christians made a good many of the people of Jerusalem believe that it was the merits of this servant of God which held off the thunderbolt which was ready to burst on the people. They nearly went as far as creating for him as for Jesus, a legend founded upon biblical passages, where they pretended that the prophets had spoken of him in parables.

The image of Jesus in this Christian family became smaller year by year, whilst in the Churches of Paul it took more and more colossal proportions. The Christians of James were simple, pious Jews-- hasidim--believing in a Jewish mission of Jesus; the Christians of Paul were good Christians in the sense which has prevailed ever since. The Law, the temple, sacrifices, high priests, all became indifferent to them. Jesus has replaced everything else, abolished everything else; to attach a meaning of sanctity to what has been before, is to do injury to the merits of Jesus. It was natural that to Paul, who had not seen Jesus, the wholly human figure of the Galilæan Master should transform itself into a metaphysical type much more easily than for Peter and the others who had talked with Jesus. To Paul, Jesus is not a man who has lived and taught; he is Christ who has died for our sins, who saves us, who justifies us; He is an altogether Divine being: we partake of him; we communicate with Him in a wonderful manner; He is for man Wisdom and Righteousness, Santification and Redemption; He is the King of Glory, All Powerful in Heaven and Earth, which is soon to be delivered to Him; He is only inferior to God the Father. If this school only had written the Scriptures, we should not touch upon the person of Jesus, and we might doubt its existence. But those who know Him, and who guarded His memory, possibly wrote about this time the first notes upon which these Divine writings (I speak of the Gospels) which have made the fortune of Christianity, and which have transmitted to us the essential features of the most important character which has ever been known.

CHAPTER XI

TROUBLES IN THE CHURCHES OF GALATIA

The emissaries of James, having left Antioch, bent their steps towards the Churches of Galatia. The Jerusalemites had for a long time known of the existence of these Churches; it was even with regard to them that the question of the circumcision was first raised, and that what was called the Council of Jerusalem was held. James had probably recommended his confidential agents to attack this important point, it being one of the centres of Paul's power.

Success was easy for them. These Galatians were men readily seduced; the last one who had come to speak to them in the name of Jesus was almost certain to be right. The Jerusalemites had soon persuaded a great number of them that they were not good Christians. They incessantly repeated to them that they ought to be circumcised, and to observe all the Law. With the puerile vanity of fanatical Jews, the deputies represented circumcision as a corporal advantage; they were proud of it, and did not admit that one could be as much a man without this privilege as he ought to be. The habit of ridiculing the Pagans, representing them as inferior beings and badly brought up, introduced these grotesque ideas. The Jerusalemites poured out at the same time against Paul a flood of invective and disparagement. They accused him of posing as an independent Apostle, although he had received his mission from Jerusalem, or else they had seen him at different times betake himself to the school of the Twelve, as a disciple. Was not his coming to Jerusalem a recognition of the superiority of the Apostolic College? What he knew he had learned from the Apostles; he had accepted the rules which they had drawn up. This missionary who pretended to dispense with circumcision, knew very well the need of preaching and of practising it. Turning his concessions against him, they alleged cases when they had seen him recognise the necessity of Jewish practices; perhaps they did not recall in particular the facts relative to the circumcision of Titus and Timothy. How could he, who had never seen Jesus, dare to speak in the name of Jesus? It was Peter, it was James, who ought to be held to be the true Apostles--the depositaries of revelation.

The consciences of these good Galatians were troubled. One party abandoned the doctrine of Paul, yielded to the new doctors, and were circumcised; the other party remained faithful to their first master. The trouble, in all these cases, was profound: they said the harshest things to each other.

This news on reaching Paul filled him with anger. Jealousy, which formed the basis of his character, and susceptibility, often already put to the test, were excited in the highest degree. It was the third time that the Pharisaical party of Jerusalem attempted to demolish his work as he accomplished it. The kind of cowardice which there is in attacking weak, docile men without defence, and who only lived in confidence on their master, revolted him. He could restrain himself no longer. At the same time, the daring and vehement Apostle dictated that admirable epistle, that may well be compared, except for the art of writing, with the most beautiful classical works, and in which his impetuous nature is painted in letters of fire. The title of "Apostle" that he had at first taken timidly, he now took as assumed in defiance, to reply to his adversaries, and in the maintenance of what he believed to be the truth.

"Paul an Apostle (not of men, neither by man, but by Jesus Christ, and God the Father, who raised him from the Dead); and all the brethren which are with me, unto the Churches of Galatia:

"Grace be to you and peace from God the Father, and from our Lord Jesus Christ, who gave himself for our sins, that he might deliver us from this present evil world, according to the will of God and our Father: to whom be glory for ever and ever. Amen.

"I marvel that ye are so soon removed from him that called you into the grace of Christ unto another gospel: which is not another; but there be some that trouble you, and would pervert the gospel of Christ. But though we, or an angel from heaven, preach any other gospel unto you than that which we have preached unto you, let him be accursed. As we said before, so say I now again, if any man preach any other gospel unto you than that ye have received, let him be accursed. For do I now persuade men, or God? or do I seek to please men? for if I yet pleased men, I should not be the servant of Christ.

"But I certify you, brethren, that the gospel which was preached of me is not after man. For I neither received it of man, neither was I taught it, but by the revelation of Jesus Christ. For ye have heard of my conversation in time past in the Jews' religion, how that beyond measure I persecuted the Church of God, and wasted it: and profited in the Jews' religion above many my equals in mine own nation, being more exceedingly zealous of the traditions of my fathers. But when it pleased God, who separated me from my mother's womb, and called me by his grace, to reveal his Son in me, that I might preach him among the heathen; immediately I conferred not with flesh and blood: neither went I up to Jerusalem to them which were Apostles before me; but I went into Arabia, and returned again unto Damascus. Then after three years I went up to Jerusalem to see Peter, and abode with him fifteen days. But other of the Apostles saw I none, save James, the Lord's brother. Now the things which I write unto you, behold, before God, I lie not.

"Afterwards I came into the regions of Syria and Cilicia; and was unknown by face unto the Churches of Judæa which were in Christ; but they had heard only, that he which persecuted us in times past, now preacheth the faith which once he destroyed And they glorified God in me.

"Then, fourteen years after, I went up again to Jerusalem with Barnabas, and took Titus with me also. And I went up by revelation, and communicated unto them that gospel which I preach among the Gentiles, but privately to them which were of reputation, lest by any means I should run, or had run in vain. But neither Titus, who was with me, being a Greek, was compelled to be circumcised; and that because of false brethren unawares brought in, who came in privily to spy out our liberty which we have in Christ Jesus, that they might bring us into bondage, to whom we gave place by subjection, no, not for an hour: that the truth of the gospel might continue with you. But of these who seemed to be somewhat (whatsoever they were, it maketh no matter to me. God accepteth no man's person), for they who seemed to be somewhat in conference added nothing to me; but contrariwise, when they saw that the gospel of the uncircumcision was committed onto me, as the gospel of the circumcision was unto Peter (for he that wrought effectually in Peter to the apostleship of the circumcision, the same was mighty in me toward the Gentiles), and when James, Cephas and John, who seemed to be pillars, perceived the grace that was given unto me, they gave to me and Barnabas the right hands of fellowship; that we should go unto the heathen, and they unto the circumcision. Only they would that we should remember the poor; the same which I also was forward to do.

"But when Peter was come to Antioch, I withstood him to the face, because he was to be blamed. For before that certain came from James, he did eat with the Gentiles; but when they were come, he withdrew and separated himself, fearing them which were of the circumcision. And the other Jews dissembled likewise with him; insomuch that Barnabas also was carried away with their dissimulation. But when I saw that they walked not uprightly according to the truth of the gospel, I said unto Peter, before them all, If thou, being a Jew, livest after the manner of the Gentiles, and not as do the Jews, why compellest thou the Gentiles to live as do the Jews? We, who are Jews by nature, and not sinners of the Gentiles, knowing that a man is not justified by the works of the law, but by the faith of Jesus Christ, even we have believed in Jesus Christ, that we might be justified by the faith of Christ, and not by the works of the law; for by the works of the law shall no flesh be justified. But if, while we seek to be justified by Christ, we ourselves also are found sinners, is therefore Christ the minister of sin? God forbid. For, if I build again the things which I destroy, I make myself a transgressor. For I through the law am dead to the law, that I might live unto God. I am crucified with Christ; nevertheless I live; yet not I, but Christ Liveth in me; and the life which I now live in the flesh I live by the faith of the Son of God, who loved me and gave himself for me. I do not frustrate the grace of God, for if righteousness come by the law, then Christ is dead in vain.

"O foolish Galatians, who hath bewitched you, that ye should not obey the truth, before whose eyes Jesus Christ hath been evidently set forth, crucified among you? This only would I learn of you, Received ye the Spirit by the works of the law, or by the hearing of faith? Are ye so foolish? Having begun in the Spirit are ye now made perfect by the flesh? Have ye suffered so many things in vain? if it be yet in vain. He therefore that ministereth to you the Spirit, and worketh miracles among you, doeth he it by the works of the law, or by the hearing of faith? Even as Abraham believed God, and it was accounted to him for righteousness. Know ye therefore that they which are of faith, the same are the children of Abraham. And the scripture, foreseeing that God would justify the heathen through faith, preached before the gospel unto Abraham, saying, In thee shall all nations be blessed. So then they which be of faith are blessed with faithful Abraham. . . . . . But before faith came, we were kept under the law, shut up unto the faith which should afterwards be revealed. Wherefore the law was our schoolmaster, to bring us unto Christ, that we might be justified by faith, but after that faith has come we are no longer under a school-master. For ye are all the children of God by faith in Christ Jesus. For as many of you as have been baptised into Christ have put on Christ. There is neither Jew nor Greek, there is neither bond nor free, there is neither male nor female; for ye are all one in Christ Jesus. And if ye are Christ's, then are ye Abraham's seed, and heirs according to the promise. Now I say that the heir, as long as he is a child, differeth nothing from a servant, though he be lord of all; but is under tutors and governors until the time appointed of the father. Even so we, when we were children, were in bondage under the elements of the world: but when the fulness of the time was come God sent forth his Son made of a woman, made under the law, to redeem them that were under the law, that we might receive the adoption of sons. And because ye are sons, God hath sent forth the Spirit of his Son into your hearts, crying, Abba, Father, Wherefore thou art no more a servant but a son, and if a son then an heir of God through Christ.

"Howbeit then when ye knew not God, ye did service unto them which by nature are no gods. But now, after that ye have known God, or rather are known of God, how turn ye again to the weak and beggarly elements, whereunto ye desire again to be in bondage? Ye observe days, and months, and times, and years. I am afraid of you, lest I have bestowed upon you labour in vain.

"Brethren, I beseech you, be as I am; for I am as ye are; ye have not injured me at all. Ye know how through infirmity of the flesh I preached the gospel unto you at the first. And my temptation, which was in my flesh ye despised not, nor rejected; but received me as an angel of God, even as Christ Jesus. Where is then the blessedness ye spake of? for I bear you record, that, if it had been possible, ye would have plucked out your own eyes, and have given them to me. Am I therefore become your enemy, because I tell you the truth? They zealously affect you, but not well; yea, they would exclude you, that ye might affect them. But it is good to be zealously affected always in a good thing, and not only when I am present with you. My little children, of whom I travail in birth again until Christ be formed in you, I desire to be, present with you now, and to change my voice; for I stand in doubt of you. . . . . .

"Stand fast therefore in the liberty wherewith Christ hath made us free, and be not entangled again with the yoke of bondage. Behold, I, Paul, say unto you that, if ye be circumcised, Christ shall profit you nothing. For I testify again to every man that is circumcised, that he is a debtor to do the whole law. Christ is become of no effect unto you, whosoever of you are justified by the law: ye are fallen from grace. For we, through the Spirit, wait for the hope of righteousness by faith. For in Jesus Christ neither circumcision availeth anything, nor uncircumcision, but faith, which worketh by love.

"Ye did run well; who did hinder you that ye should not obey the truth? This persuasion cometh not of him that calleth you. A little leaven leaveneth the whole lump. I have confidence in you through the Lord, that ye will be none otherwise minded; but he that troubleth you shall bear his judgment, whosoever he be. And I, brethren, if I yet preach circumcision, why do I yet suffer persecution? Then is the offence of the cross ceased? I would they were even cut off which trouble you.

"For, brethren, ye have been called unto liberty: only use not liberty for an occasion to the flesh, but by love serve one another. For all the law is fulfilled in one word, even in this: Thou shalt love thy neighbour as thyself. But if ye bite and devour one another, take heed that ye be not consumed one of another. This I say then, Walk in the Spirit, and ye shall not fulfil the lust of the flesh. For the flesh lusteth against the Spirit, and the Spirit against the flesh: and these are contrary the one to the other, so that ye cannot do the things that ye would. But if ye be led of the Spirit, ye are not under the law. Now, the works of the flesh are manifest, which are these: Adultery, fornication, uncleanness, lasciviousness, idolatry, witchcraft, hatred, variance, emulations, wrath, strife, seditions, heresies, envyings, murders, drunkenness, revellings, and such like; of the which I tell you before, as I have also told you in times past, that they which do such things shall not inherit the kingdom of God. But the fruit of the Spirit is love, joy, peace, long-suffering, gentleness, goodness, faith, meekness, temperance: against such there is no law. And they which are Christ's have crucified the flesh with the affections and lusts. . . . ."

Paul wrote this epistle at a single sitting, as if filled with an interior fire. According to his habit, he wrote with his own hand, in postscript, "Ye see how large a letter I have written unto you with mine own hand."

It seems natural that he should finish with the usual salutation; but he was too much animated: his fixed idea possessed him. The subject being exhausted, he again returns to it with some keen remarks:--

"As many as desire to make a fair shew in the flesh, they constrain you to be circumcised; only lest they should suffer persecution for the cross of Christ. For neither they themselves who are circumcised keep the law, but desire to have you circumcised that they may glory in your flesh. But God forbid that I should glory, save in the cross of our Lord Jesus Christ, by whom the world is crucified unto me, and I unto the world. For in Christ Jesus neither circumcision availeth anything, nor uncircumcision, but a new creature. And as many as walk according to this rule, peace be upon them, and mercy, and upon the Israel of God. From henceforth let no man trouble me, for I bear in my body the marks of the Lord Jesus. Brethren, the grace of our Lord Jesus Christ be with your spirit. Amen."

Paul despatched this letter at once. If he had taken an hour's reflection, it is doubtful whether he would have let it be sent. We do not know to whom it was entrusted; Paul doubtless had it carried by one of his disciples, whom he charged with a journey into Galatia. The epistle, in fact, is not addressed to a particular community; each of those little Churches of Derbe, of Lystra, of Iconium, of Antioch in Pisidia, was not considerable enough to serve as a metropolis to the others; the Apostle, on the other hand, gives no instruction to the receivers as to the manner of circulating his letter. The effect that the letter produced upon the Galatians is also unknown. Without doubt it confirmed the party of Paul; it probably, however, did not entirely extinguish the opposite party. Almost all the Churches henceforward will be divided into two camps. The Church of Judæa will maintain its pretensions until the fall of Jerusalem (A.D. 70). It is only at the end of the first century that a true reconciliation will come about, partly at the expense of Paul's glory, which will during nearly a hundred years be cast into the shade, but for the full triumph of its fundamental ideas. The Judæo-Christians from this moment will only be a sect of old fanatics, dying out slowly and obscurely, and only ending towards the close of the fifth century in the remoter districts of Syria. Paul, in revenge, will be nearly disavowed. His title of Apostle, refused him by his enemies, will be feebly defended by his friends. The Churches which notoriously owe their foundation to him, will wish it to be thought that they were founded by him and by Peter. The Church of Corinth, for example, will do the most flagrant violence to history to show that she owes her origin to Peter as well as to Paul. The conversion of the Gentiles will pass for the collective work of the Twelve; Papias, Polycrates, Justin, Hegesippus, seem to labour to suppress the share of Paul in the work, and nearly ignore his existence. It is only when the idea of a canon of new sacred writings will be established that Paul will regain his importance. His epistles will then emerge in some way from the archives of the Churches to become the base of Christian theology, which they will renew from age to age.

At the distance at which we now stand, the victory of Paul appears complete. Paul recounts to us, and perhaps exaggerates, the injuries that have been done to him. Who will tell us the injuries of Paul? The mean intention which he attributes to his adversaries of following in his footsteps to carry away for themselves the affection of his disciples and to glorify themselves afterwards over the circumcision of these simple men, is not this a travesty? May not the recital of his relations with the Church of Jerusalem, different as it is from that of the Acts, be a little arranged for the needs of the moment? The pretence of having been an Apostle by divine right from the very day of his conversion, is it not historically inaccurate! in this sense, that the conviction of his own apostleship slowly took possession of him, and arrived at its completion only after his first great mission. Was Peter really so much to be blamed as Paul asserted? The conduct of the Galilean Apostle, on the contrary, was not it that of a conciliatory man, preferring brotherliness to principle, wishing to content everybody, yielding to avoid scandal, and blamed by all, precisely because he was right. We have no means of answering these questions. Paul was very egotistical; it is not impossible that he more than once attributed to a private revelation what he had learnt from his elders. The Epistle to the Galatians is so extraordinary a work, the Apostle there paints himself with so much artlessness and truth, that it would be absolutely unjust to turn against him a document which does so much honour to his talent and his eloquence. The cares of a narrow orthodoxy are not ours; to others belong the right of explaining how one can be a saint, whilst abusing the ancient Cephas. Paul is not degraded from the companionship of great men when he is proved to be sometimes hasty, passionate, pre-occupied with his own defence, and fighting his enemies. In everything that is truly Protestant, Paul has the faults of a Protestant. It requires time and much experience to enable him to see that each dogma is not worth the trouble of violent resistance and of wounding charity. Paul is not Jesus. How far we are from thee, dear Master. Where is thy tenderness, thy poesy? Thou who didst consider the lilies, dost thou recognise as thy disciples these disputants, these men who are so bitter about precedence, who wish that every body should originate with them alone. They are men, thou wast a God. Where should we be, if thou wert known to us only by the simple letters of him who calls himself thy Apostle. Happily, the perfumes of Galilee still live in some faithful memories. Perhaps already the Sermon on the Mount is written on some secret sheet. The unknown disciple who bears this treasure truly bears the future.

CHAPTER XII

THIRD JOURNEY OF PAUL--FOUNDATION OF THE CHURCH AT EPHESUS

Less great, less possessed by the sacred genius whicn had seized upon him, Paul was made use of in these barren disputes. To reply to little minds, he was obliged to make himself as mean as they were: these miserable quarrels had absorbed him. Paul scorned them as a man of superior genius should. He went straight forward, and left time to decide between him and his enemies. The first rule for a man devoted to great things, is to refuse mediocre men the power of turning him aside from his way. Without discussing with the delegates of James as to whether it were right or wrong to preach to the Gentiles and to convert them, Paul only thought of beginning again, even at the risk of encountering new anathemas. After some months passed at Antioch he departed on a third mission, on this occasion to his dear Galatian Churches. At times he was in great perplexity with regard to these Churches; he regretted having grieved them by using harsh language to them; he wished to change his tone, to correct by the gentleness of his words the asperity of his letter. Paul wished above all things to dwell at Ephesus, which he had only touched at first in order to constitute a preaching centre such as there was at Thessalonica and Corinth. The field of that third mission was thus very nearly that of the second. Asia Minor, Macedonia, and Greece were the provinces that Paul in some sort assigned to himself.

He set out from Antioch, accompanied probably by Titus. He followed the same track as on his second journey, and visited for the third time the Churches of the centre of Asia Minor--Derbe, Lystra, Iconium, Antioch in Pisidia. He speedily regained his authority, and soon effaced such false impressions as still remained, and which his enemies had sought to raise against him. At Derbe he took as assistant a new disciple, named Gaius, who followed him. These good Galatians were full of docility, but weak in the faith. Paul, accustomed to express himself with firmness, treated them with a severity that sometimes even he himself was afraid they would take for harshness. He had scruples; he was afraid that he had spoken to his children in a manner that perhaps did not express clearly enough the affection there was for them in his heart.

The motives that had made him in his second journey abstain from preaching the gospel to pro-consular Asia existing no longer, Paul, after having finished his tour in Galatia, set out for Ephesus. This was in the middle of the summer. From Antioch in Pisidia, the most natural route to follow should have led him to Apamea-Cibotus, and thence into the basin of the Lycus, to the three neighbouring towns of Colosse, of Laodicæa, of Hierapolis. These three towns for some years will form an active centre of Christian work, and Paul will be in close communication with them. But for the moment he did not stop here, and made acquaintance with no one. Going round the rock of Cadmas, he passed into the valley of Meander, towards the inns of Carura, a great highway of the roads of Asia. Thereçe, a beautiful and easy route, leads, in three days, by Nysa, Tralles, and Magnesia, to the summits of the chain which separates the waters of the Meander from those of the Caystrus. A ravine, where the ancient road and the torrent dispute the narrow space, descends into "the prairie of Asia," sung of by the Homerides, that is to say, into the plain where the Caystrus forms a lagoon before reaching the sea. It is a beautiful Greek site, with a clear horizon, formed sometimes of from five to six mountain heights, or bounded by low hills. The swans and the beautiful birds which met there at that time even as now gave all the charm of antiquity. There, partly in the marshes, partly hanging to the declivities of Mount Coressus, supported, besides, by Mount Prion and its surroundings on another little isolated hill, rose the immense town destined to be the third capital of Christianity after Jerusalem and Antioch.

We have already had occasion several times to remark that Christianity was most readily accepted in the smaller towns of the Roman Empire. The policy of that Empire had been to multiply isolated municipalities; isolated as regards race, religion, and patriotism. Ephesus was like Alexandria, Antioch, and Corinth, a typical town of this kind. It is easy thus to imagine what are still, in our days, the great towns of the Levant. What strikes the traveller when he goes through these labyrinths of infectious bazaars, of narrow and filthy courtyards, of temporary structures, which do not seem expected to last long?--it is the litter of a noble, of a political, and even of a municipal spirit. In these swarms of men, vulgarity and good instincts, idleness and activity, impertinence and amiability, meet each other: everything is found there excepting what constitutes an old local aristocracy; I would say glorious remembrances cultivated in common. With all that, there is much gossiping, prattling, levity; nearly everybody knows everybody else, and the people for ever occupy themselves with each other's business; there is something active, passionate, unsteady,--a vain curiosity of frivolous folk, greedy after the smallest novelty, ever ready to follow the fashion, never capable of setting it. Christianity was a fruit of that species of fermentation which usually arises in societies of this kind, where men, freed from the prejudices of birth and race, take up more readily the philosophical attitude which calls itself cosmopolitan and humanitarian, than the peasant, the burgess, the noble, or feudal citizen can do. Like the Socialism of our days, like all new ideas, Christianity germinates in what may be called the corruption of great towns. This corruption, in fact, is often only a plainer and freer life, a greater indication of the hidden forces of humanity.

Formerly, as now, the Jews in such mixed towns held a very conspicuous position. That place was, to a small extent, what Smyrna and Salonica are at the present day. Ephesus especially possessed a very populous Jews' quarter. The Pagan inhabitants were fanatical enough, as happens in all towns which are centres of pilgrimages and famous rites. The devotion to Artemis of Ephesus, spreading over the entire world, supported several considerable industries. But the importance of the town as the capital of Asia, the movement of business, the wealth of the people, of every race, made Ephesus a very useful centre for the diffusion of Christian ideas. These ideas found nowhere a better reception than in the populous commercial cities, full of strangers, visited by Syrians, Jews, and that population of uncertain origin who from time to time have commanded all the ports of the Mediterranean.

For centuries Ephesus had been nothing more than a purely Hellenic town. Formerly Ephesus had shone in the first rank, the least artistic among the Greek cities; but now and then she had allowed herself to be seduced by the manners of Asia. The town always had a bad reputation among the Greeks. Corruption, the introduction of luxury, was, according to the Greeks, a result of the effeminate manners of Ionia; at this time, and in this way, Ephesus was the centre and the abridgment of Ionia. The domination of the Lydians and of the Persians had destroyed energy and patriotism alike. Ephesus, like Sardis, was the most advanced point of Asiatic influence upon Europe. The excessive importance which the worship of Artemis took there, extinguished the scientific spirit, and favoured the over-flowing of all superstitions. It was an almost theocratic town; the fêtes there were numerous and splendid; the right wing of the temple peopled the town with courtesans. The scandalous sacerdotal institutions maintained there appeared each day more devoid of all sense of shame. That brilliant country of Heraclites, of Parhasius, perhaps of Apella, was only a town of porticoes, of stadia, of gymnasia, of theatres, a town of common-place sumptuosity, in spite of the masterpieces of painting and of sculpture that she still guards.

Although the gate had been spoilt by the engineers of Attains Philadelphus, the town increased rapidly, and became the principal emporium of the region on this side of the Taurus. It was the port of landing for what came from Italy and Greece, a sort of hostelry or mart on the threshold of Asia. Produce of every kind was heaped together there, and the town became a cosmopolitan one, where the socialistic ideas gained ground among the men who had lost all idea of patriotism. The country was extremely rich; the commerce immense; but nowhere was public spirit at a lower ebb. The inscriptions breathed the most shameful servility, the most absolute submission to the Romana.

It has been called the meeting-place of harlots and their prey. The town swarmed with magicians, diviners, mummers, and flute players; eunuchs, jewellers, sellers of amulets and medals, and romancers. The title of "Ephesian novels" designated, like that of "Milesian fables," a species of literature, Ephesus being one of the towns which was especially chosen as the scene of love romances. The softness of the climate, in fact, put aside serious things: dancing and music remained the sole occupation. Public life degenerated into bacchanalian festivities: there was no such thing as study. The most extravagant miracles of Apollonius are reputed to have happened at Ephesus. The most celebrated Ephesian of the time at which we have now arrived was an astrologer named Balbilas, who possessed the confidence of Nero and Vespasian, and who appears to have been a scoundrel. A beautiful Corinthian temple, whose ruins can be seen at the present day, was raised about the same period. It was perhaps a temple dedicated to poor Claudius, whom Nero and Agrippa had just "drawn to heaven with a hook," according to the happy word of Gallio.

Ephesus had already been reached by Christianity when Paul went to sojourn there. We have seen that Aquila and Priscilla had remained there, after having set out from Corinth. This pious couple, to whom, by a singular destiny, it was reserved to figure in the origin of the Churches of Rome, of Corinth, of Ephesus, formed a little nucleus of disciples. Of this number, doubtless, was that Epasnetus whom St Paul calls "the first-fruits of Achaia unto Christ," and whom he loved so much. Another much more important conversion was that of a Jew named Apollonius or Apollos, originally of Alexandria, who had settled at Ephesus a little after the first journey of Paul. He had acquired in the Jewish schools of Egypt a profound knowledge of the Scriptures, an ingenious manner of interpreting them, a sublime eloquence. He was a kind of Philo, in quest of new ideas which then dawned on all parts of Judaism. In his journeys, he found himself of the same belief with the disciples of John the Baptist, and had received their baptism. He had also heard them speak of Jesus, and it seems certain that from that time he accorded to the latter the title of Christ; but his idea of Christianity was incomplete. On his arrival at Ephesus he betook himself to the synagogue, where he had much success by his lively and inspired delivery. Aquila and Priscilla heard him, and were enraptured to receive such an auxiliary. They took him aside, instructed him more fully, and gave him more precise ideas upon certain points. As they were not very clever theologians themselves, they did not dream, it seems, of re-baptising him in the name of Jesus. Apollos formed around him a little group, whom he taught his doctrine, corrected by Aquila and Priscilla, but on whom he merely bestowed the baptism of John, the only one he knew. After some time he wished to pass into Achaia, and the brethren of Ephesus gave him a very warm letter of recommendation to those of Corinth.

It is under these circumstances that Paul arrived at Ephesus. He lodged with Aquila and Priscilla, as he had already done at Corinth; associated himself anew with them, and worked in their shop. Ephesus was justly celebrated for its tents. The artisans of this trade probably inhabited the poor suburbs which extended from Mount Prion to the steep hill of Aia-Solouk. There doubtless was the first Christian household; the apostolic basilicas were there, the venerated graves of all Christianity. After the destruction of the temple of Artemis, Ephesus having exchanged its Pagan celebrity for an equally celebrated Christianity, and having become a town of the first order in the memories and legends of the new worship. Byzantine Ephesus was wholly grouped round a hill which had the advantage of possessing the most precious monuments of Christianity. The old site being exchanged from an infectious marsh, where an active civilisation had ceased to regulate the course of the waters, the old town had been abandoned little by little; its gigantic monuments, in consequence of their nearness to navigable canals and the sea, had been made use of as quarries, and thus the town had been displaced for nearly a league. Perhaps the choice of a domicile which some poor Jews in the reign of Claudius or Nero had made was the first cause of this removal. The most ancient Turkish conquest continued the Byzantine tradition; a great Mussulman town succeeded to the Christian town, which still exists in the midst of so many memories of ruin, fever, and oblivion.

Paul was not here, as he was in his first missions, in the midst of a synagogue, ignorant of the new mystery, which he must endeavour to gain over. He had before him a Church which had been formed in the most original and spontaneous fashion, with the aid of two good Jewish merchants, and of a strange doctor, who was still only half a Christian. The company of Apollos was composed of about twelve members. Paul questioned them, and perceived that their faith was still incomplete: in particular, they had never heard of the Holy Ghost. Paul completed their instruction, re-baptised them in the name of Jesus, and "laid his hands on them." The Spirit immediately descended on them; they spake with tongues, and prophesied like perfect Christians.

The Apostle sought to enlarge this little circle of believers. He was not afraid of finding himself here in the presence of the intellectual and scientific spirit which had stopped him short at Athens. Ephesus was not a great intellectual centre. Superstition reigned there without any control; everybody lived in foolish preoccupations of demonology and theology. The magic formulas of Ephesus (Ephesia Grammata) were celebrated, books of sorcery abounded, and a number of men employed their time in these foolish puerilities. Apollonius of Tyana was at Ephesus about this time.

Paul, according to his habit, preached in the synagogue. During the space of three months, he did not cease each Sabbath to teach the Kingdom of God. He had little success. They did not come against him with riotings or severities, but they received his doctrine with insulting and scornful words. He then resolved to renounce the synagogue, and re-united himself to part of his disciples in a place which they called Σχολὴ Τυράννου, "The school of one Tyrannus." Perhaps it was a public spot there, one of those scholæ or semicircular vaults (or apses) which were so numerous in ancient towns, and which served as xystes for conversation and free instruction. Perhaps, on the other hand, it served as a private hall of a personage--of a grammarian, for example--named Tyrannus. In general, Christianity profited very little by these scholæ, which nearly always formed parts of the hot baths and gymnasia. The favourite place of the Christian propaganda, after the synagogue, was the private house, the chimney corner, In this vast metropolis of Ephesus. preaching might, however, be done openly. During two years, Paul did not cease to speak in the Schola Tyranni. This prolonged teaching in a public place, after a little time, made noise enough. The Apostles supplemented it by frequent visits to the houses of those who had been converted or touched. All pro-consular Asia heard the name of Jesus, and several Churches, subordinate to Ephesus, were established around. They also spoke of certain miracles effected by Paul. His reputation as a worker of miracles had reached such a point that people eagerly sought for the "hand-kerchiefs and aprons" which had touched his garment, to apply them to the sick. They believed that a medical virtue was exhaled from his body, and was so transmitted.

The taste of the Ephesians for magic introduced episodes still more shocking. Paul was believed to have a great power over devils. It appears that the Jewish exorcists sought to steal his charms and to exorcise "in the name of Jesus whom Paul preacheth." There is a legend of the misadventure of these quacks, who pretended to be sons or disciples of a certain High Priest named Scæva. Having wished to drive out an evil spirit by means of the aforesaid formula, they were grossly insulted by the possessed man, who not content with that, threw himself upon them, tore their clothes in pieces, and beat them soundly. The degradation of the popular mind was such, that many Jews and many Pagans believed in Jesus for such a poor motive. These conversions took place above all among the men who occupied themselves with magic. Struck by the superiority of Paul's formula, the lovers of occult sciences came to him to exchange confidences concerning their practices. Many even brought their books of magic and burnt them; they valued at fifty thousand pieces of silver (drachmæ) the price of the Ephesia Grammata burnt in this manner.

Let us turn our eyes away from these sad shadows. All that is done by the popular ignorant masses is spotted with unpleasantness. Illusion, chimera, are the conditions of the great things created by the people. It is only the work of wise men which can be pure; but wise men are usually powerless. We have a physiology and a medicine very superior to that of Paul; we are disengaged from a crowd of errors of which he partook, alas! and it is to be feared that we may never do a thousandth part of what he did. It is only when humanity as a whole shall be instructed, and reach a certain point of positive philosophy, that human affairs will be led by reason. One would never understand the history of the past if one did not refuse to treat as good and great movements in which many mean and equivocal features are mixed up.

CHAPTER XIII

PROGRESS OF CHRISTIANITY IN ASIA AND PHRYGIA

The ardour of Paul during his stay at Ephesus was extreme. There were difficulties every day, numerous and animated adversaries. As the Church of Ephesus was not purely a foundation of Paul, it counted in its bosom the Judæo-Christians, who, upon important points, resisted energetically the Apostle of the Gentiles. They were like two flocks accusing each other, and denying to each other the right of speaking in the name of Jesus. The Pagans, for their part, were discontented with the progress of the new faith, and already manifested themselves as dangerous. On one occasion, in particular, Paul ran so grave a danger that he compares the position in which he was on that day to that of a man exposed to wild beasts. Perhaps the incident happened at the theatre, which would render the expression altogether just. Aquila and Priscilla saved him, and risked their heads for him.

The Apostle forgot all, however, for the word of God had become fruitful. All the western part of Asia Minor, especially the basins of the Meander and the Hermus, was covered with Churches at this time, of which, without doubt, Paul was in a manner more or less directly the founder. Smyrna, Pergamos, Thyatira, Sardis, Philadelphia, probably Tralles, thus received the germs of the faith. These towns had already important Jewish colonies. The gentleness of manners, and the great tediousness of provincial life, in the heart of a rich and beautiful country, dead for centuries to all political life, and pacified nearly to a level, had prepared many souls for the joys of a pure life. The softness of the Ionian manners, so inimical to national independence, was favourable to the development of moral and social questions. These good populations, without military spirit, effeminate, if I dare say it, were naturally Christian. The family life appears to have been very strong among them; the habit of living in the open air, and, for the women, upon the threshold of their doors, in a delicious climate, had developed great sociability. Asia, with its Asiarchs, presidents of the games and spectacles, seemed a pleasure company, an association of diversions and fêtes. The Christian population even to-day has the charm of gaiety; the women have the clear complexion, the vague and sweet eyes, beautiful blonde hair, a retiring and modest disposition, involving the sentient life of their beauty.

Asia became thus, in some sort, the second province of the kingdom of God. The towns of this country, apart from its monuments, did not perhaps differ essentially then from what they are to-day clusters of wooden houses without order, with open balconies covered with an inclined roof; quarters often placed in tiers one upon the other, and always intermingled with beautiful trees. The public buildings necessary in a hot country to a life of pleasure and repose were of a surprising grandeur. There were not here, as in Syria, artificial constructions, very little adapted to comfort, walled towns, rendered necessary by the predatory habits of the Bedouin. Nowhere does the fulness of a sure and satisfied civilisation show itself in more imposing forms than in the ruins of these "magnificent cities of Asia." Every time that the beautiful countries of which we speak are crushed into pieces by fanaticism, war, or barbarity, they will become mistresses of the world by richness; they hold nearly all the sources of it, and thus force the great number of the more noble people to mass themselves up among them. Ionia, in the first century, was very populous, and covered with towns and villages. At this period, the misfortunes of the civil wars were forgotten. With powerful associations of workmen (ἐργασίαι, συνεργασαι, συμβιώσεις), analogous to those of Italy and Flanders in the Middle Ages, they name their dignitaries, raise public monuments, erect statues, construct works of public utility, found charitable institutions, give every kind of sign of prosperity, of welfare, of moral activity. Side by side with the manufacturing towns, such as Thyatira, Philadelphia, Hieropolis--principally engaged in the great industries of Asia, carpets, the dyeing of cloth, the wool, leather--was developed a prosperous agriculture. The varied products of the districts of the Hermus and the Meander, the mineral riches of Imolus and of Messogio sources of the treasures of the old Assyrian town Lydia, had produced at Tralles above all an opulent middle-class, which contracted alliances with the kings of Asia, almost even became itself royal. These upstarts ennobled themselves in a more honourable manner by their literary labours and their generosity. It is true that we must not look in their works for either delicacy or Hellenic perfection. We feel, in contemplating such parvenu monuments, that all nobleness was lost when these people were raised. The municipal spirit, however, was still very energetic. The citizen who had become king, or reached Cæsar's favour, contended for an official position in the city, and expended his fortune in embellishing it. This movement of construction was in full force in the time of St Paul, partly on account of the earthquakes which, notably in the reign of Tiberius, had desolated the country, and which necessitated much repairing.

A rich province of Southern Phrygia, in particular the little basin of the Lycus, a tributary of the Meander, was soon formed into active Christian centres. Three towns close to each other--Colossus or Colosse, Laodicæa upon the Lycus, and Hieropolis--there diffused the Word of Life. Colosse, which had formerly been of most importance, seemed to decline; it was an old city which remained faithful to the ancient manners, and which would not change them. Laodicæa and Hieropolis, on the contrary, became, under the Roman rule, very considerable towns. The summit of this beautiful country is Mount Cadmas, the father of all the mountains of Eastern Asia, massive and gigantic, full of dark precipices, and crowned with snow throughout the year. The waters which flow from it nourish upon the slopes of the valleys orchards full of fruit trees, which are traversed by rivers abounding in fish, and brightened by tame storks. The other side exhibits the strangest freaks of nature. The petrifying quality of the water of one of the tributaries of the Lycus, and the enormous mineral stream which falls in a cascade from the mountains of Hieropolis, have sterilised the plain and formed crevasses, grotesque caverns, beds of subterranean rivers, of fantastic basins, like petrified snow, serving as a reservoir to the waters, which glisten with all the colours of the rainbow; deep trenches through which roll a series of resounding cataracts. On this side the heat is extreme, the soil being simply a vast plain paved with limestone; but upon the heights of Hieropolis the purity of the air, the splendid light, the view of the Cadmas, floating like an Olympus in a dazzling atmosphere, the burning summits of Phrygia vanishing in the blue of heaven in a rosy hue, the opening of the Meander, the oblique sections of Messogio, the distant snowy summits of the Imolus, are absolutely dazzling. Saint Philip lived there; Paphas also; there Epictetus was born. All the valley of the Lycus offers the same character of dreamy mysticism. The population was not originally Greek; it was partly Phrygian. There was also, it would appear, around the Cadmas an ancient Semitic establishment, probably an annexe of Lydia. This peaceful valley, separated from the rest of the world, became for Christianity a place of refuge. Christianity underwent, as we shall see, grave trials.

The evangelist of these regions was Epaphroditus or Epaphras of Colosse, a very zealous man, a friend and fellow-worker with Paul. The Apostle had only passed through the valley of the Lycus; he had never remained there; but these Churches, composed chiefly of converted Pagans, were not less completely dependent on him. Epaphras exercised upon the three villages a sort of episcopacy. Nymphadore, or Nymphas, who gathered a Church in his house at Laodicæa; the rich and benevolent Philemon, who, at Colosse, presided over a similar conventicle; Appia, deaconess of this town, perhaps the wife of Philemon; Archippus, who also filled an important function there, recognised Paul as chief. The last appears even to have worked directly with Paul. The Apostle called him his "companion in arms." Philemon, Appia, and Archippus must have been relatives or in intimate connection with each other.

Paul's disciples travelled constantly, and reported to their master. Each one, though hardly converted, was a zealous catechist, spreading around him the faith with which he was filled. The delicate moral aspirations which prevailed in the country propapagated the movement like a train of gunpowder. The catechists went everywhere; as soon as they were received, they were jealously guarded; all and each tried to supply their wants. A cordiality, a joy, an infinite benevolence, prevailed by degrees, and touched the hearts of all. Judaism, besides, had preceded Christianity in these regions. Jewish colonies had been founded there by exiles from Babylon two centuries and a half before, and had perhaps carried there some of those industries (carpet-making, for example) which under the Roman emperors produced in the country so much wealth and so many strong associations.

Did the preaching of Paul and his disciples reach Great Phrygia, the region of Azanes, of Synnades, of Colia, of Docimius? We have seen that in his two first journeys, Paul preached in Phrygia Parorea; that in his second journey he traversed Phrygia, Epicteta, without preaching; that in his third journey he traversed Apamea, Cibotos, and Phrygia, called at a later date Pacatiana. It is extremely probable that the remainder of Phrygia, as well as Bithynia, owed to Paul's disciples the seeds of Christianity. About the year 112, Christianity appears in Bithynia as a worship which had taken root, which had penetrated all the ranks of society, which had invaded the villages and the rural districts, as well as the towns and cities, and had brought about a long cessation of the official worship, so that the Roman authority was reduced by it to command the restoration of Pagan sacrifices. Some of the proselytes returned to the temples, and the victims, now made slaves, found buyers here and there. About the year 112, some men, on being asked if they were Christians, replied that they had been, but they had ceased to be "more than twenty years ago"--a clear proof that the first Christian preaching took place during the lifetime of Paul.

Phrygia was thenceforward, and remained for three hundred years, an essentially Christian country. There first begins the public profession of Christianity; there, from the third century, are to be found upon monuments exposed to every one's eyes, the word ΧΡΗΣΤΙΑΝΟΣ or ΧΡΙΣΤΙΑΝΟΣ: these epitaphs, without openly avowing Christianity, exhibit Christian dogmas in a veiled form: there, from the time of Severus the Second, great towns adopted upon their coins biblical symbols, or, rather, assimilated their old traditions to biblical story. A large number of the Ephesian and Roman Christians came from Phrygia. The names which are shown oftenest upon the Phrygian monuments are old Christian names--names belonging specially to the Apostolic age, those which fill the martyrology. It is very probable that this prompt adoption of the doctrine of Jesus was natural to the race and to the former religious institutions derived from the Phrygian people. Apollonius of Tyana had, it is said, temples among these simple populations: the idea of gods clothed in human form appeared very natural to them. What remains of ancient Phrygia often breathes something of religion, of morality, of depth, of something analogous to Christianity. Some good workers, near to Cotia, made a vow "to the saintly and just God;" not far from there, another vow is addressed to "the holy and just God." Such an epitaph in verses of this province, not very classical in style, incorrect and bad in form, seems imprinted with a very modern sentiment of a touching kind of romance. The country itself differs much from the rest of Asia. It is sad, austere, sombre, bearing the profound imprint of old geological catastrophes, burnt, or rather incinerated, and agitated by frequent earthquakes.

Pontus and Cappadocia heard the name of Jesus at about the same time. Christianity illuminated all Asia Minor like a sudden fire. It is probable that the Judæo-Christians laboured on their part to spread the Gospel there. John, who belonged to this party, was received in Asia as an Apostle with authority superior to that of Paul. The Apocalypse, addressed in the year 68 to the Churches of Ephesus, of Smyrna, of Pergamos, of Thyatira, of Sardis, of Philadelphia, and of Laodicæa-upon-the-Lycus, is obviously written for Judæo-Christians. Without doubt, between the death of Paul and the composition of the Apocalypse, there was in Ephesus and in Asia a second Judæo-Christian mission. Otherwise, if Paul had been during ten years the sole chief of the Churches of Asia, we should find it difficult to understand why he had been so quickly forgotten there. St Philip and Paphias, the glories of the Church of Hieropolis; Miletum, the glory of that of Sardis, were Judæo-Christians. Neither Paphias nor Polycrates of Ephesus quote Paul; the authority of John has absorbed everything, and John is for these Churches a great Jewish priest. The Churches of Asia in the second century, the Church of Laodicæa especially, are the scene of a controversy which attacks the vital question of Christianity, and the traditional party of which shows itself very distant from the ideas of Paul. Montanism is a kind of return towards Judaism in the heart of Phrygian Christianity. In other words, in Asia, as in Corinth, the memory of Paul, after his death, appears to have suffered during one hundred years a kind of eclipse. The very Churches which he had founded abandoned him, as one who had gone too far, so that in the second century Paul appears to have been discarded.

This reaction must have set in shortly after the Apostle's death, perhaps even before. The second and third chapters of the Apocalypse are a cry of hate against Paul and his friends. This Church of Ephesus, which owes so much to Paul, is praised be-cause "it cannot bear with them which are evil," for having known how to "try them which say they are apostles and are not, and have found them liars," for hating "the deeds of the Nicolaitans, which I also hate," adds the celestial voice. The Church of Smyrna is congratulated on being the object of the insults of men "which say they are Jews, and are not, but are the synagogue of Satan." "But I have a few things against thee," says the Divine voice to the Church of Pergamos, "because thou hast there them that hold the doctrine of Balaam, who taught Balak to cast a stumbling-block before the children of Israel,--to eat things sacrificed unto idols, and to commit fornication. So hast thou also them that hold the doctrine of the Nicolaitans." "Notwithstanding I have a few things against thee," says the same voice to the Church of Thyatira, "because thou sufferest that woman Jezebel, which calleth herself a prophetess, to teach and to seduce my servants to commit fornication, and to eat things sacrificed unto idols. And I gave her space to repent of her fornication; and she repented not . . . But unto you I say, and unto the rest in Thyatira, as many as have not this doctrine, and which have not known the depths of Satan, as they speak; I will put upon you none other burden." And to the Church of Philadelphia, "Behold, I will make them of the synagogue of Satan, which say they are Jews, and are not, but do lie; behold, I will make them to come and worship before thy feet, and to know that I have loved thee." Perhaps the vague reproaches addressed by the All-Seeing to the Churches of Sardis and Laodicæa included also some allusions to the great debate which broke up the Church of Jesus.

Let us say, then, if Paul had been the only missionary of Asia, one could not conceive that, so soon after his death (even supposing that he was dead when the Apocalypse appeared), his adherents could be represented as in a minority in the Churches of this country; one could not conceive that the Church of Ephesus, of which above all he was the principal founder, would have bestowed upon him an insulting nickname. Paul, as a rule, refused to trespass on the ground of others, to preach to, and to work in, the Churches which he had not established. But his enemies did not observe the same discretion. They followed him step by step, and applied themselves to destroy his works by insults and calumny.

CHAPTER XIV

SCHISMS IN THE CHURCH OF CORINTH--APOLLOS--FIRST SCANDALS

At the same time that he took his share in the vast propaganda which gained Asia to the worship of Jesus, Paul was absorbed by the gravest pre-occupations. The care of all the Churches that he had founded, weighed upon him. The Church of Corinth especially inspired him with the gravest disquiet. During the three or four years which had elapsed since the departure of the Apostle from the port of Cenchrea, trouble of every kind had incessantly agitated this Church. Greek levity had indeed produced certain phenomena which had nothing to do with the points that Christianity had touched.

We have seen that Apollos, after a short stay at Ephesus, where Aquila and Priscilla had worked at his Christian education, had set out for Corinth, with urgent letters from the brethren in Asia to those of Achaia, The knowledge and the eloquence of this new doctor were much admired by the Corinthians. Apollos equalled Paul in his knowledge of the Scriptures, and he greatly surpassed him in his literary culture. The Greek which he spoke was excellent, whilst that of the Apostle was extremely defective. He had also, it seems, the exterior gifts of the orator, which failed in Paul, the imposing attitude, the easy eloquence. What is quite certain is, that at Corinth he had remarkable success. His arguments with the Jews upon the question of knowing if Jesus was the Messiah, were regarded as very strong, and he made many conversions.

Apollos and St Paul appeared, among the new sect, in different aspects. They were the only well-instructed Jews in the Jewish manner who had embraced the doctrine of Jesus. But they came from different schools. Paul came from the Pharisaism of Jerusalem, corrected by the liberal tendencies of Gamaliel. Apollos came from the Judæo-Hellenic school of Alexandria: such things we know by Philo; perhaps he was already instructed in the theories of the logos, and was the introducer of these theories into Christian theology. Paul had the kind of feverish ardour, the intense fanaticism, which characterises the Jew of Palestine. Natures like that of Paul only change once in their life; the direction of their fanaticism once found, they press on without ever deviating or examining anything. Apollos, more curious and more critical, was ready to inquire into everything. He was a man of talent rather than an Apostle. But everything makes one believe that he joined to this talent great sincerity, and that he was a very affectionate man. At the time of his arrival at Corinth he had not seen St Paul. It was only by Aquila and Priscilla that he knew the Apostle of whom soon, without wishing it, he was going to be the rival.

Among the light-hearted and brilliant populations of the shores of the Mediterranean, factions, parties, divisions are a social necessity. Life without that appears tedious. These people are bent on procuring for themselves the satisfaction of hating and of loving, of excitement, of jealousy, of triumphing over an opponent, even in the most trivial matters. The object of the division is insignificant; it is the division that is wanted, and that is sought for its own sake. Personal questions become, in societies of this kind, all important. When two teachers or two doctors meet in a little town of the south, the town divides into two parties on the merits of each of them. The two preachers, the two doctors, may be warm friends; they will not prevent their names from becoming the signal of keen contests, the banners of two opposing camps.

It was thus at Corinth. The talent of Apollos turned all heads. His manner was absolutely different from that of Paul. The latter charmed by his boldness, his passion, the keen impression of his ardent soul; Apollos by his speech, which was elegant, correct, and assured. Some people, who did not greatly love Paul. and who perhaps did not owe their conversion to him, highly preferred Apollos. They treated Paul as an unpolished man, without education, a stranger to philosophy and polite learning. Apollos was their doctor; they swore only by Apollos. The disciples of Paul, doubtless, replied eagerly, and under-valued the new doctor. Although Paul and Apollos were in no wise enemies, although they regarded themselves as fellow-labourers, and although there was no difference of opinion between them, their names became thus the ensigns of two parties, who quarrelled, in spite of the two doctors, with quite sufficient vivacity. The bitterness continued, even after the departure of Apollos. He, in fact, fatigued perhaps by the zeal displayed for him, and showing himself above all these petty rivalries, left Corinth, and returned to Ephesus. He there found Paul, with whom he had long conversations, and consolidated a friendship which, without being that of the disciple or of the intimate friend, was one of two great souls, worthy of understanding and of loving each other.

That was not the only cause of trouble. Corinth was a place much frequented by strangers. The port of Cenchrea saw great numbers of Jews and Syrians disembark every day, many of whom were already Christians, but of another school than that of Paul, and by no means well disposed to the Apostle. The emissaries of the Church of Jerusalem, whom we have already met at Antioch and in Galatia, upon the footsteps of Paul, had reached Corinth. These new-comers, great orators, full of boasting, fortified with letters of recommendation from the Apostles of Jerusalem, rose against Paul, scattered suspicions upon his honesty, questioned or denied his title of Apostle, and pushed their indelicacy so far as to maintain that Paul himself did not believe that he was really an Apostle, since he did not profit by the ordinary privileges of an Apostle. His disinterestedness was made use of against him. They represented him as a vain, frivolous, inconstant man, speaking and menacing without much effect; they reproached him with glorifying himself whenever opportunity offered, and of appealing to pretended favours from Heaven. They scoffed at his visions. They dwelt upon the fact that Paul had not known Jesus,--that he had not, in consequence, any right to speak of him.

At the same time, they represented the Apostles of Jerusalem, especially James and Peter, as the true Apostles, the arch-apostles, in some way. The new-comers, simply because they were of Jerusalem, claimed a relationship with Christ after the flesh, considering the bond that they had with James and with those whom Christ had chosen in his lifetime. They held that God had established a single Doctor, who is Christ, who had instituted the Twelve. Proud of their circumcision and of their Jewish descent, they sought to impose as much as possible the yoke of legal observances. There was thus at Corinth, as there was nearly everywhere else, a "party of Peter." The division was profound. "I am of Paul," said some; "I am of Apollos," said others; "I am of Cephas," said others still. Some people, finally wishing to pose as superior spirits to these quarrellers, created a very spiritual title for themselves. They invented as the name by which they would designate themselves, that of the "party of Christ." When the discussion got warm, and when the names of Paul, Apollos, Peter (Cephas) crossed them in the battle, they intervened with the name of that One whom they forgot. "I am of Christ," said they, and, as these juvenilities did not exclude at the bottom a truly Christian spirit, the remembrance of Jesus had a powerful effect in restoring concord. The name of this "party of Christ" involved nevertheless something of hostility against the Apostle, and a certain ingratitude, since those who were opposed to the "party of Paul" seemed to wish to efface the trace of an apostleship to which it owed its knowledge of Christ.

Contact with the Pagans caused to the young Church no small dangers. These dangers came from Greek philosophy, and from bad morals, which everywhere assailing the Church in some degree, here penetrated it and undermined it. We have already seen that at Athens philosophy had stopped the progress of the preaching of Paul. Corinth was far from being a town of as high culture as Athens; there were, however, many well-instructed men there, who received the new doctrines very ill. The cross, the resurrection, the approaching restoration of all things, appeared to them follies and absurdities. The faith of many was shaken, and the attempt to bring about an impossible reconciliation altered the gospel. The irreconcilable struggle between positive science and the supernatural elements of the Christian faith began. This contest will only finish by the complete extinction of positive science in the Christian world in the sixth century; the same contest will be revived with positive science on the threshold of modern times.

The general immorality of Corinth produced upon the Church the most disastrous effects. Many Christians had not been able to break themselves away from loose habits, which, from being common, had almost ceased to be thought culpable. They talked of strange and almost unheard of scandals even in the assembly of the saints. The bad habits of the town crossed the threshold of the Church, and corrupted it. The Jewish rules about marriage, which all parts of the Christian Church proclaimed imperative and absolute, were violated: Christians even lived publicly with their mothers-in-law. A spirit of vanity, of frivolity, of disputation, of foolish pride, reigned among many. It seemed as if there was not another Church in the world, so much did this community walk in its own ways without caring for others. The gifts of the Spirit, speaking with tongues, prophesying, the gift of miracles, formerly subjects of so much edification, degenerated into shocking scenes. Hence arose strange disorders in the Church. The women, formerly so submissive, were here very bold, almost claiming equality with the men. They wished to pray aloud, to prophesy in the Church, and that without a veil, their long hair disordered, making the assembly witness of their ecstasies, of their drunken effeminacy, of their pious lubricities.

But it was the agapes (love feasts) or mystic feasts above all which gave an opportunity for the most crying abuses. The scenes of rioting which followed the Pagan sacrifices were there reproduced. Instead of all things being common, each ate the part that he had brought; some went nearly drunk, others very hungry. The poor were covered with shame; the rich seemed by their abundance to insult those who had nothing. The remembrance of Jesus, and of the high significance which he had given to this repast, appeared forgotten. The corporal state of the Church was for the rest bad enough; there were many sick, and several had died. Death, in the state in which the mind of the faithful then was, caused much surprise and hesitation; sickness was held as a trial of faith or as a chastisement.

Had four years then sufficed to take all the virtue out of the work of Jesus? Certainly not. There were still edifying families, in particular that of Stephanas, who was entirely devoted to the service of the Church, and was a model of evangelical activity. But the conditions of Christian society were already much changed. The little Church of saints of the latter day was thrown into a corrupted, frivolous world very little given to mysticism. There were already bad Christians. The time was gone by when Ananias and Sapphira were struck dead for having kept back some little property. The sacred feast of Jesus had become a debauch, and the earth did not open to devour him who went out drunk from the table of the Lord.

These evil tidings reached Paul one upon another, and filled him with sadness. The first rumours only mentioned some faults against good morals. Paul wrote on this subject an epistle that we no longer have. He therein forbade to the faithful all communication with persons whose life was not pure. Some ill-intentioned men affected to give to this order a meaning which rendered it impossible to be executed. "Are we at Corinth then," said they, "to have communications with irreproachable people only? . . . . But what is he thinking of? It is not only from Corinth, it is from the world that we must depart." Paul was obliged to revert to this order, and explain it.

He knew the divisions which agitated the Church a little later, probably in April, by the brothers whom he called "them which are of the house of Chloe." Just at this moment he thought of leaving Ephesus. Some motives which we do not know detained him there for some time. He sent into Greece before him, with powers equal to his own, his disciple Timothy, accompanied by several brothers, amongst others a certain Erastus, probably another than the treasurer of the town of Corinth, who bore the same name. Although the principal object of their journey was Corinth, they passed through Macedonia. Paul intended to take this journey himself, and, according to his custom, he caused his disciples to precede him to announce his arrival.

Shortly after the message of Chloe, and before Timothy and his companion had arrived at Corinth, new envoys from this town came to find Paul. These were the deacon Stephanas, Fortunatus, and Achaicus, three men very dear to the Apostle. Stephanas was according to the Apostle's expression, "the first fruits of Achaia," and since the departure of Aquila and Priscilla he had held the first rank in the community, or at least in the party of Paul. The envoys brought a letter asking for explanations with regard to the former epistle of Paul, and for solutions of divers cases of conscience, in particular touching marriage, the meats sacrificed to idols, spiritual exercises, and the gifts of the Holy Ghost. The three envoys added by word of mouth details of the abuses which had been introduced. The annoyance of the Apostle was extreme, and, regardless of consolation that the pious messengers gave him, he lost his temper in the presence of such feebleness and levity. He had fixed his departure for after Easter, which was probably two months later on; but he wished to pass through Macedonia. He could not even now be at Corinth in less than three months. He immediately resolved to write to the sick Church, and to reply to the questions they had addressed to him. As Timothy was not with him, he took as a secretary a disciple unknown to the others, named Sosthenes, and, by a delicate attention, he wished that the name of this disciple should figure in the subscription of the letter along with his own.

He began by an appeal to concord, and, under the appearance of humility, by an apology for his preaching,--

"Now this I say, that every one of you saith, I am of Paul; and I of Apollos; and I of Cephas; and I of Christ. Is Christ divided? was Paul crucified for you? or were ye baptised in the name of Paul? I thank God that I baptised none of you but Crispus and Gaius; lest any should say that I baptised in mine own name. And I baptised also the household of Stephanas: besides I know not whether I baptised any other. For Christ sent me not to baptise, but to preach the gospel: not with wisdom of words, lest the cross of Christ should be made of none effect. For the preaching of the cross is to them that perish, foolishness; but unto us which are saved it is the power of God. For it is written, I will destroy the wisdom of the wise, I will bring to nothing the understanding of the prudent. Where is the wise? where is the scribe? where is the disputer of this world? hath not God made foolish the wisdom of this world? For after that in the wisdom of God the world by wisdom knew not God, it pleased God by the foolishness of preaching to save them that believe. For the Jews require a sign, and the Greeks seek after wisdom. But we preach Christ crucified, unto the Jews a stumbling-block, and unto the Greeks foolishness; but unto them which are called, both Jews and Greeks, Christ the power of God and the wisdom of God. Because the foolishness of God is wiser than men; and the weakness of God is stronger than men. For ye see your calling, brethren, how that many wise men after the flesh, not many mighty, not many noble, are called: but God hath chosen the foolish things of the world to confound the wise; and God hath chosen the weak things of the world to confound them which are mighty; and base things of the world, and things which are despised, hath God chosen, yea, and things which are not, to bring to nought things that are: that no flesh should glory in his presence. . . .

"And I, brethren, when I came to you, came not with excellency of speech or of wisdom, declaring unto you the testimony of God. For I determined not to know anything among you, save Jesus Christ and him crucified. And I was with you in weakness, and in fear, and in much trembling. And my speech and my preaching was not with enticing words of man's wisdom, but in demonstration of the Spirit and of power; that your faith should not stand in the wisdom of men, but in the power of God. Howbeit we speak wisdom among them that are perfect; yet not the wisdom of this world, nor of the princes of this world, that come to nought, but we speak the wisdom of God in a mystery, even the hidden wisdom, which God ordained before the world unto our glory; which none of the princes of this world knew; for had they known it they would not have crucified the Lord of glory. But as it is written, Eye hath not seen, nor ear heard, neither have entered into the heart of man, the things which God hath prepared for them that love him. But God hath revealed them unto us by his Spirit; for the Spirit searcheth all things, yea, the deep things of God. For what man knoweth the things of a man, save the spirit of man which is in him? even so the things of God knoweth no man, but the Spirit of God. Now we have received, not the spirit of the world, but the spirit which is of God; that we might know the things that are freely given to us of God. Which things also we speak, not in the words which man's wisdom teacheth, but which the Holy Ghost teacheth; comparing spiritual things with spiritual. But the natural man receiveth not the things of the Spirit of God: for they are foolishness unto him: neither can he know them, be-cause they are spiritually discerned. But he that is spiritual judgeth all things, yet he himself is judged of no man. . .

"And I, brethren, could not speak unto you as unto spiritual, but as unto carnal, even as unto babes in Christ. I have fed you with milk, and not with meat; for hitherto ye were not able to bear it, neither yet now are ye able. For ye are yet carnal: for whereas there is among you envying, and strife, and divisions, are ye not carnal, and walk as men? For when one saith, I am of Paul, and another, I am of Apollos, are ye not carnal? Who then is Paul, and who is Apollos, but ministers by whom ye believed, even as the Lord gave to every man? I have planted, Apollos watered; but God gave the increase. So then neither is he that planteth anything, neither he that watereth, but God, that giveth the increase . . . For we are labourers together with God; ye are God's husbandry, ye are God's building. According to the grace of God which is given unto me, as a wise master-builder, I have laid the foundation, and another buildeth thereon. But let every man take heed how he buildeth thereupon. For other foundation can no man lay than that is laid, which is Jesus Christ. . . . Know ye not that ye are the temple of God, and that the Spirit of God dwelleth in you? . . . Let no man deceive himself. If any among you seemeth to be wise in this world, let him become a fool, that he may be wise. For the wisdom of this world is foolishness with God. For it is written, He taketh the wise in their own craftiness. And again, The Lord knoweth the thoughts of the wise, that they are vain. Therefore let no man glory in men. For all things are yours; whether Paul, or Apollos, or Cephas, or the world, or life, or death, or things present, or things to come, all are yours; and ye are Christ's; and Christ is God's.

"Let a man so account of us, as of the ministers of Christ, and stewards of the mysteries of God. . . . But with me it is a very small thing that I should be judged of you, or of man's judgment; yea, I judge not mine own self . . . but he that judgeth me is the Lord. . . . Therefore judge nothing before the time, until the Lord come, who both will bring to light the hidden things of darkness, and will make manifest the counsels of the hearts: and then shall every man have praise of God.

"And these things, brethren, I have in a figure transferred to myself and to Apollos for your sakes that no one of you be puffed up for one against another . . . Now ye are full, now ye are rich, ye have reigned as kings without us: and I would to God ye did reign, that we also might reign with you. For I think that God hath set forth us, the Apostles, last, as it were, appointed to death: for we are made a spectacle unto the world, and to angels, and to men. We are fools for Christ's sake, but ye are wise in Christ; we are weak, but ye are strong; ye are honourable, but we are despised. Even unto this present hour we both hunger, and thirst, and are naked, and are buffeted, and have no certain dwelling-place; and labour, working with our own hands; being reviled, we bless; being persecuted, we suffer it; being defamed, we entreat; we are made as the filth of the world, and are the offscourings of all things unto this day!

"I write not these things to shame you, but as my beloved sons I warn you. For though ye have ten thousand instructors in Christ, yet have ye not many fathers; for in Christ Jesus I have begotten you through the gospel. Wherefore I beseech you, be ye followers of me. For this cause have I sent unto you Timotheus, who is my beloved son, and faithful in the Lord, who shall bring you into remembrance of my ways, which be in Christ, as I teach everywhere in every Church. Now some are puffed up, as though I would not come to you. But I will come to you shortly, if the Lord will, and will know, not the speech of them which are puffed up, but the power. For the Kingdom of God is not in word, but in power. What will ye? Shall I come unto you with a rod, or in love, and in the spirit of meekness?"

After this general apology, the Apostle approaches each of the abuses which had been pointed out to him, and the questions which had been put to him. It is for the incestuous an extreme severity.

"It is reported commonly among you that there is fornication among you, and such fornication as is not so much as named among the Gentiles, that one should have his father's wife. And ye are puffed up, and have not rather mourned, that he hath done this deed might be taken away from you. For I verily, as absent in body, but present in spirit, have judged already, as though I were present, concerning him that hath so done this deed. In the name of our Lord Jesus Christ, when ye are gathered together, and my spirit, with the power of our Lord Jesus Christ, to deliver such an one unto Satan for the destruction of the flesh, that the spirit may be saved in the name of the Lord Jesus."

There can be no doubt: it is a sentence of death that Paul pronounces. Terrible legends were circulated as to the effect of the excommunications. It is to be remembered, besides, that Paul seriously believed in the working of miracles. By only delivering to Satan the body of the blameable, he doubtless believed himself to be indulgent.

The order that Paul had given in a preceding letter (lost) to the Corinthians, to avoid the shameless, had brought about mistakes. Paul developed his idea. The Christian has not to judge the world without, but to be severe only upon those who are within. A single spot on the purity of life ought to be sufficient to exclude one from the Christian society; it is forbidden so much as to eat with a delinquent. Thus it may seem in a convent, a congregation of pious persons, occupied in watching and judging each other, much more than in a church, in the modern sense of the word. The whole Church, in the eyes of the Apostle, is responsible for the faults committed within its bosom. This exaggeration of severity had its reason for its existence in ancient society, which sinned in so many other ways. But we feel that such an idea of sanctity is narrow-minded, illiberal, contrary to the morality of him whom we formerly called "a good fellow;" a morality whose fundamental principle is to busy oneself as little as possible with other people's conduct. The question is only to know if society can exist without censuring bad manners, and if the future will not bring back something analogous to the ecclesiastical discipline that modern liberalism has so jealously suppressed.

The ideal type of moral perfection, according to Paul, is a man, gentle, honest, chaste, sober, charitable, unfettered by riches. Humility of condition and poverty are almost necessary for one who would be a Christian. The words "miser, greedy one, thief," are nearly synonymous; at least the vices which they designate are liable to the same reproach. The antipathy of this little world for the great profane society was strange. Paul, following in that the Jewish tradition, reproves as an act unworthy of the faithful any reference to the courts of law.

"Dare any of you, having a matter against another, go to law before the unjust, and not before the saints? Do ye not know that the saints shall judge the world? and if the world be judged by you, are ye unworthy to judge the smallest matters? . . . Know ye not that we shall judge angels? How much more things that pertain to this life? If then ye have judgments of things pertaining to the life, set them to judge who are least esteemed in this church. I speak to your shame. Is it so, that there is not a wise man among you? No, not one that shall be able to judge between his brethren? But brother goeth to law with brother, and that before the unbelievers. Now therefore there is utterly a fault among you, because ye go to law one with another. Why do ye not rather take wrong? Why do ye not rather suffer yourselves to be defrauded? Nay, ye do wrong, and defraud, and that your brethren!"

The relations of the sexes were a matter of the gravest difficulty. The Apostle was occupied with them constantly when he wrote to the Corinthians. The coldness of Paul gives to his morality something sensible, but at the same time monastic and narrow. The sexual attraction is in his eyes an evil, a shame. Since it cannot be suppressed, it must be regulated. Nature, for Saint Paul, is evil, and grace consists in contradicting and mastering it. He has, nevertheless, beautiful expressions as to the respect that man owes to his body: God will raise it, the bodies of the faithful are the temples of the Holy Ghost, the members of Christ. What a crime then it is to take the members of Christ to make them the members of a harlot! Absolute chastity is most valuable, virginity is the perfect state; marriage has been established as a lesser evil. But, from the time when it is contracted, the two parties have equal rights over each other. The interruption of conjugal relations ought only to be admitted for a time and in view of religious duties. Divorce is forbidden, save in the case of mixed marriages, where the unbeliever first retires.

Marriages contracted between Christians and unbelievers may be continued. "For the unbelieving husband is sanctified by the wife, and the unbelieving wife is sanctified by the husband," in the same manner that the children are sanctified by the parents. One can, moreover, hope that the faithful spouse will convert the unfaithful. But new marriages can only be between Christians. All these questions will present themselves under the most singular light, since the end of the world was believed to be at hand. In the state of crisis which existed, pregnancy and the begetting of children appeared anomalies. There is little marrying in the sect, and one of the most untoward consequences for those who had associated these was the impossibility of establishing their daughters. Many murmured, finding that thing unbecoming and contrary to custom. To prevent greater evils, and out of regard for the fathers of families, who had on their hands marriageable daughters, Paul permitted marriage, but he did not conceal the contempt and disgust which he had for that estate, which he found disagreeable, full of trouble, and humiliating.

"The time is short; it remaineth, that both they that have wives be as though they had none; and they that weep, as though they wept not; and they that rejoice, as though they rejoiced not; and they that buy, as though they possessed not; and they that use this world, as not abusing it, for the fashion of this world passeth away. But I would have you without carefulness. He that is unmarried careth for the things that belong to the Lord, how he may please the Lord: but he that is married careth for the things of the world, how he may please his wife. There is a difference also between a wife and a virgin. The unmarried woman careth for the things of the Lord, that she may be holy both in body and in spirit: but she that is married careth for the things of the world, how she may please her husband. And this I speak for your own profit; not that I may cast a snare upon you, but for that which is comely, and that ye may attend upon the Lord without distraction."

Religious exaltation always produces such sentiments. Orthodox Judaism, which, however, showed itself opposed to celibacy, and which treated marriage as a duty, had doctors who reasoned like Paul. "Why should I marry?" said Rabbi ben Azai. "I am in love with the Law; the human race can be perpetuated by others." Later on, as will appear, Paul expressed upon this subject much juster thoughts, and saw in the union of man and wife a symbol of the love of Christ for his Church; he placed as the supreme law of marriage the love of the man on the one hand, and the submission of the woman on the other; he recalled the admirable chapter of Genesis in which the mysterious attraction of the two sexes is explained by a philosophical fable of a divine beauty.

The question of the meats offered to idols is resolved by St Paul with great good sense. The Judæo-Christians held that total abstinence from such meats was a duty, and it appears that it had been agreed at the Council of Jerusalem that they should be generally forbidden. Paul has broader views. According to him, the circumstance of a piece of meat having been part of a sacrificed beast is insignificant. The false gods being nothing, the meat which is offered to them is not defiled. Any meat exposed in the market may be bought freely, without there being any need for asking questions as to the origin of each morsel. A reserve, however, ought to be made: there are scrupulous consciences which take that for idolatry; and the enlightened man ought to be guided not only by principle, but also by charity. He ought to forbid himself the things which are permitted, if weak brethren are scandalised by it. Knowledge exalts, but charity edifies. "All things are lawful unto you, but all things are not expedient; but all this edify not. Let no man seek his own, but every man another's wealth." It is one of the favourite ideas of Paul, and the explanation of several episodes of his life, in which one sees him subdue himself out of regard for timorous persons, to observances which he did not consider of the least value. "If the meat that I eat," says he, "innocent as it is, scandalises my brother, I will renounce eating it for ever."

Some faithful people, however, went a little further. Constrained by family relationships, they took part in the festivities which followed the sacrifices, and which took place in the temples. Paul blames this custom, and, according to a method of reasoning familiar to him, starts on a different principle from that which he had just before admitted. The gods of the nations are devils; to participate in their sacrifices, is to have commerce with devils. One cannot at the same time participate at the table of the Lord and at the table of devils, or drink the cup of the Lord and the cup of devils. The feasts which are held in the houses are not of the same importance: it is not necessary to go there, nor to disquiet oneself about the providing of meats; if you are told that any meat has been sacrificed to the gods, from a scandal which must result, abstain from it. In general, avoid that which can be a stumbling-block for the Jew, the Pagan, the Christian; subordinate in practice one's own liberty to that of others, all the while maintaining one's rights; in everything seek to please all.

"Follow my example," he continues. "Am I not an apostle? am I not free? have I not seen Jesus Christ our Lord? are not ye my work in the Lord? If I be not an apostle unto others, yet, doubtless, I am to you: for the seal of mine apostleship are ye in the Lord. Mine answer to them that do examine me is this, Have we not power to eat and to drink? Have we not power to lead about a sister, a wife, as well as other apostles, and as the brethren of the Lord, and Cephas? Or I only and Barnabas, have not we power to forbear working? Who goeth a warfare anytime at his own charges? who planteth a vineyard, and eateth not of the fruit thereof? or who feedeth a flock, and eateth not of the milk of the flock? . . . If we have sown unto you spiritual things, is it a great thing that ye shall reap your carnal things? If others be partakers of this power over you, are not we rather? Nevertheless, we have not used this power; but suffer all things, lest we should hinder the gospel of Christ. . . . What is my reward then? Verily, that, when I preach the gospel, I may make the gospel of Christ without charge, that I abuse not my power in the gospel. And unto the Jews I became as a Jew, that I might gain the Jews; to them that are under the law, as under the law; to them that are without law, as without law (being not without law to God, but under the law to Christ), that I might gain them that are without law. To the weak became I as weak, that I might gain the weak: I am made all things to all men, that I might by all means save some. . . . Know ye not that they which run in a race run all, but one receiveth the prize. So run, that ye may obtain. And every man that striveth for the mastery is temperate in all things. Now they do it to obtain a corruptible crown; but we an incorruptible. I therefore so run, not as uncertainly; so fight I; not as one that beateth the air: but I keep under my body, and bring it into subjection: lest that by any means, when

I have preached to others, I myself should be a castaway."

As for the question of the place of women in the church, we can easily see that the Apostle will decide it with his unyielding harshness. He blames the bold efforts of the Corinthian women, and recalls them to the practice of other communities. Women ought not to speak or even ask questions in church. The gift of tongues is not for them. They ought to be submissive to their husbands. If they wish to know anything, let them ask their husbands at home. It is also shameful for a woman to appear without a veil in church, unless she be shorn or shaven. The veil is, moreover, necessary "because of the angels." It was supposed that the angels present at divine service are capable of being tempted by the sight of the hair of women, or at least of being distracted by this sight from their duty, which is to bear to God the prayers of the saints. "The head of every man is Christ; and the head of the woman is the man; and the head of Christ is God. . . . For a man indeed ought not to cover his head, forasmuch as he is the image and glory of God; but the woman is the glory of the man. For the man is not of the woman; but the woman of the man . . . but all things of God."

The related observations on the "Supper of the Lord" have an immense historical interest. This feast became more and more the essential part of Christian worship. More and more also is spread abroad the idea that Jesus himself was eating there. That, without doubt, was metaphorical; but the metaphor in the Christian language of this time was not openly distinct from the reality. In every case this sacrament was in a great degree a sacrament of union and of love.

"The cup of blessing which we bless, is it not the communion of the blood of Christ? The bread which we break, is it not the communion of the body of Christ? For we being many are one bread, and one body: for we are all partakers of that one bread. Behold Israel after the flesh; are not they which eat of the sacrifices partakers of the altar? . . . For I have received of the Lord that which also I delivered unto you, That the Lord Jesus the same night in which he was betrayed took bread: And when he had given thanks, he brake it, and said, Take, eat: this is my body, which is broken for you: this do in remembrance of me.' After the same manner also he took the cup, when he had supped, saying, This cup is the new testament in my blood: this do ye, as oft as ye drink it, in remembrance of me.' For as often as ye eat this bread, and drink this cup, ye do shew the Lord's death till he come. Wherefore whosoever shall eat this bread, and drink this cup of the Lord, unworthily, shall be guilty of the body and blood of the Lord. But let a man examine himself, and so let him eat of that bread, and drink of that cup. For he that eateth and drinketh unworthily, eateth and drinketh damnation to himself, not discerning the Lord's body."

The penalty incurred by not acknowledging the high sanctity of the Supper of the Lord is not eternal damnation--there are temporal trials, or even death--death being often an expiation which saves the soul. "There are perhaps," adds the Apostle, "among you many feeble men, sick, and numerous deaths. If we judge ourselves, we shall not be judged. But the judgments of the Lord are corrections which preserve us from being judged with the world," that is to say, condemned in eternity. For the moment the Apostle limits himself to ordaining that those who come to the agapes shall wait for each other, that they must eat at home to satisfy their appetite, and that they must guard the mystical significance of the Lord's Supper. He will "set the rest in order" when he comes to them.

The Apostle then traces the theory of the manifestations of the Spirit. Under the badly-defining names of "gifts," "services" (offices), and "powers," he arranges thirteen functions, constituting all the hierarchy and all the forms of supernatural activity. Three functions are openly designated and subordinated to each other. They are, 1st, the function of an apostle; 2d, that of a prophet; 3d, that of a teacher. Then come gifts, services, or powers which, without conferring so elevated a permanent character, serve for perpetual manifestations of the Spirit. These are, 1st, the word of wisdom; 2d, the word of knowledge; 3d, faith; 4th, the gifts of healing; 5th, the power of working miracles; 6th, the discerning of spirits; 7th, the gift of speaking in divers kinds of tongues; 8th, the interpretations of tongues thus spoken; 9th, the works of charity; 10th, the cares of administration. All these functions are good, useful, necessary; they ought neither to undervalue nor to envy each other. All have the same source. All the "gifts" come from the Holy Ghost, all the "services" come out from Christ, all the "powers" come from God. The body has several members, and yet is one; the division of functions is necessary in the Church as in the body. These functions can no more be divided from each other than the eye can be divided from the hand, or the head from the feet. All jealousy between them is therefore misplaced. Without doubt they are not equal in dignity, but they are justly the most feeble members which are the most necessary; they are the feeblest members which are the most honoured, the most carefully surrounded, God having wished to establish in this way a compensation, so that there might be neither schism nor jealousy in the body. The members ought to be careful of each other; if one suffers, all suffer. The advantages and the glory of one are the advantages and the glory of the other. To what good besides are these rivalries? There is a way open to all, the gift which has an immense superiority over all others.

Borne along by a truly prophetical inspiration beyond the confused ideas and blundering which he had just exposed, Paul then wrote this admirable passage, the only one in all Christian literature which can be compared to the discourses of Jesus.

"Though I speak with the tongues of men and of angels, and have not charity, I am become as sounding brass, or a tinkling cymbal. And though I have the gift of prophecy, and understand all mysteries and all knowledge; and though I have all faith, so that I could remove mountains, and have not charity, I am nothing. And though I bestow all my goods to feed the poor, and though I give my body to be burned, and have not charity, it profiteth me nothing. Charity suffereth long, and is kind; charity envieth not; charity vaunteth not itself, is not puffed up, doth not behave itself unseemly, seeketh not her own, is not easily provoked, thinketh no evil; rejoiceth not in iniquity, but rejoiceth in the truth; beareth all things, believeth all things, hopeth all things, endureth all things. Charity never faileth; but whether there be prophecies, they shall fail; whether there be tongues, they shall cease; whether there be knowledge, it shall vanish away. For we know in part, and we prophesy in part. But when that which is perfect is come, then that which is in part shall be done away. When I was a child, I spake as a child, I understood as a child, I thought as a child; but when I became a man, I put away childish things. For now we see through a glass darkly, but then face to face; now I know in part, but then shall I know even as also I am known. And now abideth faith, hope, and charity, these three; but the greatest of these is charity."

Versed in experimental psychology, Paul went a little further. He had said,--"Brethren, leave illusions. These inarticulate stammerings, these ecstasies, these miracles, are the dreams of your infancy. That which is not visionary--that which is eternal--is what I have just preached to you." But then if he had not been of his time, he would not have done what he did. Is it not already a great deal to have indicated this capital distinction of eternal religious truths, which are infallible, and of those which, like the dreams of the first age, come to nought? Has he not done enough for immortality by having written this sentence, "The letter killeth, but the Spirit giveth life?" Woe to him who would stop on the surface, and who, for the sake of two or three visionary gifts, would forget that in this strange enumeration--among the diaconies and the charismata of the primitive Church, are the care of those who suffer, the administration of charitable funds, reciprocal assistance! Paul enumerates these duties in the last place, and as humble things. But his piercing glance can still read the truth here. "Take care," says he, "that our humblest members are justly the most honoured." Prophets, speakers with tongues, doctors, you will pass. Deacons, devoted widows, administrators of the good of the Church, you will remain: you build for eternity."

In the laying down of rules relative to spiritual exercises, Paul shows his practical spirit. He puts preaching highly above the gift of tongues. Without absolutely denying the reality of the gift of tongues, he makes on this subject reflections which are equivalent to blaming it. The gift of tongues does not speak to men; it speaks to God. No one can understand it; it only edifies him who is speaking. Preaching, on the contrary, serves for the edification and consolation of all. The gift of tongues is only good if it be interpreted--that is to say, if other faithful people specially endowed for that intervene, and know that they hold the sense of it. By itself, it is like indistinct music; we hear the sound of the flute or cithara, but know not the piece that these instruments are playing. It is like a badly-blown trumpet: it makes a great noise, but as it says nothing clear, nobody obeys the uncertain signal or prepares for the combat. If the tongue does not give clearly articulated sounds, it does but beat the air; a discourse in a tongue that no one understands has no meaning. Thus much of the gift of tongues is without interpretation. Moreover, the gift of tongues in itself is barren; the meaning of it remains without fruit.

"Else when thou shalt bless with the Spirit, how shall he that occupieth the room of the unlearned say Amen at thy giving of thanks, seeing he understandest not what thou sayest? For thou verily givest thanks well, but the other is not edified. I thank my God I speak with tongues more than ye all; yet in the Church I had rather speak five words with my understanding, that by my voice I might teach others also, than ten thousand words in an unknown tongue. Brethren, be not children in understanding; howbeit in malice be ye children, but in understanding be men. . . . If therefore the whole Church be come together into one place, and all speak with tongues, and there come in those that are unlearned, or unbelievers, will they not say that ye are mad? But if all prophesy, and there come in one that believeth not, or one unlearned, he is convinced of all, he is judged of all; and thus are the secrets of the heart made manifest; and so falling down on his face he will worship God, and report that God is in you of a truth. How is it then, brethren? When ye come together, every one of you hath a psalm, hath a doctrine, hath a tongue, hath a revelation, hath an interpretation. Let all things be done unto edifying. If any man speak in an unknown tongue, let it be by two, or at the most by three, and that by course; and let one interpret. But if there be no interpreter, let him keep silence in the Church, and let him speak to himself and to God. Let the prophets speak two or three, and let the other judge. If anything be revealed to another that sitteth by, let the first hold his peace. For ye may all prophesy one by one, that all may learn and all may be comforted. And the spirits of the prophets are subject to the prophets. For God is not the author of confusion, but of peace, as in all churches of the saints. . . . Wherefore, brethren, covet to prophesy, and forbid not to speak with tongues. Let all things be done decently and in order."

Some strange noises, which were called the gift of tongues, and in which were mixed Greek,

Syriac, the words anathema maran atha, the names of "Jesus, of Lord," greatly embarrassed simple men. Paul, when consulted on this subject, practised what was called "the discerning of spirits," and to distinguish in this confused jargon what might come from the spirit and what might not.

The fundamental dogma of the primitive Church, the resurrection, and the approaching end of the world, hold a considerable place in this epistle. The Apostle returns to it eight or nine different times. The renewal will be by fire. The saints will be the judges of the world, even of the angels. The resurrection, which of all Christian dogmas was the most repugnant to the Greek spirit, is the object of particular attention. Many, whilst admitting the resurrection of Jesus, his approaching appearance, and the restoration that he was about to accomplish, did not believe in the resurrection of the dead. When there was a death in the community, it was to them a scandal and an embarrassment. Paul had no difficulty in showing them their illogical position: "If the dead be not raised, neither is Christ raised any the more--all hope is vain." Christians have much more cause to complain than other men; the truly wise are those who say, "Let us eat and drink, for to-morrow we die." The resurrection of Jesus is the guarantee of the resurrection of all. Jesus has made the first step, his disciples will follow him in the day of his glorious manifestation. Then will begin the reign of Christ: all other power but his will be destroyed. Death will be the last enemy that he will vanquish: all will be submitted to him, God alone excepted, who has submitted all things to him. The Son, in fact, will be eager to render homage to God, and to submit himself to him, that God may be all in all.

"But some man will say, How are the dead raised up? and with what body do they come? Thou fool, that which thou sowest is not quickened except it die: And that which thou sowest, thou sowest not that body that shall be, but bare grain, it may chance of wheat, or of some other grain: but God giveth it a body as it hath pleased him, and to every seed his own body. All flesh is not the same flesh: but there is one kind of flesh of man, another flesh of beasts, another of fishes, and another of birds. There are also celestial bodies, and bodies terrestrial: but the glory of the celestial is one, and the glory of the terrestrial is another. There is one glory of the sun, and another gory of the moon, and another glory of the stars: for one star differeth from another in glory. So also is the resurrection of the dead. It is sown in corruption, it is raised in incorruption; it is sown in dishonour, it is raised in glory; it is sown in weakness, it is raised in power: It is sown a natural body, it is raised a spiritual body. . . . Behold, I shew you a mystery; we shall not all sleep, but we shall be changed, in a moment, in the twinkling of an eye, at the last trump: for the trumpet shall sound, and the dead shall be raised incorruptible, and we shall be changed. For this corruptible must put on incorruption, and this mortal must put on immortality. So when this corruptible shall have put on incorruption, and this mortal shall have put on immortality, then shall be brought to pass the saying that is written, Death is swallowed up in victory. death, where is thy sting? O grave, where is thy victory? . . . But thanks be to God, which giveth us the victory through our Lord Jesus Christ."

Alas, the Christ came not. All died one after another. Paul, who was believed to be one of those who would live till near the great appearance, died in his turn. We shall see how neither faith nor hope stopped for that. No experience, however desolating it may be, appears decisive to humanity, when it is concerned with these sacred dogmas in which it finds, not without reason, its consolation and joy. It is easy for us to find that after a time that these hopes were exaggerated; it were well, nevertheless, that those who have partaken of them had not been so clear sighted. Paul tells us candidly that, if he had not counted upon the resurrection, he would have led the life of a peaceable citizen, wholly occupied with his vulgar pleasures. Some sages of the first order--Marcus Aurelius, Spinoza, for example--have gone further, and have practised the highest virtue without hope of reward. But the crowd is never heroic. It has needed a generation of men persuaded that they would not die, it has needed the attraction of an immense immediate reward, to draw from man that enormous sum of devotion and of sacrifice which has founded Christianity. The great chimera of the approaching kingdom of God has been thus the maternal and creative idea of the new religion. We shall soon assist at the transformation that the necessity of things will bring about in this belief. About the years 54-58 it had attained its highest degree of intensity. All the letters of Paul written about this time are, so to speak, impregnated with it. The two Syriac words Maran atha--"The Lord is at hand," were the passwords amongst Christians,--the lively and short expression that they used to each other to encourage one another in their hopes

CHAPTER XV

CONTINUATION OF THE THIRD JOURNEY OF PAUL--THE GREAT CONTRIBUTION-- DEPARTURE FROM EPHESUS

Paul, according to his habit, added to the end of the letter,--

"The salutation of me, Paul, with mine own hand. If any man love not the Lord Jesus Christ, let him be anathema. Maran atha."

He confided his letter to Stephanas, Fortunatus, and Achaicus, who had brought that of the Corinthians to him. Paul thought the three deputies would reach Corinth in nearly the same time as Timothy. He feared that the youth and timidity of his disciple were badly received in the mocking society of Corinth, and that they did not accord him enough authority. The Apostle recommended them in the most pressing way to treat Timothy as himself, and expressed a desire to see him again as soon as possible. He did not wish to leave Ephesus without his valuable companion, whose presence had become a sort of necessity to him.

Paul strongly urged Apollos to join Stephanas, and to return to Corinth, but Apollos wished rather to postpone his departure. From this moment we lose sight of him. Tradition, however, continues to regard him as a disciple of Paul. It is probable, in truth, that he continued his apostolic career, putting to the service of the Christian doctrine his Jewish erudition and his elegant style.

Paul, however, revolved in his mind boundless projects, in which he believed, according to his constant habit, that he saw the dictates of the Spirit. There happened to Paul, what often happens to persons accustomed to a species of activity. He could not leave what had been the occupation of his life. Travelling had become necessary to him: he sought occasions for it. He wished to revisit Macedonia, Achaia, then to visit Jerusalem anew, then to set out to try new missions in countries farther off, and not yet reached by the faith, such as Italy and Spain. The idea of going to Rome tormented him. "I must see Rome," he often said. He foresaw that the centre of Christianity would one day be there, or at least that decisive events would happen there. The journey to Jerusalem was another project which greatly pre-occupied him far more than a year.

To calm the jealous feelings of the Church of Jerusalem, and to fulfil one of the conditions of the peace which was signed at the time of the interview of the year 51, Paul had prepared a great contribution in the Churches of Asia Minor and of Greece. We have already seen that one of the bonds which marked the dependence of the provincial Churches on those of Judlea, was the obligation of alms. The Church of Jerusalem, partly through the fault of those who composed it, was always in distress. Mendicants abounded there. In the earliest ages, the leading characteristic of Jewish society was that there was neither poverty nor riches. For two or three centuries, there had been at Jerusalem rich, and consequently poor, people. The true Jew, turning his back on Gentile civilisation, became day by day more destitute of resources. The public works of Agrippa II. had filled the town with starving masons; buildings were demolished merely for the sake of not leaving thousands of workmen without work. The Apostles and their companions suffered like every one else by this state of things. It was necessary that the suffering Churches, active, laborious, should save these holy men from dying of hunger. Whilst supporting impatiently the pretensions of the brethren of Judæa, their supremacy and their titles of nobility were not doubted in the provinces. Paul had for them the greatest regard. "You are their debtors," said he to his faithful ones; "for if the Gentiles have been made partakers of spiritual things with the saints of Judæa, their duty is all the more to minister to them in carnal things." It was, moreover, an imitation of the custom which had for a long time obtained among the Jews of all parts of the world, to send contributions to Jerusalem. Paul thought a large alms, which he would himself carry to the Apostles, would cause him to be much better received by the old college who pardoned him with so much reluctance for doing great things without their assistance, and would be, in the eyes of these hungry nobles, the best mark of submission. How could they treat as schismatics and rebels those who gave such substantial proofs of generosity, and of fraternal and respectful sentiment?

Paul began the gathering about the year 56. He wrote of it first to the Corinthians, then to the Galatians, and without doubt to other Churches. He returned to it in his new letter to the Corinthians. There were in the Churches of Asia Minor and Greece people in easy circumstances, but none with large for-tunes. Paul knew the economical habits of the world in which he had lived. The insistence with which he presents his maintenance as a heavy charge with which he was not desirous of burdening the Churches, proves that he himself suffered from the petty embarrassments of poor men, obliged to be careful about trifles. He thought that if, in the Churches of Greece, they waited his arrival before collecting the alms, the business would be a failure. He still wished each one on Sunday to put aside an amount, proportioned to his means, for this pious end. This little treasure of charity thus constantly added to, must wait his arrival. Then, the Churches would elect deputies, whom Paul would send with letters of recommendation to bear the offering to Jerusalem. Perhaps even, if the result was worth the trouble, Paul would go in person, and in that case the deputies would accompany him. So much honour, and so much happiness, to go to Jerusalem, to travel in company with Paul, greatly agitated the believers. An emulation in well-doing, skilfully encouraged by the great master in the art of the direction of souls, kept everybody on the alert. This contribution was, during some months, the thought which sustained life, and made all hearts to beat.

Timothy soon returned to Ephesus, as Paul had desired him. He brought the news later than that of the departure of Stephanas; but there is reason to believe that he had left the town before Stephanas went there on his return; for it is by Titus that Paul learnt later the effect that his new letter had produced. The situation at Corinth was always very strained. Paul modified his projects, resolved to touch first at Corinth, to remain there a little time, afterwards to accomplish his journey from Macedonia, to make a second and longer sojourn at Corinth, and afterwards, resuming his first plan, to set out for Jerusalem, accompanied by Corinthian deputies. He believed that he ought to inform the Church of Corinth immediately of his change of resolution. He charged Titus with a message and the most delicate communications for the rebellious Church. The disciple was at the same time to press for the realisation of the contribution that Paul had ordered. Titus, it would seem, at first declined; he feared, like Timothy, the giddy and inconsiderate temper of the men of Corinth. Paul reassured him,-- told him what he thought of the qualities of the Corinthians, extenuated their faults, dared to promise him a warm reception. He gave him for a companion a "brother" whose name is not known to us. Paul was near the last days of his stay at Ephesus; nevertheless it was agreed that he should wait in this town for the return of Titus.

But new trials had just compelled him anew to modify his designs. Few periods in the life of Paul were so troubled as this. For the first time he found the limit overrun, and avowed that all his strength had departed. Jews, Pagans, Christians, hostile to his supremacy, appeared to be sworn together against him. The situation of the Church of Corinth gave him a kind of fever; he sent messenger after messenger to it; he daily changed his resolution with regard to it. Sickness, probably, befell him there: he believed he was about to die. A riot which had taken place at Ephesus still further complicated the situation, and obliged him to set out without awaiting the return of Titus.

The temple of Diana offered a terrible obstacle to the preaching of the new cult. This gigantic establishment, one of the wonders of the world, was the life and reason for existence of the entire town, by its colossal riches, by the number of strangers whom it attracted, by the privileges and celebrity which it conferred upon the city, by the splendid festivals of which it was the occasion, by the trades which it maintained. Superstition had here the most sure of guarantees, that of material interest, never so happy as when it can disguise itself under the pretext of religion.

One of the industries of the town of Ephesus was that of the silversmiths, who made little shrines of Diana. Strangers carried away with them these objects, which, placed afterwards upon their tables or in the interior of their houses, represented to them the celebrated sanctuary. A great number of craftsmen were employed in this work. Like all manufacturers living by the piety of pilgrims, these workmen were very fanatical. To preach a religion opposed to that which had enriched them, appeared to them a piece of frightful sacrilege; it was as if in our days one were to declaim against the worship of the Virgin at Fourvières or La Salette. One of the formulas in which were summed up the new doctrine was: "The gods made with hands are not gods." This doctrine had become sufficiently public to cause anxiety to the silversmiths. Their chief, named Demetrius, excited them to a violent manifestation, maintaining that he himself acted before all for the honour of the temple that Asia and the whole world worshipped. The workmen rushed into the streets, crying, "Great is Diana of the Ephesians!" and in a short time all the town was filled with confusion.

The crowd was borne along to the theatre, the ordinary place of assembly. The theatre of Ephesus, whose immense outline, despoiled of nearly all its completeness--still to be seen on the flanks of Mount Prion--was perhaps the greatest in the world. It is estimated that it must have held at least 56,000 people. As the immense seats were formed in the side of the hill, an enormous crowd could in an instant spread itself over from the top and completely inundate it. The lower part of the theatre, moreover, was surrounded by colonnades and open porticoes; and being in the neighbourhood of the forum, of the market, of several gymnasia, the whole place was always open. The tumult was at its height in an instant. Two Christians of Thessalonica, Caius and Aristarchus, who had joined Paul at Ephesus, and were attached to him as companions, were in the hands of the rioters. Great was the trouble among the Christians. Paul wished to enter into the theatre and harangue the people; his disciples begged him to do nothing of the kind. Some of the rulers who knew him also persuaded him not to commit such an imprudence. The most diverse cries were heard in the theatre; the majority did not know why they had come. There were many Jews, who put forward a certain Alexander, who made a sign with his hand demanding silence; but when they recognised him as a Jew, the noise was redoubled; during two hours, no other cry was heard but "Great is Diana of the Ephesians!" It was with difficulty that the chancellor of the town could make them listen to him. He represented the honour of the great Diana as beyond all reproach; besought Demetrius and his workmen to have a trial of those who he believed had displeased them, begged everybody to return to the legal ways, and showed the consequences that such seditious movements might bring upon the town, if they could not justify themselves in the eyes of the Roman authority. The crowd dispersed. Paul, who had fixed his departure some days from that time, did not wish to prolong this perilous situation. tie resolved to take his departure as soon as possible.

In terms of the letter which he had sent by Titus to the Christians of Corinth, Paul would first of all embark for that town. But he was cruelly perplexed: the anxieties that he had because of Achaia rendered him undecided. At the last moment, he again changed his route. The time did not appear to him opportune for a visit to Corinth; there was much discontent, and a disposition to proceed with vigour. Perhaps his presence might provoke revolt and schism. He did not know what effect his letter had produced, and he was very anxious about it. He believed himself, moreover, to be stronger at a distance than near at hand: his presence impressed people very little; his letters, on the contrary, were his triumph. In general, men who have a certain timidity prefer to write rather than speak. He preferred then not to go to Corinth until he had seen Titus again, but rather to write anew to the indocile Church. Thinking that severity is exercised better at a distance, he hoped that his new letter would bring his adversaries to a better state of mind. The Apostle resumed, therefore, his former plan of travelling. He summoned the faithful, addressed his farewells to them, gave orders that, when Titus should arrive, he should be sent to Troas, and set out for Macedonia, accompanied by Timothy. Perhaps he took, as assistants from thence, the two deputies of Ephesus, Tychicus and Trophimus, charged to bear to Jerusalem the offerings of Asia. This must have been in the month of June in the year 57. Paul's sojourn at Ephesus had lasted three years.

During so long an apostleship, he had had time to give to this Church a strength proof against all trials. Ephesus will be henceforth one of the metropolitan cities of Christianity, and the place in which its most important transformations will occur. It was necessary, moreover, that this Church should be exclusively Pauline, like the Churches of Macedonia, and the Church of Corinth. There were those who worked against him at Ephesus, enemies there were for certain, and in ten years we shall see the Church of Ephesus cited as a model for having known how to do justice to "those who call themselves apostles without being so," for having unmasked their imposture, and for the vigorous hate that it bore to the "Nicolaitans," that is to say, to the disciples of Paul. The Judæo-Christian party existed without doubt at Ephesus from the first year.

Aquila and Priscilla, the assistants of Paul, continued after his departure to be the centre of the Church. Their house, in which the Apostle had dwelt, was the place of meeting of all that was most pious and zealous. Paul was pleased to celebrate every-where the merits of this respectable couple, to whom he recognised that he owed his life. All the Churches of Paul had for them a great veneration. Epænetus, the first Ephesian whom they converted, came after them; then a certain Mary, who appears to have been a deaconess, an active and devoted woman; then Urbane, whom Paul names his co-operator; then Apelles, to whom Paul gives the title "approved in Christ;" then Rufus, "chosen in the Lord," who had an aged mother, whom the Apostle, out of respect, called "My mother." Besides Mary, other women, true sisters of charity, were vowed to the service of the faithful. These were Tryphena and Tryphosa, "who labour in the Lord;" then Persis, particularly dear to Paul, and who had valiantly worked with him. There were still Ampliatus or Amplias, the Jew Herodion, Stachys, beloved by Paul; a Church or conventicle composed of Asyncritus, Phlegon, Hermas, Patrobas, Hermes, and many others; another Church or a little society composed of Philologus and Julia, of Nereus and "his sister" (that is to say, probably his wife), of Olympas, and of several others. Two great houses of Ephesus, those of Aristobulus and of Narcissus, counted among their slaves several of the faithful. Finally, two Ephesians, Tychicus and Trophimus, were attached to the Apostle, and were henceforth in the number of his companions. Andronicus and Junia were also at this time at Ephesus. These were members of the primitive Church of Jerusalem; St Paul had the greatest respect for them "because they had been in Christ before him." He calls them "of note among the Apostles." It is a new detail that in the trial that Paul calls "his battle against the beasts," they probably had shared of his prison.

At a much more perilous time appeared Artemas, who is said to have been a companion of Paul; Alexander the coppersmith, Phygellus Hermogenus, who seems to have left an evil reputation behind him,--provoked schisms or excommunications, and to have been considered as traitors in the school of Paul; Onesiphorus and his house, who, on the contrary, would have shown themselves more than once full of love and devotion towards the Apostle.

Several of the names which have just been enumerated are the names of slaves; thus much we see in their peculiar designations, in which is the ironical emphasis which make them so like to the grotesque names that are given to negroes in the colonies. It is not improbable that there were already among the Christians many persons of servile condition. Slavery, in many cases, did not induce so complete an attachment to the master's house as our modern domesticity. The slaves of certain categories were free to mix together, to associate to a certain extent, to form brotherhoods, a kind of tontine or club, in view of their funerals. It is not impossible that several of the pious men and women who had given themselves up to the service of the Church were slaves, and that the hours that they gave to the diaconate were those that their masters allowed them. At the time in which these events happened, the servile class comprised many polished, resigned, virtuous, well-instructed persons. The highest lessons on morality came from slaves; Epictetus passed a great part of his life in servitude. The Stoics, the sages, spoke as did St Paul to the slave: "Remain as thou art; do not think of setting thyself free." It is not necessary to judge of the lower classes in the Greek towns by our populace of the same age, dull, brutal, sensual, incapable of distinction. This refined, delicate, polished something that one feels in the relations of the first Christians is a tradition of Greek elegance. The humble workmen of Ephesus, whom St Paul salutes with so much cordiality, were without doubt persons of a gentle nature, with a touching honesty, relieved by excellent manners, and by the peculiar charm that there is in the civility of the poorer classes. Their serenity of soul, their content, were perpetual sermons. "See how these Christians love one another!" was the exclamation of the Pagans, surprised at this innocent and tranquil air, at this profound and attractive gaiety. After the preaching of Jesus, it is the divine work of Christianity; it is his second miracle,--a miracle drawn truly from the living forces of humanity, and of that in it which is best and most holy.

CHAPTER XVI

CONTINUATION OF THE THIRD JOURNEY OF PAUL--SECOND STAY OF PAUL IN MACEDONIA

Paul, on leaving Ephesus, probably went by land, for at least part of the way. He had calculated, in fact, that Titus, going by sea from Ephesus to Troas would have reached this latter point before him. This calculation was not verified. Arrived at Troas, he did not meet Titus there, which caused him a lively concern. Paul had already passed by Troas; but it does not appear that he had preached there. This time he found very favourable dispositions. "A door was opened unto me of the Lord." Troas was a Latin town in the style of Antioch in Pisidia and of Philippi. A certain Carpus welcomed the Apostle, and lodged him at his house; Paul employed the days during which he was waiting for Titus in founding a Church. He succeeded admirably, for, some days afterwards, a company of the faithful accompanied him to the shore, when he set out for Macedonia. It was about five years since he had embarked from the same port, at the demand of a Macedonian man whom he had seen in a vision. Never assuredly had a dream counselled greater things or brought about more beautiful results.

This second stay of Paul in Macedonia must have occupied six months, from June to November 57. Paul employed himself all this time in confirming his beloved Churches. His principal residence was at Thessalonica; he was constrained, however, to dwell also for some time at Philippi and at Berœa. Troubles which had filled the last months of his stay at Ephesus seemed to pursue him. During the first days after his arrival he had no rest. His life was a continual struggle: the gravest apprehensions stood in his way. These cares and afflictions did not assuredly come from the Churches of Macedonia. There could not be more perfect Churches, more generous, more devoted to the Apostle; nowhere had he met with so much heart, nobleness, and simplicity. He found a good many bad Christians--sensual, earthly-- on whose account the Apostle expressed himself with much vivacity, calling them "enemies of the Cross of Christ whose end is destruction, whose God is their belly, and whose glory is in their shame, who mind earthly things," and upon whom he denounces eternal ruin; but it is doubtful if they belonged to the actual flock of the Apostle. It is from the side of the Church of Corinth that these great anxieties come. He fears more and more lest his letter may not have stirred up the indifferent, and may have armed his enemies.

Titus at last rejoined him, and consoled him for all his griefs. He brought, in a word, good news, although the clouds were far from being wholly dissipated. The letter had produced the most profound effect. At its reading, Paul's disciples had listened in tears. Nearly all had testified to Titus, whilst shedding tears, the profound affection that they bore for the Apostle, sorrow for having grieved him, the desire of seeing him again, and of obtaining pardon from him. These Greek natures, unsteady and inconstant, came back to the right path as quickly as they had left it. His expressions frightened them. They supposed that the Apostle was armed with the most terrible powers; before his threats, all those who owed their faith to him, trembled and sought to exculpate themselves. They had not indignation enough against the guilty; each sought by his zeal against others to justify himself, and to turn aside the severity of the Apostle. Titus was overwhelmed by Paul's disciples with the most delicate attentions. He came back enchanted by the reception that they had given him, by the fervour, by the docility, by the goodwill that he had found in the spiritual family of his master. The subscription was not much advanced, but there was a hope that it would be fruitful. The sentence pronounced against the incestuous had been softened, or rather Satan, to whom Paul had given them up, did not execute the decree. The sinner was allowed to live on; the Apostle had the credit of giving an indulgent consent to what was after all a mere following of the course of nature. They did not even chase him absolutely from the Church, but they avoided having relations with him. Titus had conducted all this business with consummate prudence, and as skilfully as Paul would have done it himself. The Apostle never experienced keener joy than at the reception of this news. During some days, he altogether lost his self-command. He repented of having grieved such good souls; then, on seeing the admirable effect that his severity had produced, he became full of joy.

This joy was not unmixed. His enemies were far from yielding; the epistle had exasperated them, and they made the keenest criticisms upon it. They noted that it was hard and insulting to the Church; they accused the Apostle of pride and vanity; "His letters," said they, "are severe and energetic; but his figure is mean, and his speech without authority." They attributed to personal hate his rigour towards the incestuous. They treated him as a foolish, extravagant, conceited, and indiscreet man. The changes in his plans of journey were presented as proofs of instability. Agitated by this double news, the Apostle set about dictating to Timothy a new letter, destined, on the one hand, to lessen the effect of the first, and to bear to his beloved Church, which he believed himself to have wounded, the expression of his paternal sentiments; on the other, to reply to the adversaries who had failed for the moment to carry away the hearts of his children from him.

As for his enemies, Paul knew that he had not disarmed them. At each instant there are lively and smart allusions to these people "which corrupt the word of God," above all, to those letters of recommendation which they have turned to his detriment. His enemies are false apostles, deceitful workers, who disguise themselves as the apostles of Christ. Satan sometimes changes himself into an angel of light; therefore is it astonishing if his ministers transform themselves into ministers of righteousness? Their end shall be according to their works. They pretend that he has not known the Christ. He does not agree with them; because for him his vision on the road to Damascus has been a true personal relationship with Jesus. But, after all, what does it matter? Since Christ is dead, all are dead with Christ, to carnal considerations. For himself, he no longer knows any one according to the flesh. If he has known Christ after the flesh, he knows him no more. Let them not force him to be other than he is. When he is amongst them, he is humble, timid, embarrassed; but he hopes they will not oblige him to use the arms which have been given to him to destroy every fortress opposed to Christ, to destroy all scorners who raise themselves against the knowledge of God, and to submit every thought to the yoke of Jesus; it is easy to see that he knows how to punish disobedience. Those who describe themselves as of the party of Christ ought to remember, that he, Paul, is also of the school of Christ. The power that the Lord has given him to edify, do they wish to oblige him to use it to destroy? They try to make the Corinthians believe that he seeks to frighten them by his letters. Let those who use this language take care lest he be forced to write to them in even severer terms. It is not of the number of men who vaunt themselves and who have just hawked about right and left their letters of recommendation. His letter of recommendation is the Church of Corinth. This letter, he bears in his heart; it is legible for all; it is not written in ink, but by the Spirit of the living God, not upon tables of stone, but upon the tables of the heart. He only measures it in its proper proportion, he only compares it himself. He only arrogates to himself authority over the Churches which he has founded; he is not like men who wish to extend their power over countries in which they have not shown themselves in their own person, and who, after having yielded to him, Paul, the Gospel of the Circumcision, have just now gathered the fruit of a work which they had at first opposed. Each to his own ground. He need not boast of the works of others, nor vaunt him-self verbosely and without measure; the portion that God apportioned to him is beautiful enough, since it has been his lot to bear the Gospel to Corinth; and still he hopes to go farther away. But it is in God alone that he finds his glory.

This modesty was not feigned. But it is difficult for a man of action to be modest; he runs the risk of being taken literally. The least egotistical of the Apostles is incessantly compelled to speak of himself. He calls himself an abortion, the least of the saints, the least of the Apostles, unworthy of that name, since he has persecuted the Church of God; but do not believe that for all that he resigns his prerogative.

"But by the grace of God I am what I am: and His grace which was bestowed upon me was not in vain; but I laboured more abundantly than they all: yet not I, but the grace of God which was with me. . . ."

"For I suppose I was not a whit behind the very chiefest Apostles. But though I be rude in speech, yet not in knowledge; but we have been thoroughly made manifest among you in all things. Have I committed an offence in abasing myself that ye might be exalted, because I have preached to you the gospel of God freely? I robbed other Churches, taking wages of them to do you service. And when I was present with you, and wanted, I was chargeable to no man: for that which was lacking to me, the brethren which came from Macedonia supplied: and in all things I have kept myself from being burdensome unto you, and so will I keep myself. As the truth of Christ is in me, no man shall stop me of this boasting in the regions of Achaia. Wherefore? because I love you not? God knoweth. But what I do, that I will do, that I may cut off occasion from them which desire occasion; that wherein they glory, they may be found even as we. . . ."

Arming himself with the accusation of madness, that his adversaries raised against him, he accepts for a moment this position which they have lent him, and, under the mask of oratorical irony, he makes the madman throw in the face of his adversaries the harshest truths.

[2] "I am a fool, it is agreed; very well, bear with my folly for a moment. You that are wise, ought to be indulgent to fools. And then, you shew so much tolerance for men who put you into servitude, who devour you, who extort your money, and who, after that, are puffed up with pride, and strike you in the face. Let us go on, since it is the fashion to sing one's own glory, let us sing ours. All that can be said in this kind of folly, I can say like them. They are Hebrews; so am I. They are Israelites; so am I They are

of the race of Abraham; so am I. They are ministers of Christ (ah I speak as a fool), I am more. In labours more abundant, in stripes above measure, in prisons more frequent, in deaths oft. Of the Jews five times received I forty stripes save one. Thrice was I beaten with rods, once was I stoned, thrice I suffered shipwreck, a night and a day I have been in the deep; in journeyings often, in perils of waters, in perils of robbers, in perils by mine own countrymen, in perils by the heathen, in perils in the city, in perils in the wilderness, in perils in the sea, in perils among false brethren; in weariness and painfulness, in watchings often, in hunger and thirst, in fastings often, in cold and nakedness. And outside of these accidents, snail I recall my daily anxieties, the care of all the Churches? Who is weak, and I am not weak? Who is offended, and I burn not? . . . . But I only wish to glory in my infirmities . . . . it is in our infirmities that the strength of Christ is more manifest. That is why I glory in my infirmities, in my injuries, in my necessities, in my persecutions, in my sufferings for Christ, for when I am weak in the flesh I am strong in Christ.

"Truly I am become a fool in glorying; you have compelled me. I should have been exempt from it, if you had wished to charge yourselves with my apology to those who attack me. I am nothing; but I yield in nothing to the very chiefest Apostles. Truly I have wrought the signs of an Apostle among you in all patience, in signs, and wonders, and mighty deeds. For what is it wherein ye were inferior to other Churches, except it be that I myself was not burdensome to you? Forgive me this injustice. It is the third time that I have announced my approaching arrival to you. This time I will not be burdensome to you; for I seek not yours, but you. For the children ought not to lay up for the parents, but the parents for the children. And, I will very gladly spend and be spent for you; though the more abundantly I love you the less I be loved.

"But if it be so, it may be said I have not been directly in your charge, but, crafty rogue that I am, I have skilfully swindled you of the silver that I refused to accept. Did I gain anything by any of those whom I have sent to you? I sent Titus to you, and with him a brother whom you know. Did Titus make a profit out of you? Walked we not in the same spirit and in the same steps? . . . For I fear lest, when I come, I shall not find you such as I would, and that I shall be found unto you such as ye would not: lest there be debates, envyings, wraths, strifes, backbitings, whisperings, swellings, tumults. And lest when I come again, my God will humble me among you, and that I shall bewail many which have sinned already, and have not repented of the uncleanness and fornication and lasciviousness which they have committed. This is the third time I am coming unto you . . . I told you before, and warn you, absent as present, the second time; and being absent now I write to them which heretofore have sinned, and to all other, that, if I come again, I will not spare: since ye seek a proof of Christ speaking in me . . . Therefore I write these things being absent, lest being present I should use sharpness, according to the power which the Lord hath given me."

Paul, we see, had reached that great state of exaltation in which the religious founders of the first order lived. His thoughts lifted him out of himself. The manner in which to execute the contribution for the poor of Jerusalem was at this time his consolation. Macedonia showed an exemplary zeal in it. Those excellent souls gave with a joy, with an eagerness, which ravished the Apostle. Nearly all the members of the sect had suffered in their little way through having adhered to the new doctrine; but in their poverty they still knew how to find something for a work which the Apostle designated as excellent. The hopes of Paul were more than fulfilled; the faithful nearly went down on their knees, to beg the Apostle to accept the necessarily small donations which they were able to offer. They would have given themselves, if the Apostle would have accepted them. Paul, pushing his delicacy almost to exaggerated refinement, and wishing, as he said, to be irreproachable not only before God but before men, requiring that they should choose at the election deputies charged to carry the offering of each Church, carefully sealed, so as to disperse the suspicions that malevolence would certainly cast upon him concerning his management of considerable funds. These deputies followed him already everywhere, and formed around him a kind of escort always ready to execute his missions. They were those whom he calls "the envoys of the Churches, the glory of Christ"

Cleverness, suppleness of language, the epistolary dexterity of Paul, were employed entirely in this work. He employed to recommend it to the Corinthians the most moving and tenderest phrases; he commanded nothing; but, knowing their charity, he allowed himself to give them advice. It was a year since they had begun; he was now anxious himself to finish; goodwill did not suffice. It is not a question of worrying oneself to put others at ease. The rule in such affairs is equality, or rather reciprocity. For the moment, the Corinthians are rich and the saints of Jerusalem are poor, it is for the former to help the latter, the latter will help the former in turn. Thus he himself will verify the saying: "He that gathered much had nothing over, and he that gathered little had no lack."

Paul prayed the faithful Titus to return to Corinth and to continue the work of charity there which he had so well begun. Titus had desired this mission, and received it with eagerness. The Apostle gave him two companions, whose names we do not know. One was of the number of the deputies who had been elected to bear the offering from Macedonia to Jerusalem; "his praise," says Paul, "is in the Gospel throughout all the Churches." The other was a brother "whom Paul had oftentimes proved diligent in many things, but now much more diligent, upon the great confidence which he had in the Church of Corinth." Neither of those indications suffices to settle who is meant. Paul prayed the Corinthians to keep up the good opinion which he had tried to give of them to these three persons, and employs to excite their generosity a little charitable manoeuvre which raises a smile.

"For I know the forwardness of your mind, for which I boast of you to them of Macedonia, that Achaia was ready a year ago; and your zeal hath provoked very many. Yet have I sent the brethren, lest our boasting of you should be vain in this behalf; that, as I said, ye may be ready: lest haply if they of Macedonia come with me, and find you unprepared, we (that we say not, ye) should be ashamed in this confident boasting. Therefore I thought it necessary to exhort the brethren, that they would go before unto you and make up beforehand your bounty, whereof ye had notice before, that the same might be ready as & matter of bounty, not as of covetousness. But this I say, he which soweth sparingly, shall reap also sparingly; and he which soweth bountifully, shall reap also bountifully. Every man according as he purposeth in his heart, so let him give; not grudgingly, or of necessity: for God loveth a cheerful giver. . . . Now he that ministereth seed to the sower both minister bread for your food, and multiply your. seed sown, and increase the fruits of righteousness. . . . For the administration of this service not only supplieth the want of the saints, but is abundant also by many thanksgivings unto God; whilst by the experiment of this ministration they glorify God for your professed subjection unto the Gospel of Christ, and for your liberal distribution unto them, and unto all men; and by their prayer for you, which long after you for the exceeding grace of God in you. Thanks be unto God for His unspeakable gift!"

This letter was carried to Corinth by Titus and by the two brethren who accompanied him. Paul remained still for some months in Macedonia. The times were still very hard. Scarcely ever has there been a Church which has not had to contend with ever-recurring difficulties. Patience is the recommendation that the Apostle addresses the oftenest. "Tribulations, distresses, pangs, cudgellings, prisons, bad treatment, vigils, fastings,--purity, long-suffering, honesty, sincere charity, such is our life; sometimes honoured, sometimes despised, sometimes slandered, sometimes respected; held as impostors, as well as truthful ones; as unknown, yet well known (of God); as dying, whilst we live; as men whom God chastises and yet we do not die; as sorrowful, yet always rejoicing; for poor, yet making many rich; as having nothing, and yet possessing all things." Joy, concord, hope without limit, made suffering light, and inaugurated that delicious reign of "the God of love and peace" that Jesus had announced. Above a thousand meannesses, the spirit of Jesus shines in these groups of saints with infinite brightness and sweetness.

Footnotes:

2. This is the latter part of the 2d Epistle to the Corinthians, freely rendered. No literal translation gives the sense.--Trans.

CHAPTER XVII

CONTINUATION OF THE THIRD MISSION--SECOND STAY OF PAUL AT CORINTH--THE EPISTLE TO THE ROMANS

Paul, according to our calculation, set out from Macedonia, and came to Greece at the end of November or the beginning of December 57. He had with him the delegates chosen by the Churches of Macedonia to accompany him to Jerusalem, and to carry himself and the alms of the faithful, amongst others Sopater or Sosipater, son of Pyrrhus of Beræa, a certain Lucius, a certain Tertius, Aristarchus, and Secundus of Thessalonica. Jason of Thessalonica, his host since his first voyage, accompanied him also, it seems. Perhaps, finally, the deputies of Asia--Tychicus, and Trophimus of Ephesus, Gaius from Derbe, were already with him. Timothy about this time did not leave him. All these made a kind of apostolic caravan of a very imposing aspect. When they had rejoined Titus and the two brothers who had accompanied him, Corinth really possessed all the leaders of the new movement. Paul, conformably to his former plan, which he had several times modified, but which he finished by carrying out in its essential lines, passed in this town three months of the winter 57-58 (December 57, January and February 58). The Church of Athens was so small that Paul, according to all appearance, did not visit it, or at least hardly stopped there.

The Apostle, not having any longer at his disposal the kindly hospitality of Aquila and Priscilla, lodged this time at the house of Caius, whose house served for the meetings of the whale Church, and to whom he was attached by a bond then held very sacred. Stephanas was perhaps dead or absent. Paul always observed at Corinth much reserve, for he did not feel himself to be on very firm ground. Seeing the danger that association with the world offered in a town so corrupted, he reverted always to broad principles, and advised avoiding all relations with the Pagans. The welfare of the souls at such a time was his only rule, the only end which he proposed to himself.

It is probable that the presence of Paul at Corinth calmed altogether the dissentients, who, for several months, gave him much anxiety. A bitter allusion which he made about this time to "those who vaunt themselves of works that Christ has not done by them," and of others, "who build upon another man's foundations," shows, however, that a vivid impression of the evil works of his adversaries remained with him. The business of the subscription had gone forward as he desired--Macedonia and Achaia had contributed a large sum. The Apostle had at last an interval of repose; he utilised it by writing, always under the form of an epistle, a kind of summing up of his theological doctrine.

As this great document interested all Christianity equally, Paul addressed it chiefly to the Churches which he had founded, and with which he could communicate at this time. The Churches favoured with such an address were four in number at the least. One was the Church of Ephesus; a copy was also sent into Macedonia; Paul even had an idea of addressing this piece to the Church of Rome. In all his copies the body of the epistle was nearly the same; the moral recommendations and the salutations varied. In the copy destined for the Romans, in particular, Paul introduced some varied readings suited to the taste of this Church, which he knew was very much attached to Judaism. It is the copy addressed to the Church of Rome which served as the basis of the constitution of the text when the collection of the epistles of St Paul was made. Hence the name that the epistle in question bears to-day. The publishers (if we may be permitted so to call them) only copied at one time the parts common to all; however, as they would themselves be scrupulous not to lose anything which came from the pen of the Apostle, they gathered together at the end of the copy princeps, the parts which varied in the different copies, or which they themselves found in more than one of them.

This precious writing, the foundation of all Christian theology, is mainly that in which the ideas of Paul are exposed in better order. There appears in full daylight the great idea of the Apostle: there the law is put on one side; works are of no value; salvation comes only from Jesus, Son of God, raised from the dead. Jesus, who, in the eyes of the Judæo-Christian school, is a great prophet, come to fulfil the law, is, in the eyes of Paul, a divine apparition, rendering useless all that has preceded him, even the Law. Jesus and the Law are for Paul two opposite things. He who accords to the Law excellence and efficacy is a traitor to Jesus. To overthrow the Law, is to exalt Jesus. Greeks, Jews, Barbarians, all are equal; the Jews are first called, then the Greeks: all are saved only by faith in Jesus.

What can man do, indeed, if he be left to himself? One thing only--he can sin. And at first, in that which concerns Pagans, the spectacle of the visible world and the natural law written in their hearts would suffice to reveal to them the true God and their duties. By a voluntary and inexcusable blindness, they have not worshipped the God whom they knew well; they have lost themselves in their vain thoughts; their pretended philosophy has only been idle speculation. To punish them, God has abandoned them to the most shameful vices, to sins against nature. The Jews are no more innocent; they have received the Law, but they have not observed it. Circumcision does not make the true Jew; the Pagan who observes the natural law well is worth much more than the Jew who does not observe the Law of God. Have not the Jews then some prerogative? Without doubt, they have one: it is to them that the promises have been made; the unbelief of many among them does not prevent these promises from being fulfilled. But the Law by itself cannot bring about the reign of justice; it has served merely to create the offence and to put it in evidence. In other words, the Jews, like the Gentiles, have lived under the dominion of sin.

Whence then does justification come? From faith in Jesus, without distinction of race. All men were sinners; Jesus has been the propitiatory victim; His death has been the redemption that God has accepted for the sins of the world, the works of the law not having been able to justify the world. God is not only the God of the Jews, He is also the God of the Gentiles. It was by faith that Abraham was justified, since it is written, "He believed, and it was accounted to him for righteousness." Justification is free; one has no right to it by merit; it is an imputed grace and an all-merciful act of the Divinity.

The fruit of justification is peace with God, hope, and consequently patience, which enables us to show our glory and our happiness in tribulation, according to the example of Christ, who has died for sinners, and by whose blood we have been justified. If God has so loved men that He has given His son to die for them when we were sinners, what will He not do now that they are reconciled?

Sin and death were brought into the world by one man, Adam, in whom all have sinned. Grace and salvation were brought into the world by one Man, Christ, in whom all are justified. Two typical men have existed, "the first Adam," or the earthly Adam, the origin of all disobedience; "the second Adam," or the heavenly Adam, the origin of all justice. Humanity divides itself between these two leaders of the human race, some following the earthly Adam, others the spiritual Adam. The Law has served only to multiply offences, and to make sinners conscious of them. It is grace which, superabounding where offence has abounded, has effaced all, so that one may almost say that, thanks to Jesus, sin has been happiness, and has only served to bring to light the mercy of God.

But, it will be said, let us sin then that grace may abound; let us do evil, that good may come. That, says Paul, is what they assert of me, thus falsifying my doctrine. Nothing is further from my thoughts. Those who have been baptised in Christ are dead to sin, buried with Christ, to rise again and live with Him--that is to say, lead a new life. Our "old man," that is to say, the man that we were before baptism, has been crucified with Christ. Because the Christian is not under the Law, it does not follow that he may sin. From the slavery of sin, he has passed to the service of righteousness; from the way of sin unto death, to the way of life. The Christian, moreover, is dead to the Law; for the Law created sin. In itself, it was good and holy, but it made sin known; it aggravated it, so that the commandment which should have created life, created death. A woman is an adultress if, whilst living with her husband, she fails to keep her marriage vow; but after the death of her husband, adultery is no longer possible. Christ, in breaking down the letter of the Law, has taken us from under the Law, and won us to himself. Dead to the flesh, which was in sin, being dead to the Law, he who cast off sin, the Christian has only to serve God "in newness of spirit, and not in the oldness of the letter." The Law was spiritual, but man is carnal. There are two parts in man--one which loves and wishes to do well, the other which does evil, without that other man wishing to do it. Does it not often happen that we do not that we would, while the evil that we would not, that we do? Is it that sin, innate in man, acts in him without his wishing it. "The inner man," that is to say, reason, would obey the law of God; but concupiscence is ever at war with reason and the law of God. "O wretched man that I am! Who shall deliver me from the body of this death? I thank God through Jesus Christ our Lord."

The true Christian, being delivered from the Law and from concupiscence, is then safe from damnation, by the mercy of God, who has sent His only Son to take upon Him a body of sinful flesh like our own, to destroy sin. But this deliverance does not take place if he destroy not his life according to the flesh, and live according to the Spirit. The wisdom of the flesh is the great enemy of God; it is even death. The Spirit, on the contrary, is life. By Him we have been made the adopted sons of God, whereby we cry Abba, that is to say, "Father." But, if we are the sons of God, we are also His heirs, and joint heirs with Christ. After having partaken of His sufferings, we shall also partake of His glory. What are all the sufferings of this present time compared with the glory that shall be revealed in us? The whole creation waits for this great revelation of the sons of God. It hopes, I say, to be delivered from the bondage under which it groans, subject as it is to infirmity and corruption, and to pass into the glorious liberty of the sons of God. We also, who have received the first-fruits of the Spirit, even we ourselves groan within ourselves, waiting for the moment in which our elevation to the position of the sons of God shall be complete, and when our body shall be delivered from its frailty. It is hope which saves us;

but we do not hope for that which we see. Let us persevere patiently in this hope for the invisible, with the help of the Spirit. We know not what we should pray for; but the Spirit makes up for our weakness, and makes intercession for us with God with groanings which cannot be uttered. God, who seeth the heart, knoweth how to divine the desires of the Spirit, and to separate its indistinct and inarticulate sighs.

What a motive of assurance, moreover! It is by a direct act of God that we are destined for the metamorphosis which will make us like His Son, and who will make of all living a body of brethren of whom Jesus will be the first born. By His foreknowledge, God knows His elect beforehand; those whom He knows, He predestinates; those whom He predestinates, He calls; those whom He calls, He justifies; those whom He justifies, He glorifies. Let us be tranquil: if for us God has not spared His only Son, but has delivered Him to death, what can He refuse us? Who will be in the day of judgment the accuser of the elect? God, who has justified them? Who will condemn them? Christ, who has died and risen again, who is seated at the right hand of God, who intercedes for us? Impossible! "Who shall separate us from the love of Christ? shall tribulation, or distress, or persecution, or famine, or nakedness, or peril, or sword? For I," adds Paul, "am persuaded that neither death, nor life, nor angels, nor principalities, nor powers, nor things present, nor things to come, nor height, nor depth, nor any other creature, shall be able to separate us from the love of God, which is in Christ Jesus our Lord."

We see to what a complete rupture with Judaism Christianity has reached in the hands of Paul. Jesus has not been so far off assuredly. Jesus has boldly proclaimed that the reign of the Law is ended, that the worship in spirit and in truth of God the Father only remains. But, with Jesus, poetry, sentiment, imagery, and style are essentially Jewish. He continues in a direct line Isaiah, the psalmists, the prophets of the time of the captivity, the author of the Song of Songs, and sometimes the author of Ecclesiastes. Paul only continues Jesus, not as he was by the side of the lake of Gennesareth, but Jesus such as he conceives him, such as he has seen him in his inner vision. For his old co-religionists he has only pity. The "perfect" Christian, the "enlightened" Christian, is in his eyes the one who knows the vanity of the Law, its uselessness, the frivolity of its pious practices. Paul would wish to be anathema for his brothers in Israel; it is for him a great sadness, a continual heartache to dream of this noble race, raised so high in glory, which had the privilege of adoption, of alliance, of the Law, of the true worship, of the promises,--which has had patriarchs out of whom Christ has come in the flesh. But God will not fail in His promises. Even though one is of the seed of Israel, he is not necessarily a true Israelite; he is heir to the promises by the choice and calling of God, not by the accident of birth. There is no injustice in that. Salvation is the result, not of human efforts, but of the mercy of God. God is free to have mercy on whom He will, and to deal hardly with whom he will. Who will dare to ask of God the reason for His choice? Can the vessel of clay say to the potter: Why hast thou made me thus? Hath not the potter the power, with the same lump, to make two vessels, one for honourable uses, the other for dishonourable? If it please God to prepare man to show His power by crushing him, as He did Pharaoh, He is the master, the rather that thereby He shows forth His mercy towards those whom He has prepared and called to glory. But He makes this choice, without stopping for any consideration of race or of blood.

If the Jewish people, moreover, see themselves supplanted, it is their own fault. They have too much confidence in the works of the Law; they believe that they will by these works be justified. The Gentiles, disembarrassed of this stone of stumbling, have entered more easily into the true doctrine of salvation by faith. Israel has sinned by too much zeal for the Law, and by having placed too much reliance upon the personal justification which it acquires by works. Thus it has been made to forget that justification is from God only,--that it is the fruit of grace and not of works; which has made it misunderstand the instrument of that justification which is Jesus.

Has God then cast off his people? No. God, it is true, has found it good to blind and to harden the greater part of the Jews. But the corner-stone of the elect has been taken out of the breasts of Israel. Besides, the perdition of the Hebrew people is not definitive. This perdition has had for its only object the salvation of the Gentiles and the creation of a salutary emulation between the two branches of the elect. It is a happiness for the Gentiles that the Jews had for a time failed in their vocation, since it is through their fault, and thanks to their weakness, that the Gentiles have been substituted for them. But if the falling away of the Jewish people, if a moment of delay on its part has been the salvation of the world, what will be its introduction in a mass into the Church? This will truly be the resurrection. If the first-fruits be holy, the whole mass is holy also; if the root be holy, the branches are holy also. Some branches have been cut off, and in their place have been grafted branches of the wild olive, which have thus become partakers of the root and of the sap of the olive tree. Take care, O wild olive! lest thou grow proud at the expense of the branches which have been cut off! It is not thou that bearest the root; it is the root that bears thee! Yes, thou wilt say, but the branches have been cut off so that I may be grafted. Doubtless; they have been cut off for want of faith; it is to faith that thou owest all; beware lest thou grow proud; tremble. If thou dost not persevere, thou also wilt be cut off. If they come to the faith, God is perfectly well able to regraft them on their own trunk. Israel has been blinded till the crowd of the Gentiles can be received into the Church; but after that, Israel will be saved in turn. The gifts of God are without repentance. The friendship of Israel and of God has suffered an eclipse, so that the Gentiles may in the interval receive the Gospel; but the calling of Israel, the promises made to the patriarchs, will have their effect none the less. God will use the incredulity of some for the salvation of others; then those whom He has rendered faithless, He will save in their turn; all which goes to prove that salvation on His part is purely an act of mercy, and not a result at which one will arrive by right of birth, or by works, or by the free choice of his reason. God will not take counsel of any one; He has not any account to render to any one. "O the depth of the riches, both of the wisdom and knowledge of God! How unsearchable are His judgments, and His ways past finding out! For who hath known the mind of the Lord? or who hath been His counsellor? . . . For of Him, and through Him, and to Him are all things: to whom be glory for ever. Amen."

The Apostle, according to his habit, ends by moral applications. The worship of the Christian is the worship of reason, without other sacrifice than that of himself. Each must present to God a pure sacrifice, and worthy of being favourably accepted. The spirit of the Church must be modesty, concord, mutual responsibility; all the gifts, all the duties are intimately associated with it. The body has many members; all the members have not the same office, but all have need of each other. Prophets, deacons, doctors, preachers, benefactors, superiors, delegates, for works of mercy are equally necessary, provided that they exhibit in the discharge of their functions the simplicity, zeal, and cheerfulness that these functions require. Charity without hypocrisy, brotherly kindness, politeness and kind attentions, activity, fervour, joy, hope, patience, amiability, concord, humility, pardon for injuries, love of our neighbours, eagerness to assist the needs of the saints; to bless those who persecute you, to rejoice with those who rejoice, to weep with those who weep, to conquer evil, not by evil, but by good: such is the moral, in part inculcated in the ancient Hebrew books, that Paul preached after Jesus. It would seem that at the period in which Paul wrote this epistle, various Churches, above all the Church of Rome, reckoned amongst their number certain disciples of Judah the Gaulonite, who denied the legitimacy of the Roman tribute, and who preached revolt against the Roman authority; possibly also the Ebionites, who absolutely opposed the reign of Satan and the reign of the Messiah to each other, and who identified the present world with the empire of the devil. Paul replied to them, as a true disciple of Jesus:

"Let every soul be subject unto the higher powers. For there is no power but of God: the powers that be are ordained of God. Whosoever therefore resisteth the power, resisteth the ordinance of God: and they that resist shall receive to themselves damnation. For rulers are not a terror to good works, but to the evil. Wilt thou then not be afraid of the power? do that which is good, and thou shalt have praise of the same: for he is the minister of God to thee for good. But if thou do that which is evil, be afraid: for he beareth not the sword in vain: for he is the minister of God, a revenger to execute wrath upon him that doeth evil. Wherefore ye must needs be subject, not only for wrath, but also for conscience' sake. For, for this cause pay ye tribute also: for they are God's ministers, attending continually upon this very thing. Render therefore to all their dues; tribute to whom tribute is due; custom to whom custom; fear to whom fear; honour to whom honour."

This was written in the fourth year of Nero. This prince had not yet afforded a reason for every subject to curse him. His government had been the best since the death of Augustus. At the moment when Paul, with much good sense, took up the defence of the tax against the Jewish theocracy, Nero softened its rigour, and even sought to apply to it the most radical reforms. The Christians at this date had not themselves complained of him, and it may readily be believed that at a time when the Roman authority served his plan rather than made an obstacle to it, Paul had sought to prevent tumultuous movements which might lose all, but to which the Jews of Rome were much inclined. These seditions, the arrests, and the punishments which were its consequences, threw the new sect into the greatest disfavour, and made the adepts confound them with thieves and the disturbers of public order. Paul had too much tact to be a rioter: he wished that credit should be given to the name of Christian, that a Christian should be a man of order, in good odour with the police, of good reputation in the eyes of Pagans. This was what made him write that page, equally singular in the eyes of a Jew and of a Christian. Yet in it may be seen, however, with a rare simplicity, that there was in the very essence of this nascent Christianity some-thing politically dangerous. The theory of the divine right of all the powers that be is candidly laid down. Nero has been proclaimed by St Paul a minister, an officer of God, a representative of Divine authority. The Christian, whilst he is allowed to practise his religion openly, will be a subject, by no means a citizen. I do not intend to utter any censure here; but no one can do two things at once; policy is not everything, and the true glory of Christianity is to have created a whole world out of itself. But see to what we expose ourselves with these absolute theories! "The minister of God," of whom all honest men must seek approbation, whose sword is only terrible to the wicked, will become in a few years the Beast of the Apocalypse, the Anti-Christ, the persecutor of the saints.

The strange situation of the spirits, the persuasion which they held that the end of the world was close at hand, explain for the remainder this haughty indifference.

"And that, knowing the time, that now it is high time to awake out of sleep: for now is our salvation nearer than when we believed. The night is far spent, the day is at hand: let us therefore cast off the works of darkness, and let us put on the armour of light. Let us walk honestly, as in the day; not in rioting and drunkenness, not in clambering and wantonness, not in strife and envying. But put ye on the Lord Jesus Christ, and make not provision for the flesh, to fulfil the lusts thereof."

The contest of Paul against his adversaries, who were more or less Ebionites, can be traced in part in his letter relating to the abstinence from meats, and to the observance of new moons, of Sabbaths, and of days. Ebionism, which at this period had its principal centre at Rome, held greatly to these external practices, which were in truth only a continuation of the practices of the Essenes. They were scrupulous, ascetic persons, who not only practised the legal ordinances with regard to meats, but who obliged themselves to eat only vegetables and to drink no wine. It is necessary to remember that Christianity recruited itself among very pious persons, and, as such, much given to devotional practices. In becoming Christians, these persons remained faithful to their ancient habits; or rather, the adoption of Christianity was for them only an act of devotion (religio) the more. Paul, in this new epistle, remained faithful to the excellent rules of conduct which he had already traced among the Corinthians. In themselves, these practices are perfectly vain. But what is of the greatest importance, is not to offend these feeble consciences, not to trouble them, not to argue with them. He whose conscience is enlightened must not despise him whose conscience is feeble. The timorous conscience must not be permitted to judge the large conscience. Let each follow his own judgment, the right thing is what one believes to be right before God. How shall one dare to judge his brother? It is Christ who will judge us all; each will only have to answer for him-self. The distinction of meats rests upon nothing; all things are pure. But what is of importance is that no one should cause scandal to his brother. If, in eating the permitted meats, you aggrieve your brother, take care; for the sake of the question of meats, do not lose a soul for whom Christ died. The kingdom of heaven has nothing to do with eating and drinking; it sums itself up in justice, peace, joy, edification.

The disciples of Paul were occupied for several days in copying this manifesto, addressed to different Churches. The epistle to the Churches of Macedonia was written by Tertius. The Macedonians who accompanied Paul, and the Corinthians who had relations with the Churches of the north of Greece, profited by the occasion to salute their brethren. The Epistle to the Ephesians contained the nominal salutation of Paul to nearly all the Christians of this great Church. As there was little communication between Corinth and Macedonia on the one hand, and Ephesus on the other, the Apostle does not speak to the Ephesians of the world which surrounds him; but he vigorously recommends to them Phoebe, who probably carried the letter to them. This poor woman set out on a painful voyage in winter across the archipelago, without any other resource than the recommendation of Paul. The Church of Ephesus was begged to receive her in a manner worthy of the saints, and to provide for all her needs. Paul had probably some anxieties about the intrigues of the Judæo-Christian party at Ephesus; for, at the end of the letter, he added in his own handwriting:--

"Now I beseech you, brethren, mark them which cause divisions and offences contrary to the doctrine which ye have learned; and avoid them. For they that are such serve not our Lord Jesus Christ, but their own belly; and by good words and fair speeches deceive the hearts of the simple. For your obedience is come abroad unto all men. I am glad, therefore, on your behalf: but yet I would have you wise unto that which is good and simple concerning evil. And the God of peace shall bruise Satan under your feet shortly. The grace of our Lord Jesus Christ be with you. Amen."

We have seen that St Paul in writing this most important epistle had intended to send it to the Church of Rome. This Church had reformed itself since the Edict of Claudius, and much that was good had been said of it. It was not very numerous, and was chiefly composed of Ebionites and Judæo-Christians; it also contained in its ranks Proselytes and converted Pagans. The idea of addressing a dogmatic writing to a Church which he had not founded, was bold, and altogether contrary to the habit of Paul. He much feared lest they should see in his attempt something indiscreet; he forbade himself all that might recall the tone of a master speaking with authority; he made no personal salutations. With these precautions, he thought that his title, henceforth recognised as the Apostle of the Gentiles, gave him the right to address a Church which he had never seen. The importance of Rome as capital of the Empire pre-occupied him: for several years he nourished the project of betaking himself thither. Not being able to execute his design as yet, he wished to give a mark of sympathy to this illustrious Church, which contained a class of the faithful of whom he considered himself the pastor, and announced to it the good news of his future arrival.

The composition and despatch of the epistle written "to the Romans" occupied the greatest part of the three months of the winter, which Paul passed this year at Corinth. They were, in a sense, the best employed weeks of his life. This epistle became, later on, the summing up of dogmatic Christianity, the declaration of war by theology against philosophy, the chief inducement to a class of eager spirits to embrace Christianity as a means of setting reason at defiance, whilst proclaiming the sublimity and credibility of the absurd. It is the application of the merits of Christ which justifies; it is God who works in us to will and to do of His good pleasure. Here is the overthrow of reason, which, essentially

Pelagian, has for its fundamental dogma, liberty, and the personality of merit. Very well, then, the doctrine of Paul, opposed to all merely human sense, has been really liberty and salvation. It has separated Christianity from Judaism; it has separated Protestantism from Catholicism. Pious observances, persuading the devotee that by them he is justified, have a double disadvantage: in the first place, they kill morality by making the devotee believe that there is a sure and easy way of entering Paradise in despite of God. The hardest-hearted Jew--a selfish and malicious usurer, let us say-- imagined that by observing the Law he would force God to save him. The Catholic of the time of Louis XI. imagined that with masses he took proceedings against God as by a bailiff's summons, so that, rogue though he might be, he had the game in his own hands, he could compel Almighty God to admit him into His company. To this impiety, in which Judaism was upset by Talmudism, in which Christianity was upset by the Catholicism of the Middle Ages, Saint Paul has adminstered the most efficient antidote. According to him, we are justified, not by works, but by faith; it is faith in Jesus which saves. That is why this doctrine, apparently so paltry, has been that of all the reformers--the lever by means of which Wycliff, John Huss, Luther, Calvin, St Cyran, have overthrown the ancient tradition of blind confidence in the priest, and in a kind of exterior justice, which has nothing to do with a change of heart.

The other practical inconvenience is the multiplication of scruples. Practices, supposed to have a value by themselves, ex opere operato, independently of the state of the soul, open the door to all the subtleties of a meticulous casuist. Legal work becomes a prescription, the success of which depends upon its punctual execution. Here again Talmudism and Catholicism are agreed. The despair of the Jewish devotees of the time of Jesus and of St Paul was the fear of not observing the whole Law--the apprehension of not being in order. It was believed that the holiest man sins,--that it is impossible not to prevaricate. They almost regretted that God had given the Law, since it only served to bring about transgressions; they confessed to the singular idea, that God had laid down all these laws with the sole purpose of creating sin, and making all the world sinful. Jesus, in the opinion of his disciples, had made easy the entrance to this kingdom of God which the Pharisees had made so difficult, to enlarge the door of that Judaism which they had narrowed so much. Paul, at least, does not imagine any other way of sup-pressing sin than by suppressing the Law. His reasoning has something of that of the Probabilists: to multiply obligations is to multiply offences; to relax rules, to render them as broad as possible, is to prevent offences, since we do not violate precepts by which we do not consider ourselves bound.

The great torment of delicate souls is scrupulousness: he who eases them of it is all-powerful over them. One of the most common customs of devotion amongst the pious sects in England, is to think of Jesus as of him who disemburdens the conscience, reassures the guilty, calms the sinning soul, delivers it from the thought of evil. Overwhelmed by the consciousness of sin and of condemnation, Paul in the same way finds peace in Jesus only. All are sinners, even to the last, by reason of their descent from Adam. Judaism, by its sacrifices for sin, had established the idea of accounts as it were opened between man and God,--of remission and of debts; a false enough idea, for sin does not remit itself,--it carries its punishment with it; a crime committed will last until the end of time, only the conscience which has committed it can atone for it and produce altogether contrary acts. The power of remitting sins was one of those that they believed to have been conferred by Jesus on his disciples. The Church had nothing more precious than it. To have committed a crime, to have a tormented conscience, was a motive to make oneself a Christian. "Here is a law which delivers you from sin, from which you could not be delivered by the Law of Moses." What could be more tempting to the Jews? One of the reasons which confirmed Constantine in Christianity was, it is said, the belief that Christians alone could absolve the soul of a father who had killed his son. The merciful Jesus, pardoning all, according even a kind of preference for those who have sinned, appeared in this troubled world as the great comforter of souls. They took it upon themselves to say that it was well to have sinned, that all remission was gratuitous, that faith alone justified.

One peculiarity of the Semitic tongues explains such a misunderstanding, and excuses this morally incomplete psychology. The form hiphil signifies at the same time the effective and the declarative, so that hasdik can say equally "to render justice," and "to declare justice," to remit a sin which has been committed, and to declare that he has not committed it. "Justice" is, according to this idiom, not only that he who is absolved from a sin, but that he who is calmed in his own eyes, need no more trouble himself with the sins which he may have committed, or with precepts which he may have violated unknown to himself.

When Paul despatched this terrible epistle, he had early fixed the day of his departure. The gravest anxieties assailed him: he had a presentiment of grave accidents, and he applied to himself often the verse of the psalm, "Yea, for thy sake are we killed all the day long; we are counted as sheep for the slaughter." Some very precise accounts, which were only too certain, represented to him the dangers he was likely to meet with from the Jews of Judæa. He was not even confident as to the disposition of the Church of Jerusalem. He had found this Church so many times ruled by mean prejudices, that he feared a cold reception, which, seeing the number of half-confirmed believers who accompanied him, would produce a disastrous effect. He constantly asked for the prayers of the faithful, that God would cause his offering to be favourably received by the saints. To place timid provincial neophytes thus in immediate contact with the aristocracy of the capital, was an idea of supreme temerity. Guided by his admirable integrity, Paul none the less persisted in his project. He believed himself bound by an order of the Spirit. He said with emphasis that he was going to Jerusalem to serve the saints; he represented himself as the deacon of the poor of Jerusalem. His principal disciples and the deputies, each bearing the offering of his Church, were around him, ready to set out. They were, we shall remember, Sopater of Beræa, Aristarchus and Secundus of Thessalonica, Gaius of Derbe, Tychicus and Trophimus of Ephesus, and finally Timothy.

At the moment when Paul was going to embark for Syria, the reasonableness of his fears became visible. A plot formed by the Jews was discovered to carry him off or kill him during the journey. In order to disconcert this project, Paul privately changed his route, and decided to return by Macedonia. The departure took place about the month of April of the year 58.

Thus ended this third mission, which, in the opinion of Paul, finished the first part of his apostolic projects. All the oriental provinces of the Roman Empire, from its extreme limit towards the east near to Illyria, Egypt always excepted, had heard the Gospel. Not once had the Apostle departed from his rule of preaching only in the countries where Christ had not yet been named, that is to say, where other Apostles had not passed; all his work had been original and belonged to him alone. The third mission had had for its field the same countries as the second; Paul turned a little in the same circle, and began to find himself in the right. He now delayed the accomplishment of the second part of his projects, that is to say, of proclaiming the name of Jesus in the western world, for we may say that the mystery hidden from eternity was known to all nations.

At Rome he had been anticipated, and, moreover, those of the circumcision formed the majority in the Church. It was as universal pastor of the Churches of the Gentiles, and to confirm the converted Pagans, and not as founder, that he wished to appear in the capital of the empire. He only wished to go thither that he might enjoy for a time the company of the faithful, and rest and edify himself among them, after which he would take, according to custom, new companions who should follow him in the latter part of his journey. Beyond, it was to Spain that he carried his eyes. Spain had not yet received Israelitish emigrants; the Apostle wished, this time, to abandon the rule which he had observed, until now, of following the track of the synagogues and of the earlier Jewish establishments. But Spain was considered as the western boundary of the world; so that as Paul believed himself authorised to conclude that since he had been in Achaia and in Macedonia, and that he had reached Illyria in the same way, when he will have been into Spain he would be able to say with truth that the name of Jesus has been preached in all the ends of the earth, and that the preaching of the Gospel was fully accomplished.

We shall see that circumstances independent of his will prevented Paul from realising the second part of the grand plan that he had proposed to himself. He was from forty-five to forty-eight years of age; he had certainly still found time and strength to found in this Latin world one or two of those missions that he had conducted in the Greek world with so much success; but the fatal journey to Jerusalem upset all his designs. Paul felt the perils of this journey: everybody around him felt them. He could not, nevertheless, renounce a project to which he attached much . importance. Jerusalem must lose Paul. It was one of the most unfavourable of conditions for nascent Christianity to have its capital in a home of such exalted fanaticism. The incident which, ten years later, completely destroyed the Church of Jerusalem, rendered to Christianity the greatest services that it has ever received in the course of its long history. The life-or-death question was to know if the growing sect would or would not disengage itself from Judaism. Now if the saints of Jerusalem, grouped around the temple, might always remain the aristocracy, and, so to speak, "the Court of Rome" of Christianity, this great rupture would not have occurred; the sect of Jesus, like that of John, would have died out obscurely, and Christians would have been lost amongst the sectarian Jews of the first and second century.

CHAPTER XVIII

RETURN OF PAUL TO JERUSALEM

Paul and the deputies of the Churches set out then from Cenchrea, having with them the contributions of the faithful for the poor of Jerusalem, and took their way towards Macedonia This was in some sort the first pilgrimage to the Holy Land, the first journey of a troop of converted pious people to the cradle of their faith. It seems that the ship, during a part of the voyage, was chartered at their expense, and that it obeyed their orders; but it must have been a simple decked boat. They made fifteen or twenty leagues a day; each evening they stopped to pass the night amongst the islands or the ports which bestrew the coast, and slept in the taverns near the shore. There were often many people there, and amongst the number good men who were not far from the kingdom of God. The barque, meanwhile, with its elevated poop and prow, was drawn upon the sand or anchored under some shelter.

We do not know if the Apostle touched at Thessalonica this time; but it is not probable that he did, since it would have been far out of his way. At Neapolis Paul wished to visit the Church of Philippi, which was a very short distance from it. He went forward with his companions, and asked them to wait for him at Troas. As for himself, he went to Philippi, celebrated Easter there, and rested with the persons whom he loved the most in the world, during the seven days in which they ate unleavened bread. At Philippi Paul again found the disciple who, at the time of his second mission, had directed his first steps in Macedonia, and who, most probably, was none other than St Luke. He took him with him again, and thus added to the journey a chronicler who has transmitted to us impressions of it with infinity of charm and of truth.

When the days of unleavened bread were finished, Paul and Luke re-embarked at Neapolis. They had evidently contrary winds, for they took five days to go from Neapolis to Troas. In this last town, all the apostolic company was complete. There was, as we have already said, a Church at Troas; the Apostle passed seven days with it, and consoled it much. An incident added to the general emotion. The morning of departure was a Sunday; in the evening the disciples met together according to custom, to break bread. The room in which they were was one of those lofty chambers which are so agreeable in the East, especially in the seaports. The meeting was numerous and solemn. Paul saw everywhere signs of his future trials. In his sermon he spoke much of his approaching end, and declared to those present that he bade them an eternal farewell. This was in the month of May; the window was open, and numerous lamps lighted the room. Paul spoke all the evening with an indefatigable enthusiasm; at midnight he was still speaking, and they had not broken bread, when suddenly a cry of horror was raised. A young man named Eutychus, seated upon the ledge of the window, had allowed himself to fall into a profound sleep, and dropped from the third floor upon the ground. They raised him, and they believed him to be dead. Paul, convinced of his miraculous powers, did not hesitate to do what Elisha is said to have done: he stretched himself upon the fainting man, he put his chest upon his chest, his arms upon his arms, and soon announced in an assured tone that he for whom they wept was still alive. The young man, in truth, had only been bruised by the fall; he did not take long to come to himself again. The joy was great, and all believed it a miracle. They remounted into the upper room, broke bread, and Paul continued their conversation until sunrise.

Some hours afterwards the ship set sail. The deputies and the disciples only were on board, Paul preferring to travel on foot, or at least by land, from Troas to Assos (about eight leagues). Assos was to be their meeting-place. From this time forth, Paul and his companions never separated. On the first day, they went from Assos to Mitylene, where they put in; on the second, they followed the Straits between Chios and the Peninsula of Clazomenes; on the third they touched at Samos; but, for a reason which we do not know, Paul and his companions preferred to pass the night at the anchorage of Trogyle, under the promontory of the neighbouring Cape, at the foot of Mount Mycala. They had thus passed before Ephesus without landing there. It was the Apostle who had wished it: he feared lest the friendship of the faithful of Ephesus might hinder him, and that he could not tear himself away from a town which was very dear to him; but he much wished to celebrate Pentecost at Jerusalem, and twenty-three or twenty-four days having elapsed since Easter, there was no time to be lost. On the morrow, a short sail brought the faithful company from Trogyle to one of the ports of Miletus. There Paul felt deep misgiving as to the propriety of having passed without giving any sign of his existence to his beloved community of

Ephesus. He sent one of his companions to inform it that he was some leagues from it, and to invite the elders or wardens to come to him. They came with eagerness, and when they were re-united, Paul addressed to them a touching discourse, which was a summary, and the last words of his apostolic life.

"Since the day when I first came into Asia, you know what I have been for you. You have seen me serve God in humility, in tears, in temptations, and using all my strength to preach unto the Jews and Gentiles the return to God and faith in our Lord Jesus Christ. And now, behold I go bound in the spirit unto Jerusalem. I know not what awaits me; I only know that, from town to town, the spirit announces to me that bonds and afflictions wait upon me. But it matters little to me; I am going to sacrifice my life voluntarily, provided that I finish my course, and that I accomplish the mission that I have received of the Lord Jesus, to testify the Gospel of the grace of God. Oh, you to all of whom I have preached the Kingdom of God, I know that you will no more see my face; I protest then from this day, that I am innocent of the loss of those who will perish; for I have never neglected to make known to you the will of God. Take heed therefore unto yourselves, and to all the flock over which the Holy Ghost hath made you overseers; be true pastors of the Church that the Lord has purchased with his own blood; for I know that after my departure shall grievous wolves enter in, not sparing the flock. And from the midst of you shall men arise, speaking perverse things, to draw away disciples after them. Therefore watch, and remember that by the space of three years I ceased not to warn everyone night and day with tears. And now, I recommend you to the grace of God, who is able to give you a place among the heavenly bodies. I have coveted no man's silver, or gold, or apparel. You know that these hands have ministered unto my necessities, and unto those of my companions. I have shown you how by work one can still support the weak, and to justify the words of the Lord Jesus: It is more blessed to give than to receive.'"

All then fell on their knees and prayed. Only stifled sobs were heard. The words of Paul, "You will see my face no more," had pierced them to the heart. The elders of Ephesus in turn approached the Apostle, bent their heads on his neck, and embraced him. They then conducted him to the port, and only left the shore when the ship set sail, taking the Apostle far from that Ægean sea which had been the scene of his contests, and the theatre of his prodigious activity.

A good wind abaft carried the apostolic company from the port of Miletus to Cos. On the morrow they reached Rhodes, and on the third day Patara, upon the coast of Lycia. There they found a ship loading for Tyre. The little coasting that they had done along the coast of Asia had much delayed them, and their journey would have been indefinitely protracted if they were to continue along the coasts of Pamphylia, Cilicia, Syria, and Phoenicia. They therefore preferred to take the shorter route, and, leaving their first ship there, they embarked on that which was about to sail for Phoenicia. The western coast of Cyprus was directly in their way. Paul could see from afar that Neo-Paphos, which he had visited thirteen years before, at the beginning of his apostolic career. He left it upon his left, and after a voyage of probably six or seven days, he arrived at Tyre.

Tyre had a church, dating from the first missions which followed the death of Stephen. Although Paul had had nothing to do with its foundation, he was known and loved there. In the quarrel which divided the rising sect, in that great rent between Judaism and the strange child to which Judaism had given birth, the Church of Tyre was decidedly of the party of the future. Paul was very well received, and passed seven days there. All the faithful of the place dissuaded him strongly from going to Jerusalem, and asserted that they had manifestations of the Spirit absolutely contrary to the plan. But Paul persisted, and chartered a ship for Ptolemais. On the day of his departure, all the faithful, with their wives and children, conducted him out of the town to the shore. The pious company knelt down on the sand and prayed. Paul bade them farewell; the Apostle and his companions re-embarked, and the people of Tyre returned sadly to their homes.

They reached Ptolemais the same day. There also were some brethren; he saluted them and stayed for a day with them. Then the Apostle left the sea. Going round Carmel, he reached in one day Cæsarea in Palestine. They stayed at the house of Philip, one of the seven primitive deacons, who for many years had been settled at Cæsarea. Philip had not taken, like Paul, the title of Apostle, although in reality he had exercised the functions of one. He contented himself with the name of "Evangelist," which designated apostles of the second rank, with the much more coveted title of "one of the seven."

Paul found here much sympathy, and remained several days at Philip's house. Whilst there, the prophet Agabus arrived from Judæa. Paul and he had known each other at Antioch fourteen years before. Agabus imitated the manners of the ancient prophets, and affected to act in a symbolical fashion. He entered in a mysterious manner, approached Paul, and took from him his girdle. They followed his movements with curiosity and terror. With the girdle of the Apostle that he had taken, Agabus bound his own legs and hands. Then suddenly breaking the silence, he said, in an inspired tone,--"Thus saith the Holy Ghost, so shall the Jews at Jerusalem bind the man that owneth this girdle, and shall deliver him into the hands of the Gentiles." The emotion was of the liveliest kind. The companions of Paul and the faithful of Cæsarea with one voice begged the Apostle to give up his journey. Paul was inflexible, and declared that chains could not frighten him, since he was ready to die at Jerusalem for the name of Jesus. His disciples saw plainly that he would not yield, and finished by saying,--"The will of the Lord be done." Then they began their preparations for departing. Many of the faithful of Cæsarea joined themselves to the caravans. Mnason, of Cyprus, a very old disciple, who had a house at Jerusalem, but who at this moment was at Cæsarea, was of the number. The Apostle and his following should lodge at his house. They mistrusted the welcome they would receive from the Church: there was much trouble and apprehension in all the company.

CHAPTER XIX

LAST STAY OF PAUL AT JERUSALEM--HIS APPREHENSION

Paul entered into that fatal town of Jerusalem for the last time, some days, it seems, after the feast of Pentecost (July 58). His company, formed of delegates from the Churches of Greece, of Macedonia, and of Asia, of his disciples, and of the faithful of Ceesarea who had wished to accompany him, were sufficient to give a warning to the Jews. Paul began to be well known. His arrival had been waited for by the fanatics, some had probably received from Corinth and Ephesus notice of his return. Jews and Judæo-Christians appeared to have agreed to slander him. They everywhere represented him as an apostate, as the desperate enemy of Judaism, as a man who ran all over the world to destroy the law of Moses and the biblical traditions. His doctrine upon meats sacrificed to idols everywhere excited angry passions. They maintained that he disobeyed the decrees of the Council of Jerusalem as to the observances connected with meats and marriage. They represented him as a second Balaam, sowing scandal before the sons of Israel, teaching them to practise idolatry, and to cohabit with Pagans. His doctrine of justification by faith and not by works was energetically repudiated. Whilst they admitted that converted Pagans were not obliged under the Law in its entirety, they maintained that nothing could exempt a Jew from the duties inherited by him. But Paul thought nothing of this view; he gave himself the same liberties as his converts; he was no longer a Jew in any degree.

The first brethren that the new arrivals met on the day of their arrival had welcomed them cordially. But it is already very remarkable that neither the apostles nor the elders came to meet the one man, who, accomplishing the boldest oracles of the prophets, had brought the nations and the far-off isles tributaries to Jerusalem. They waited for his visit with a coldness more politic than Christian, and Paul had to pass alone, with some humble brethren, the first evening of his last stay at Jerusalem.

St James the Great was, as we have already seen, the sole and absolute head of the Church of Jerusalem. Peter was certainly absent, and very probably established at Antioch; it is probable that John, according to his custom, had accompanied him. The Judæo-Christian party reigned thus without any counterbalances at Jerusalem. James, blinded by the respect of every one who surrounded him, proud, moreover, of the bond of relationship which united him to Jesus, represented a conservative principle of weighty solemnity, a kind of obstinate papacy in his narrow mind. Around him, a numerous party, more Pharisaical than Christian, carried the taste for the observances of the Law to nearly the same degree as the zealots, and imagined that the new movement had for its essence a redoubling of devotion. These exalted ones gave themselves the name of "the poor," Ebionim, πτωχδι, and gloried in it. There were many rich people in this community, but they were unpopular; they were considered to be as proud and tyrannical as the Sadducees. Fortunes, in the East, scarcely ever have an honest origin; of every rich man it may be said, without much chance of mistake, that he or one of his ancestors has been a conqueror, or a thief, a usurer, or a rogue. The association of ideas which, especially amongst the English everywhere collocates honesty with richness, has never been found in the East. Judæa, at least, thought of things in the opposite sense. For the saints of Jerusalem "rich" was synonymous with "enemy" and "evil-doer." The ideal of impiety was in their eyes the opulent Sadducee, who persecuted them, dragged them before the tribunals. Passing their life around the temple, they were like good little brotherhoods, occupied in praying for the people. They were, in every case, pronounced Jews and certainly Jesus would have been surprised if he could have seen what his doctrine had become in the hands of those who boasted kinship with him both in the Spirit and in the Flesh.

Paul, accompanied by the deputies of the Churches, went to see James on the morning after his arrival. All the elders were assembled in the house of St James. They gave each other the kiss of peace. Paul presented the deputies to James: they gave the money which they had brought. Then he recounted the great things that God had done in the Pagan world by his ministry; the elders gave thanks to God for them. Was the reception, however what they had a right to expect? We may doubt if it were. The author of the Acts has so completely modified, in view of his system of conciliation, the recital of the assembly of Jerusalem in 51, that one must believe that he has in like manner greatly modified in his recital the events which he himself took part in. In the first place, his inaccuracy is shown by comparing his accounts with the Epistle to the Galatians. In the second, there are grave reasons for supposing that he has in like manner sacrificed truth to the necessities of policy. At first, the apprehensions that Paul showed beforehand as to the temper with which the saints of Jerusalem would receive his offering could not have been without some foundation. In the second place, the account of the author of the Acts contains more than one suspicious feature. The Judæo-Christians are there represented as the enemies of Paul, almost as much so as the pure Jews. These Judæo-Christians have the worst opinion of him; the elders did not conceal the fact that the report of his arrival was annoying to them, and might provoke a manifestation on their part. The elders do not say that they share in these prejudices; but they excuse them, and in every case it is easy to see from their words that a great proportion of the Christians of Jerusalem, so far from being ready to welcome the Apostle, needed to be calmed and reconciled to him. It is remarkable, also, that the author of the Acts speaks only of the collection after a time and in the most indirect fashion. If the offering had been welcomed as it should have been, why does he not say so, when Paul in three of his epistles devotes entire pages to this object? It is hardly to be denied that Simon Magus, in the majority of the cases in which Christian tradition refers to him, may be the pseudonym of the Apostle Paul. The story according to which this impostor wished to buy apostolic powers with money, may very possibly be a translation of the ungracious reception accorded by the Apostles of Jerusalem to the collection of Paul. It would perhaps be dangerous to affirm so much, but it is quite conceivable that an assembly of ill-disposed elders may have represented the generous act of one who was not of their opinion as an attempt at corruption.

If the elders of Jerusalem had not been narrow-minded in the extreme, how is the strange discourse which the author of the Acts attributes to them, and which betrays all their embarrassment, to be explained? The presentation, in fact, was scarcely complete, when they said to Paul,--"Thou seest, brother, how many thousands of Jews there are which believe; and they are all zealous of the Law: and they are informed of thee that thou teachest all the Jews which are among the Gentiles to forsake Moses, saying that they ought not to circumcise their children, neither to walk after the customs. What is it therefore? From all sides they come to learn of thy arrival. Do therefore this that we say to thee: We have four men which have a vow on them; them take, and purify thyself with them, and be at charges with them, that they may shave their heads: and all may know that those things whereof they were informed concerning thee are nothing, but that thou thyself also walkest orderly, and keepest the Law."

Thus to him who brought to them the homage of a world, these narrow souls replied only by a mark of defiance. Paul ought to expiate by a mummery his prodigious conquests. It was necessary that he should give some satisfaction to this littleness of mind. He must do this in company with four mendicants, too poor to afford to have their heads shaven at their own expense. They were under a vow, and, according to the superstition, he must recognise them as his companions. Such is the strange condition of humanity, that no one need be astonished at such a spectacle. Men are too numerous for it to be possible to establish anything in this world, without making concessions to mediocrity. To conquer the scruples of the weak, one must be either utterly disinterested, or very powerful. Those whose position obliges them to reckon with the crowd are led to demand of great men independent of singular inconsequences. Every thought vigorously avowed is in the government of the world an embarrassment. Apology, proselytism themselves, when they imply a little genius, are, for conservative folk, suspected things. See those eloquent laymen who in our days have attempted to enlarge Catholicism and to reconcile it with the sympathies of a part of society which was until then closed to Christian feeling; what have they obtained from the Church to which they have brought crowds of new adherents? A disavowal. The successors of St James the Great have found it prudent to condemn them, even whilst profiting by their success. They have accepted their offering without thanks; they have said to them as to Paul, "Brethren, ye see these thousands of old believers who hold to things that you pass by in silence: when you speak to men of the world, take care, leave the novelties which scandalise them, and sanctify yourselves with us."

What was Paul to do, placed thus between his great principle of the inutility of works, and the immense interest he had in not breaking with the Church of Jerusalem? His position was cruel. To submit himself to customs that he held to be useless and almost an insult to Jesus--since if he had allowed it to be believed that salvation is obtainable by anything other than the merits of Christ, he would have to put himself in flagrant contradiction with the doctrine which he had everywhere preached, and which in his great general epistle especially he had developed with an unparalleled force. Why, besides, did they ask him to put in force a disused rite, one devoid of all efficacy, and nearly an absolute negation of the new dogma? To show that he is really a Jew,--to refute in a peremptory fashion the rumour spread abroad that he has ceased to be a Jew, that he no more holds by the Law and traditions? Now, assuredly, he admits them no more. Was not connivance at this misunderstanding unfaithfulness to Christ? All that must have caused Paul to hesitate, and agitated him profoundly. But a higher principle, which dominated his life, made him conquer his repugnance. Above his opinions and private sentiments, Paul placed charity. Christ has delivered us from the Law; but if in profiting by the liberty that Christ has given us, we offend our brother, it is much better to renounce this liberty and to return to slavery. It is in virtue of this principle that Paul, as he says, makes himself all things to all men,--a Jew with the Jews, a Gentile with the Gentiles. In accepting the proposition of James and of the elders, he applies his favourite principle; he submits himself then. Never, perhaps, in the life of the Apostle, did he make a more considerable sacrifice to his work. The heroes of practical life have other duties than those of contemplative life. The first duty of the latter is to sacrifice action to ideas, to say what they think, or do not think, in the exact measure in which they think it; the first duty of the others is frequently to sacrifice their ideas, sometimes even their most definite principles, for the good of the cause the triumph of which they have at heart.

What they asked Paul, besides, was less to shave his head and become a Nazarite himself, than to pay the expenses of four Nazarites, who had nothing wherewith to pay for the sacrifices offered on occasions of this kind. This was a work much esteemed among the Jews. There were around the temple troops of poor men who had made vows, and who expected some rich man to pay for them. "To shave a Nazarite" was an act of piety, and occasions are cited in which powerful personages, as an expressing of thankfulness for a blessing from heaven, made thousands of them shave; much the same as in the Middle Ages it was meritorious to pay men to make pilgrimages and to enter into monastic life. Paul, in the midst of the poverty which reigned in the Church of Jerusalem, passed for a rich man. He was asked as a rich devotee, and to prove publicly that he remained faithful to the practices of his country. James, much inclined towards exterior observances, was probably the inspirer of this grotesque idea. They urged, furthermore, that such observances had nothing to do with converted Pagans. His only motive in complying was that they should not allow it to be believed that the frightful scandal of a Jew not practising the Law of Moses was possible. So great was the fanaticism inspired by the Law, that such a phenomenon appeared more extraordinary than the overturning of the world and the total overthrow of creation.

Paul then placed himself in the company of the four poor men. Those who accomplished such vows began by purifying themselves, afterwards they entered into the temple, remained shut up there for a certain number of days, according to the vow that they had made--a period of from seven to thirty days--abstained from wine, and cut off their hair. When the term of days was reached, they offered sacrifices that were paid for at a sufficiently high price. Paul submitted himself to all. On the morrow of his visit to James's house, he betook himself to the temple, and got his name inscribed for seven days; and then fulfilled all the customary rites, greater during these days of humiliation, in which, by a voluntary weakness, he accomplished with men in rags an obsolete action of devotion, which when at Corinth or at Thessalonica he had denounced with all the force and independence of his genius.

Paul was already at the fifth day of his vow, when an incident which was only too easy to foresee decided the remainder of his career, and engaged him in a series of troubles, which he ended only with his death.

During the seven days which had elapsed since his arrival at Jerusalem, the hate of the Jews against him was terribly exasperated; they had seen him walk in the town with Trophimus of Ephesus, who was one of the uncircumcised. Some Jews of Asia, who recognised Trophimus, spread the rumour that Paul had introduced him into the temple. That was assuredly false, besides to have done so would have exposed him to certain death. Paul had undoubtedly not for a moment thought of making his Christians share in the religious practices of the temple. These practices were for him absolutely barren: their continuation was almost an insult to the merits of Christ. But religious hate needs little stimulus when a pretext is wanted for acts of violence. The populace of Jerusalem were soon persuaded that Paul had committed a crime which could only be washed out in blood. Like all the great revolutionists, Paul discerned the impossibility of living. The enmities that he had raised began to league themselves: the chasm was deepening around him. His companions were strangers at Jerusalem; the Christians of that city held him for an enemy, and opposed themselves to him nearly as bitterly as did the fanatical Jews. In analysing carefully certain features of the account as given in the Acts, in taking notice of the reiterated warnings which, during all his return voyage, exposed to Paul the snares prepared against him at Jerusalem, we ask ourselves if these Judæo-Christians, whose malevolent temper was asserted by the elders, and from whom they feared a hostile demonstration, did not contribute to increase the storm which was about to burst upon the Apostle. Clemens Romanus attributes the loss of the Apostle "to envy." It is frightful to think so, but it agrees well with the iron law which will rule human affairs until the day of the final triumph of God. I perhaps deceive myself, but when I read the twenty-first chapter of the Acts, an invincible suspicion rises within me; something, I do not know what, tells me that Paul was lost by these "false brethren" who overran the world in his footsteps, to oppose his work, and to represent him as another Balaam.

Be that as it may, the signal of the riot came from the Jews of Asia who had seen him with Trophimus. They recognised him in the temple whilst he accomplished the proscribed rite with the Nazarites. "Help, help! children of Israel!" cried they. "Here is the man who preaches everywhere against the Jewish people, against the Law, against this holy place. Here is the profaner of the temple-- he who has introduced Pagans into the sanctuary." The whole town was soon in an uproar. A great crowd assembled. The fanatics seized Paul; their resolute intention was to kill him. But to shed blood in the interior of the temple would have been a pollution of the holy place. They dragged Paul then outside the temple, and had scarcely got there when the Levites closed the doors behind him. They took it to be their duty to beat him. Such indeed would have been his fate if the Roman authority, who alone maintained any shadow of order in this chaos, had not intervened to tear him from the hands of the madmen.

The procurator of Judæa, ever since the death of Agrippa the First, resided habitually at Cæsarea, a Roman town, ornamented with statues, an enemy of the Jews, and opposed in all ways to Jerusalem. The Roman power at Jerusalem was, in the absence of the procurator, represented by the tribune of the cohort, who resided with all his armed force in the tower of Antonia, at the north-west angle of the temple. The tribune, at this time, was a certain Lysias, Greek or Syrian by birth, who, by protections bought with money, had obtained from Claudius the title of Roman citizen, and had since then added to his name that of Claudius. At the news of the tumult, he ran with some centurions and a detachment, by one of the staircases which placed the tower in communication with the outer courts. The fanatics then ceased to strike Paul. The tribune seized and bound him with two chains, asked him who he was, and what he had done; but the tumult prevented a word being heard. The Jewish riot was something frightful. Those strong irritated figures, those large eyes starting from their sockets, those gnashings of teeth, those vociferations, those men flinging dust into the air, tearing their clothes, or throwing themselves about convulsively, gave the looker-on the idea of demons. Although the crowd was unarmed, the Romans were not altogether free from a certain fear of such madmen. Claudius Lysias gave the order to lead Paul to the tower. The excited crowd followed them, uttering cries of death. At the foot of the staircase, the press was such that the soldiers were obliged to take Paul in their arms and to carry him. Claudius Lysias tried in vain to calm the tumult. He somewhat hastily concluded, or it was perhaps suggested by ill-informed persons, that the man whom he had arrested was the Jew of Egypt who, a short time before, had led out with him into the desert some thousands of zealots, announcing to them that he would immediately realise the kingdom of God. They did not know what had become of this impostor, and at any riot they fancied they might see him re-appear among the agitators.

When they had reached the door of the tower, Paul spoke in Greek to the tribune, and begged him to let him speak to the people. The latter, surprised that the prisoner knew Greek, and recognising at least that he was not the Egyptian false prophet, granted his request. Paul then, standing upon the staircase, made a sign with his hand that he wished to speak. Silence was obtained, and, when they heard him speak Hebrew (that is to say, Syro-Chaldean), they redoubled their attention. Paul recounted, in the form which was habitual to him, the history of his conversion and of his calling. They soon interrupted him; the cries, "Kill him! kill him!" began again; the anger was at its height.

The tribune commanded the prisoner to enter the citadel. He understood nothing of this affair; though a brutal and mean soldier, he thought to explain it by torturing him as being the cause of all the trouble. They seized Paul, and had already tied him upon the post to receive the blows of the scourge, when he declared to the centurion who presided at the torture that he was a Roman citizen. The effect of this word was always very great. The executioners receded; the centurion referred to the tribune; the tribune was very much surprised. Paul had the appearance of a poor Jew. "Is it true that thou art a Roman citizen?" Claudius asked him. "Yes." "But I paid a large sum to obtain that title." "But I was born," replied Paul. The stupid Claudius began to be afraid; his poor brain tortured itself to find any meaning in this business. Outrages against the rights of Roman citizens were punished very severely. The very fact of having tied Paul to the post with the view of flagellation was an offence,--an act of violence which would have remained unknown if it had been done by an obscure man, might now become a very grievous matter. Finally Claudius hit upon the idea of convoking for the morrow the high priest and the Sanhedrim, in order to know what complaint they made against Paul, because he himself could find none.

The high priest was Ananias, son of Nébédés, who by a rare exception had filled this high office for ten years. He was a man very much respected, in spite of his gluttonous habits, which were proverbial among the Jews. Independently of his office, he was one of the first men of the nation; he belonged to that family of Hanan, which one is sure to find upon the judicial bench whenever it is a case of condemning the Christians, the popular saints, the innovators of all kinds. Ananias presided over the assembly. Claudius Lysias ordered Paul to be released from his chains, and caused him to be brought in; he himself looking on. The discussion was extremely tumultuous. Ananias flew into a passion, and, for a word which appeared to him blasphemous, ordered his assessors to smite Paul upon the mouth. "God shall smite thee, thou whited wall," replied Paul, "for sittest thou to judge me after the law, and commandest me to be smitten contrary to the law?" "What! revilest thou God's high priest?" said the assistants. Paul, changing his mind, said, "I wist not, brethren, that he was the high priest, for if I had known I should not have spoken thus; for it is written, Thou shalt not speak evil of the ruler of thy people.'" This moderation was skilfully calculated. Paul had remarked, indeed, that the assembly was divided into two parties, animated by very diverse sentiments towards him: the high Sadducee clergy were absolutely hostile to him; but he could make himself understood to a certain point by the Pharisee middle-class. "Brethren," cried he, "I am a Pharisee, the son of a Pharisee. Do you know why they accuse me? For my hope in the resurrection of the dead." It was putting the finger upon an open sore. The Sadducees denied the resurrection, the existence of angels and of spirits; the Pharisees admitted all. The stratagem of Paul succeeded marvellously; war was soon in the assembly. Pharisees and Sadducees were more eager to fight amongst themselves than to destroy their common enemy. Many Pharisees even took up the defence of Paul, and affected to find the recital of his vision probable. "Finally," said they, "what complaint have you against this man? Who knows if a spirit or an angel has not spoken to him?"

Claudius Lysias assisted open-mouthed at this debate, utterly unmeaning as it was for him. He saw the moment when, as on the night before, Paul was about to be torn to pieces. He therefore gave orders to a squadron of soldiers to descend into the hall, to rescue Paul from the hands of those present, and to reconduct him to the tower. Lysias was much embarrassed. Paul, however, rejoiced in the glorious witness that he had just borne to Christ. The following night he had a vision. Jesus appeared to him and said, "Be of good cheer: for as thou hast testified of me in Jerusalem, so must thou bear witness to me also at Rome."

The hate of the fanatics, during this time, did not remain inactive. A certain number of these zealots or hired murderers, always ready to draw the dagger in defence of the Law, conspired to kill Paul. They bound themselves by a vow, under the most terrible anathemas, neither to eat nor to drink whilst Paul remained alive. The conspirators were more than forty in number; they took their oath on the morning of the day which followed the assembly of the Sanhedrim. To gain their ends, they went to the priests, explained to them the plan which they had formed, agreed with them to intervene with the Sanhedrim to ask the tribune for a new appearance of Paul on the morrow. The conspirators proposed to seize their opportunity and kill Paul on the way. But the secret of the plot was ill kept; it came to the knowledge of a nephew of Paul, who lived in Jerusalem. He ran to the barrack and revealed all to Paul; Paul had him led to Claudius Lysias by a centurion. The tribune took the young messenger by the hand, led him aside, obtained from him all the details of the plot, and sent him away, commanding him to keep silence.

From this time Claudius Lysias no longer hesitated. He resolved to send Paul to Cæsarea; on the one hand, to do away with all pretext for disturbances in Jerusalem, and, on the other, to extricate himself by transferring this difficult affair to the procurator. Two centurions received orders to form an escort capable of resisting any attempts at carrying Paul off. It was composed of two hundred soldiers, of seventy cavalry, and of two hundred of those policemen who served at what were called the custodia militaris, that is to say, men who guarded prisoners, fastened to them by means of a chain going from the right hand of the captive to the left hand of his guardian. Horses were also ordered for Paul, and the whole were to be ready by the third hour of the night (nine o' clock in the evening). Claudius Lysias wrote at the same time to the procurator Felix an elogium, that is to say, a letter, to explain the affair to him, declaring that, for his part, he only saw in all that some trifling questions of religion, without anything that deserved death or imprisonment; that, moreover, he had announced to the accusers that they were also to present themselves before the procurator.

These orders were promptly executed. A forced march was made in the night, and in the morning the troop reached Antipatris, which is more than half-way from Jerusalem to Cæsarea. There, all danger of surprise having disappeared, the escort divided itself: the four hundred infantry, after a halt, returned to Jerusalem; the detachment of cavalry alone accompanied Paul to Cæsarea. The Apostle thus re-entered as a prisoner (beginning of August 58) the town which he had left twelve years before, in spite of sinister forebodings that his habitual courage prevented him from listening to. His disciples rejoined him after a little time.

CHAPTER XX

CAPTIVITY OF PAUL AT CÆSAREA OF PALESTINE

Felix then governed Judæa with the powers of a king and the soul of a slave. He was the freedman of Claudius, and brother of that Pallas who had made the fortune of Agrippina, and of Nero. He had all the immorality of his brother, but not his administrative talents. Named, by the influence of Pallas, procurator of Judæa, in 52, he there showed himself cruel, debauched, greedy. Nothing was above his ambition. He was successively married to three queens, and kinsman by marriage of the Emperor Claudius. At the period at which we are, his wife was Drusilla, sister of Herod Agrippa II., whom he had carried off by infamous practices from her first husband, Aziz, King of Emesus. There was no crime of which he was not considered capable; people even went as far as accusing him of practising brigandage on his own account, and of using the dagger of the assassin to gratify his hatreds. Such were the men upon whom the highest functions had devolved since Claudius gave up everything to the freedmen. They were no longer Roman knights, grave functionaries like Pilate, or Coponius; they were covetous lackeys, proud, dissolute, profiting by the political abasement of that poor old Oriental world to gorge themselves at their ease, and to wallow in the mud. Never since has anything so horrible and so shameful been seen.

The chief of the squadron who had led Paul away, delivered up to Felix, on his arrival, the elogium and the prisoner. Paul appeared for an instant before the procurator, who asked him of what country he was. The elogium, assigned to the accused a privileged situation. Felix said that he would hear the cause when the accusers should have arrived. Whilst waiting, he commanded that Paul should be guarded, not in the prison, but in the ancient palace of Herod the Great, which had now become the residence of the procurators. At this moment, doubtless, Paul was trusted to a soldier (frumentarius), who was placed over him to guard him and to present him whenever required.

At the end of three days, the Jewish accusers arrived. The high priest Ananias had come in person, accompanied by some elders. Hardly knowing how to speak Greek and Latin, and full of confidence in the official rhetoric of the time, they had taken as an assistant a certain Tertullus, an advocate. The hearing took place immediately. Tertullus, according to the rules of his profession, began by the captatio benevolentiæ. He impudently praised the government of Felix, spoke of the happiness that they enjoyed under his administration, of the public gratitude, and he begged him to listen with his habitual kindness. Then he approached his subject, treated of Paul as a pest, as a disturber of Judaism, as the chief of the heresy of the Nazarenes, as a busybody, ever occupied in exciting sedition amongst his co-religionists throughout the world. He insisted upon the alleged violation of the temple, which constituted a capital crime, and maintained that in seeking to take possession of Paul, they had only wished to judge him according to the Law.

Upon a sign from Felix, Paul then began to speak. He argued that his conduct in the temple had been that of the most peaceful Jew,--that he had not disputed there or brought the mob together,--that he had not preached once at Jerusalem,--that he was, indeed, heretical if it be heretical to believe all that is written in the Law and the Prophets, and to hope for the resurrection of the dead; at bottom, the only crime of which they accused him was believing in the resurrection; "but," added he, "the Jews themselves believe in that. . . ." With regard to the Jews, it was a skilful apology, clever rather than sincere, since, avoiding the real difficulty, it sought to make out that there was an understanding when there was nothing of the kind, thus evading the question at issue in a fashion which has since been often imitated by Christian apologists. Felix, who interested himself very little about the dogma of the resurrection, remained indifferent. He abruptly broke up the sitting, declaring that he would not decide anything until he had been better informed, and had seen Claudius Lysias. In the meantime, he ordered the centurion to treat Paul with gentleness, that is to say, to leave him unchained, in the state of custodia libera, and to permit his disciples as well as his friends to approach him and to serve him.

Some days after, Felix and Paul again met. Drusilla, who was a Jewess, desired, it is said, to hear the Apostle expound the Christian faith. Paul spoke of justice, of temperance, of judgment to come. The subjects were not altogether agreeable to these new catechumens. Felix, himself, appears to have been afraid: "That is enough for the moment," said he to Paul; "I will make you come to me at the proper time." Having learned that Paul had brought with him a considerable sum of money, he hoped to obtain from him or his friends a heavy bribe for his release. It appears that he saw him several times, and he sought to suggest this idea to him. But the Apostle not lending himself to it, Felix wished at least to gather some profit, for his popularity was much shaken. The greatest pleasure that one could do for the Jews was to persecute those whom they regarded as their enemies. He therefore kept Paul in prison, and even put him in chains. Paul passed two years in this way.

The prison, even with the augmentation of the chain and of the soldier (frumentarius), was far from being then what it is to-day, a total privation of liberty. Every one who had pecuniary resources could arrange with his gaoler, and might attend to his business. In any case, he saw his friends, he was not rigorously confined; in short, he might do pretty much as he pleased. There is no doubt, consequently, that Paul, although a prisoner, continued his apostleship at Cæsarea. Never had he had with him such disciples. Timothy, Luke, Aristarchus of Thessalonica, Tychicus, and Trophimus, carried his orders in all directions, and helped with the correspondence that he kept up with his Churches. In particular, he charged Tychicus and Trophimus with a mission for Ephesus. Trophimus, it appears, fell ill at Miletus.

As a consequence of the stay that they thus made in Palestine, the most intelligent members of the Churches of Macedonia and of Asia found themselves in prolonged relations with the Churches of Judæa. Luke, in particular, who until then had not left Macedonia, was initiated into the traditions of Jerusalem. He was without doubt vividly impressed by the majesty of Jerusalem, and he imagined the possibility of a reconciliation between the principles maintained on the one side by Paul, on the other by the elders of Jerusalem. He thought that the best thing was to forget reciprocal injuries, to prudently veil these wrongs, and to speak no more of them. The fundamental ideas which must preside at the editing of his great manuscript probably then developed themselves in his mind. By these various contacts, a uniform tradition was established. The Gospels were elaborated by the intimate communication of all the parties which constituted the Church. Jesus had created the Church; the Church created him in its turn. That grand ideal which was to dominate humanity for centuries, truly went out from the bowels of humanity by a kind of secret agreement amongst all those to whom Jesus had bequeathed His Spirit.

Felix finally succumbed, not under the indignation that his crimes must have produced, but before the difficulties of a situation against which not even a procurator could make head. The life of a Roman governor at Cæsarea had become insupportable; the Jews and the Syrians or Greeks fought incessantly; the most honest man could hardly hold the balance between such ferocious hatreds. The Jews, according to their custom, complained at Rome. They there exercised a sufficiently strong influence, especially with Poppæa, and, thanks to the intrigues which Herod Agrippa II. directed, Pallas had lost much of his credit, above all since the year 55. He could not prevent the disgrace of his brother: he only succeeded in saving him from death. They gave as a successor to Felix a firm and just man, Porcius Festus, who arrived in the month of August of the year 60 at Cæsarea.

Three days after his disembarkation, he betook himself to Jerusalem. The high priest Ismael, son of Phabi, and all the party of the Sadducees (that is to say, the high priesthood), surrounded him, and one of the first demands that they addressed to him was relative to Paul. They wished him to be brought back to Jerusalem, and they had arranged for an ambuscade to kill him on the way. Festus replied that he was about shortly to set out for Cæsarea, that it was consequently better that Paul should remain there, but that, as the Romans never pronounced a sentence without the accused being confronted with his accusers, it would be necessary that those of the notables who wished to charge Paul should come with him. At the end of eight or ten days he returned to Cæsarea, and, on. the morrow, he caused Paul and his adversaries to appear before his court. After a confused debate, Paul maintaining that he had done nothing against the Law, or against the temple, or against the Emperor, Festus proposed to him that he should re-conduct him to Jerusalem, where he could, under his surveillance and his high jurisdiction, defend himself before a Jewish court. Festus undoubtedly did not know of the project of the conspirators; he hoped, by this dismissal, to disembarrass himself of a tedious cause, and to do an agreeable thing for the Jews, who asked from him so urgently for the transfer of the prisoner.

But Paul carefully guarded himself from accepting. He was possessed by the desire of seeing Rome. The capital of the world had for him a powerful and mysterious charm. He maintained his right to be judged by a Roman tribunal, protested that no one had any right to deliver him to the Jews, and pronounced the solemn words:--"I appeal unto Cæsar." These words pronounced by a Roman citizen, did away with all provincial jurisdictions. The citizen, in whatever part of the world he was, had the right of being taken to Rome to be judged. The governors of provinces, moreover, often referred to the Emperor and his council the causes of religious law. Festus, surprised at first by this appeal, conversed for a moment with his assessors, then replied by the formula:--"Hast thou appealed unto Cæsar? unto Cæsar shalt thou go."

The sending of Paul to Rome was from this time decided, and they only waited for an opportunity for him to set out. A singular incident occurred in the interval. Some days after the return of Festus to Cæsarea, Herod Agrippa II. and his sister Bernice, who lived with him, not without a suspicion of infamy, came to salute the new procurator. They remained for several days at Cæsarea. In the course of the conversations that they had with the Roman functionary, the latter spoke to him of the prisoner whom Felix had left him. "His accusers," said he, "have not charged against him any of the crimes that I was waiting to see established. There is nothing in all this business but subtleties relative to their superstitions, and of a certain Jesus who is dead, and whom Paul affirms to be living." "Truly," said Agrippa, "I have for a long time wished to hear this man speak." "Thou shalt hear him to-morrow," replied Festus.

On the morrow, then, Agrippa and Bernice came to the tribunal with a brilliant suite. All the officers of the army, and the chief people of the town, were present. No official procedure could take place after the appeal to the Emperor, but Festus declared that, according to his principles, the sending of a prisoner to Rome must be accompanied by a report. He pretended to wish for fuller information for the report that he had to make in this case; he alleged his ignorance of Jewish affairs, and declared that he wished to follow in this matter the advice of King Agrippa. Agrippa invited Paul to speak. Paul then made, with a certain oratorical complacency, one of those discourses that he had repeated a hundred times. He esteemed himself happy in having to plead his cause before a judge as well instructed in Jewish questions as was Agrippa. He intrenched himself more strongly than ever in his ordinary system of defence, asserted that he said nothing that was not in the Law and the Prophets,--maintained that he was persecuted only because of his belief in the resurrection, the faith which is that of all the Israelites, which gives a moving motive for their piety, a foundation for their hopes. He explained, by quotations from the Scriptures, his favourite propositions--the knowledge that Christ must suffer, that he must be the first to rise from the dead. Festus, a stranger to all these speculations, took Paul for a dreamer, a clever man in his way, but wandering and chimerical. "Paul, thou art beside thyself; much learning doth make thee mad." Paul invoked the witness of Agrippa, who was more versed in Jewish theology, knowing the prophets, and whom he supposed instructed in the facts relative to Jesus. Agrippa replied evasively. A grain of pleasantry mixed itself, it seems, in the conversation. "Almost thou persuadest me to be a Christian," said Agrippa. Paul, with his usual wit, took the tone of the court, and finished by wishing that they all resembled him. "Except these bonds," replied he, with a gentle irony.

The effect of this courteous sitting, so different from the audiences in which the Jews figured as prosecutors, was finally favourable to Paul. Festus, with his Roman good sense, declared that this man had done nothing wrong. Agrippa was of opinion that, if he had not appealed to the Emperor about it, they might have released him. Paul, who wished to go to Rome conducted by the Romans themselves, did not withdraw his appeal. They then put him, with some other prisoners, in the guard of a centurion of the cohort prima Augusta Italica, named Julius, who must have been an Italian. Timothy, Luke, and Aristarchus of Thessalonica were the only disciples who travelled with Paul.

CHAPTER XXI

PAUL'S VOYAGE AS A PRISONER

The party embarked upon a ship of Adramyttium in Mysia, which was returning thither. At one of the intermediate ports, Julius counted on finding a ship about to sail for Italy, and on taking passage in it. It was about the time of the autumnal equinox, so that they had a rough voyage in prospect.

On the second day they arrived at Sidon. Julius, who treated Paul very kindly, allowed him to go down into the town, to visit his friends and to receive their attentions. The route had been to take the open sea and to gain the south-west point of Asia Minor; but the winds were contrary. It was necessary to run to the north, sailing close to Phoenicia, then to go to the coast of Cyprus, leaving it on the port hand. They followed the channel between Cyprus and Cilicia, traversed the gulf of Pamphylia, and arrived at the port of Myra in Lycia. There they left the Adramyttium ship. Julius having found one of Alexandria which was about to sail for Italy, made a bargain with the captain, and transported his prisoners thither. The ship was very full: there were on board 276 persons.

Navigation from this time was most difficult. After several days they had only reached Cnidus. The captain wished to enter the port, but the north-east wind did not allow him, and it was necessary to allow himself to be carried under the isle of Crete. They soon recognised Cape Salmone, which is the eastern point of the island. The island of Crete forms an immense barrier, making of the portion of the Mediterranean that it covers at the south a kind of large port, sheltered from the tempest coming from the archipelago. The captain had the very natural idea of profiting by this advantage. He still followed the eastern side of the island, not without great perils; then, getting the island on the windward side, he entered the calm waters of the south. There was a little port there very deep, shut in by an islet, and bordered by two sandy beaches between which a point of rocks juts out, so that it seems divided into two parts. It is what is called Kali-Limenes (the Fair Havens); near to it was a town named Lasæa or Alassa They took shelter here; the crew and passengers were excessively fatigued, so that they made a rather pro-longed stay in this little port.

When it was a question of setting out again, the season was far advanced. The great fast of the Atonement (Kippour), in the month of Pisri (October), had passed; this fast marked for the Jews the limit after which maritime journeys were not safe. Paul, who had acquired much authority upon the ship, and who, moreover, had had long experience of the sea, gave his opinion. He predicted great dangers and disasters if they re-embarked.

"Nevertheless the centurion" (we cannot be as much surprised by the fact as the narrator of the Acts) "believed the master and the owner of the ship, more than those things which were spoken by Paul." The port of Kali-Limenes was not a good one to winter in. The general opinion was that they must try, in order to pass the winter months there, to gain the port of Phoenice, situated upon the southern coast of the island, where the men who knew those regions promised good anchorage. A day when there was a breeze from the south they believed to be the favourable one; they weighed anchor, and tacked along the side of the island, as far as Cape Littinos; then they sailed with a fair wind towards Phoenice.

The crew and the passengers believed themselves at the end of their troubles, when suddenly one of those sudden hurricanes from the east, that the sailors of the Mediterranean call Euroclydon, smote the island. The ship was soon unable to keep her head to the wind: the seamen had to run before it. They passed near a little isle named Clauda; they put themselves for a moment under the shelter of this isle, and profited by the short respite to hoist up with great difficulty the boat, which every moment ran the risk of breaking up. They then took precautions, in view of that shipwreck which all held to be inevitable. They bound the hull of the ship with cables, they struck the yards, and abandoned themselves to the wind. The second day, the tempest was quite as great; wishing to lighten the ship, they threw the cargo overboard. On the third day, they disencumbered themselves of the furniture and utensils that were not necessary for working the ship. The following days were frightful, they did not see the sun for a moment, or a single star; they did not know where they were going. Besides being strewn with islands, the Mediterranean presents between Sicily and Malta, to the west, Pelponnesus and Crete; to the east, southern Italy and Epiræus; to the north, the coast of Africa; to the south, a large square of open sea, where the wind meets with no obstacle, and rolls the sea into enormous waves. It was that place that the ancients often called the Adriatic. The general opinion of the men on board was that the ship was running upon the Syrtes of Africa, where loss of life and goods was certain. All hope seemed gone; no one dreamt of taking any food; it was, moreover, impossible to prepare it. Paul alone remained confident. He was convinced that he should see Rome, and that he would appear before the tribunal of the Emperor. He encouraged the crew and passengers; he even said, it appears, that a vision had revealed to him that not a person should perish, God having granted to him the life of all, in spite of the mistake that they had made in leaving the Fair Havens against his advice.

On the fourteenth night, indeed, after leaving this port, towards the middle of the night, the sailors believed that they recognised the land. They cast the lead, and found twenty fathoms; a short time after it was fifteen fathoms. They believed that they were about to run upon the rocks; at once four anchors were thrown from the poop; they lashed the rudders, that is to say, the two large paddles which projected from the two sides of the quarter-deck; the ship stopped; they waited anxiously for the day. The sailors then, profiting by their skill in the work, wished to save themselves at the expense of the passengers. Under the pretext of throwing the anchors from the bow, they launched the boat, and tried to get on shore. But the centurion and the soldiers, warned, it is said by Paul, of this disloyal conduct, opposed themselves. The soldiers cut the cables which held the sloop, and let it go adrift. Paul, however, spoke consolingly to all, and assured them that no one would suffer in his body. During these crises of maritime life, existence is as it were suspended; when they are ended, we perceive that we are dirty and hungry. For fourteen days scarcely any one had taken any nourishment; it might have been from emotion; it might have been from sea-sickness. Paul, in waiting for the day, advised all to eat, in order to give them-selves strength, in view of the work which remained to be done. He set the example himself, and, like a pious Jew, broke bread, according to custom, after a prayer of thanksgiving, which he offered in the presence of all. The passengers imitated him, and took heart again. They still lightened the ship, throwing into the sea all the corn which remained.

Day at last appeared, and they saw the land. It was deserted: no one could make out where he was. They had before them a bay, having at its extremity a sandy beach. They resolved to run aground upon the sand. The wind was in their favour. They then cut the cables of the anchors, and allowed them to get lost in the sea; they loosed the ropes which bound the rudders. hoisted the foresail, and steered towards the shore. The ship fell upon a neck of land beaten on two sides by the sea, and there remained. The prow sank into the sand and remained immovable; the poop, on the contrary, beaten by the waves, bumped and dislocated itself at each blow from the sea. Safety under these conditions is easy enough upon the shores of the Mediterranean, the ebb and flow of the tide being inconsiderable. The grounded ship made a shelter, and it was easy to establish communication with the land. But the presence of prisoners where there were so many passengers aggravated the situation. They might save themselves by swimming, and escape their guardians; the soldiers, therefore, proposed to kill them. The honest Julius rejected this barbarous notion. He ordered those who knew how to swim to cast themselves into the sea and to gain the land, in order to aid the escape of the others. Those who did not know how to swim escaped upon planks and wreckage of every kind; nobody was lost.

They soon learnt that they were at Malta. The island, having submitted to the Romans for a long time, and already much Latinised, was rich and prosperous. The inhabitants showed themselves humane, and lighted a large fire for the unfortunate castaways. The latter, indeed, were shivering with cold, and the rain continued to fall in torrents. A very simple incident, exaggerated by the disciples of Paul, then took place. In taking a bundle of sticks to throw into the fire, Paul at the same time took up a viper. They believed that it had bitten his hand. The idea got into their heads that this man was a murderer, followed by Nemesis, who not having been able to overtake him by means of the tempest, had pursued him on land. The men of the country, as it appears, waited to see him any moment swell and fall dead. As nothing happened, they decided, it is said, to look upon him as a god.

Near the bay in which the ship had got wrecked were the lands of a certain Publius, princeps of the municipality that the island formed with Gaul. This man came to find that the castaways, or at least a party of them, of whom were Paul and his companions, had gathered in his homestead, and he treated them during three days with much hospitality. Here soon happened one of those miracles that the disciples of Paul believed they saw at every instant. The Apostle cured, they say, the father of Publius by the imposition of hands, he suffering from fever and dysentery. His reputation of wonder-worker spread in the island, and they brought to him sick people from all sides. It is not said, however, that he founded a Church there. These low African populations could not raise themselves above their sensuality and gross superstition.

The ancient coasting trade of the Mediterranean came to a standstill during the winter. The frightful voyage that they had just made offered no encouragement to take to the sea again. They remained for three months at Malta, from the 15th of November 60 to the 15th of February 61 or thereabouts. Then Julius negotiated for the passage of his prisoners and of his soldiers upon another Alexandrian ship, the Castor and Pollux, which had wintered in the port of the island. They reached Syracuse, where they remained for three days; then sailed with a fair wind towards the straits, and touched at Rhegium. On the morrow, a good wind blew from the south, and bore the ship in two days to Puteoli.

Puteoli, as we have already said, was the port of Italy most frequented by the Jews. It was there also that ships from Alexandria discharged their cargoes. There had been formed there, at the same time as at Rome, a little Christian society. The Apostle was very warmly welcomed by it, and entreated him to stay for seven days, which, thanks to the kindness of the good centurion Julius, who was much attached to him, was possible. They subsequently set out for Rome. The rumour of Paul's arrival was spread amongst the faithful of that city, to some of whom he was already, since the sending of his epistle, a known and respected master. At the relay, at the stage called Appii Forum, forty-three miles from Rome, upon the Appian Way, the first deputation reached him. Ten miles further on, to set out from the Pontine Marshes, near a spot called "The Three Taverns," on account of the hostelries which were established there, a new group came to join. The joy of the Apostle declared itself by lively expressions of thanks. The holy flock traversed not without emotion the eleven or twelve leagues which separated "The Three Taverns" from Port Capena, and always following the Appian Way, by Aricia and Albania, the prisoner Paul entered Rome in the month of March in the year 64, in the seventh year of the reign of Nero, under the consulship of Cæsennius Pætus and Petronius Tarpilien.

CHAPTER XXII

A GLANCE OVER THE WORK OF PAUL

Paul had still three years to live, and those three years were not the least busy of his laborious existence. We shall even see that his apostolic career had in all probability an extension. But these new journeys he made in the west, not in the countries which he had already visited. These journeys, if they really took place, were, besides, without appreciable results for the propagation of Christianity. At this point we can therefore estimate the work of Paul. Thanks to him, a part of Asia Minor had received the seed of Christianity. In Europe, Macedonia has been very deeply penetrated, Greece breaks upon its borders. If we add to that Italy, from Puteoli to Rome, already furrowed by Christians, we shall have the picture of the conquests effected by Christianity in the sixteen years that this book embraces. Syria, we have seen, had previously received the word of Jesus, and possessed organised Churches. The progress of the new faith had been really marvellous, and although the world at large occupied itself very little with it, the followers of Jesus were already important to those without. We shall see them, towards the middle of the year 64, occupy the attention of the world, and play a very important part in its history.

In all this history, nevertheless, it is important to avoid a mistake which the reading of the Epistles of Paul, and the Acts of the Apostles, almost necessarily produces. One would be tempted from such a reading to imagine conversions en masse of numerous Churches of entire countries adopting the new religion. Paul, who often speaks to us of rebellious Jews, never speaks of the immense majority of Pagans who had no knowledge of the faith. In reading the journeys of Benjamin of Tudela, one would also believe that the world of his time was peopled only with Jews. Sects are subject to these optical illusions; for them, nothing exists besides themselves; the events which happen amongst them appear to them to be the only events interesting to the universe. Persons who have had relations with ancient St Simonians are struck with the facility with which they consider themselves the centre of humanity. The first Christians lived so shut up in their own (little) circle, that they knew scarcely anything of the profane world. A country was accounted evangelised when the name of Jesus had been pronounced there, and when a tenth of the people were converted. A Church often did not number more than twelve or fifteen persons. Perhaps all the converts of St Paul in Asia Minor, in Macedonia, and Greece, did not much exceed a thousand. That small number, that spirit of secret companionship, of a little spiritual family, was truly what constituted the indestructible strength of those Churches, and made of them so many fertile germs for the future.

One man contributed more than any other to the rapid extension of Christianity. That man has torn up the swaddling clothes so narrow and so prodigiously dangerous by which he was surrounded from his birth; he has proclaimed that Christianity was not a simple reform of Judaism, but that it was a complete religion, existing by itself. To say that he deserves to be placed in a very elevated rank in history, is to say what is self-evident; but it is not necessary to call him a founder. Paul well said that he was the least of the Apostles. He had not seen Jesus, he had not heard His voice. The divine logic, the parables, he scarcely knew. The Christ who personally revealed himself to him is his own ghost; he listens to himself, thinking that he hears Jesus.

Even to speak only of his exterior character, Paul must have been in his lifetime less important than we think him. His Churches were either not very solid, or else they denied him altogether. The Churches of Macedonia and of Galatia, which are truly his own work, were not very important in the second and third century. The Churches of Corinth and of Ephesus, which were not so exclusively his, went over to his enemies, or are not founded canonically enough if they have been founded only by him. After his disappearance from the scene of his Apostolic contests, we shall see him almost forgotten. His death was probably held by his enemies as the death of a firebrand. The second century hardly speaks of him, and seems systematically to seek to efface his memory. His epistles are read little, and are only considered authoritative by a much reduced group of Churches. His partisans themselves greatly weaken his pretensions. He left no celebrated disciples; Titus, Timothy, and those others who made for him a kind of court, disappear without any noise. To tell the truth, Paul had too energetic a personality to form an original school. He always crushed his disciples; they only played around him the part of secretaries, of servants, of couriers. Their respect for their master was such that they never dared to teach freely. When Paul was with his flock, he existed alone; all others were crushed or seen only through him.

In the third, fourth, and fifth centuries Paul will grow singularly: He will become the doctor in an eminent degree, the founder of Christian theology The true president of those great Greek Councils, which made of Jesus the keystone of metaphysics, was the Apostle Paul.

But in the Middle Ages, everywhere in the west, his fortune will undergo a strange eclipse. Paul will scarcely say anything to the heart of the barbarians; out of Rome, he will not be remembered. Latin Christianity will scarcely pronounce his name, except as coupled with that of his rival. St Paul, in the Middle Ages, is in some sort lost in the glory of St Peter. Whilst St Peter moved the world and made it tremble and obey, the obscure St Pou plays a secondary part in the grand Christian poesy which fills cathedrals and inspires popular chants. Scarcely anybody before the sixteenth century utters his name; he scarcely appears in monumental inscriptions; he has no devotees, they build hardly any churches to him, they burn no wax-tapers to him. His associates Titus, Timothy, Pheebe, Lydia, have little place in public worship, especially in that of the Latins. They have no legend which is worth anything. To have a legend, it is necessary to have spoken to the heart of the people--to have struck their imagination. Now, what does salvation by faith say, or justification by the blood of Christ? Paul was too little sympathetic with the popular conscience, and also perhaps too well known in history for a halo of fables to form around his head. Talk to me of Peter, who bends the necks of kings, breaks empires, walks upon the asp and the basilisk, treads under foot the lion and the dragon, holds the keys of heaven!

The Reformation opens for St Paul a new era of glory and authority. Catholicism itself returns, by studies more extended than those of the Middle Ages, to juster views upon the Apostle of the Gentiles. From the sixteenth century, the name of Paul is everywhere. But the Reformation, which has rendered so many services to science and reason, has not been known to create a legend. Rome, throwing an obliging veil upon the rudenesses of the Epistle to the Galatians, elevates Paul upon a pedestal nearly equal to that of Peter. Paul nevertheless does not become the saint of the people. What place will criticism give to him? What rank will be assigned to him in the hierarchy of those who serve the ideal.

The ideal is served by doing good, by discovering the true, by realising the beautiful. At the head of the sacred procession of humanity walks the good man, the virtuous man; the second rank belongs to the man of truth, knowledge, philosophy; then comes the man of beauty, the artist, the poet. Jesus appears to us, under his celestial halo, as an ideal of goodness and beauty. Peter loved Jesus, understood him, and was, it seems, in spite of some failings, an excellent man. What was Paul? He was not a saint. The dominating feature of his character is not goodness. He was proud, unbending, unsociable; he defends himself; self-assertive (as we say to-day); he uses harsh words; he believes himself right; he holds to his opinions; he quarrels with various people. He was not a scholar; one can even say that he has injured science by his paradoxical contempt of reason, by his eulogy of apparent folly, by his apotheosis of transcendental absurdity. Neither was he a poet. His writings; works of the highest originality, are without charm: the form is harsh and almost devoid of grace. What was he then?

He was eminently a man of action, a strong soul--invading, enthusiastic, conquering--a missionary, a propagator, all the more ardent because he had at first displayed his fanaticism on the opposite side. Now, the man of action, noble as he is when he acts for a noble aim, is less near to God than one who has lived for the pure love of truth, of the good and the beautiful. The Apostle is naturally rather narrow-minded; he wished to succeed, he made sacrifices for that end. Contact with reality always soils one a little. The first places in the kingdom of heaven are reserved to those whom a ray of grace has touched, to those who have only adored the ideal. The man of action is always- a feeble artist, for he has not for his only aim that of reflecting the splendour of the universe. He could not be a scholar, for he regulates his opinions on grounds of political utility; he is not even a very virtuous man, for he is never irreproachable, the folly and wickedness of men forcing him to make a compact with them. Above all things, he is not amiable; the most charming of virtues, reserve, is forbidden to him. The world favours the daring, those who help themselves Paul, so great, so honest, is obliged to bestow on himself the title of Apostle. He is strong in action through his faults; he is weak through his virtues. In short, the historical personage who has most analogy with St Paul is Luther. Both alike were violent in language, both displayed the same passion, the same energy, the same noble independence, the same frantic attachment to a proposition once embraced, as infallible truth.

I still persist in maintaining, that in the creation of Christianity the part of Paul ought to be treated as much inferior to that of Jesus. It is necessary even, according to my idea, to put Paul on a lower plane than Francis of Assisi, and the author of the "Imitation," who both saw Jesus very nearly. The Son of God is unique. To appear for a moment to make a sweet and profound impression, to die very young, that is the life of a god. To wrestle, to dispute, to conquer, that is the life of a man. After having been for three hundred years the Christian doctor in an eminent degree, thanks to orthodox Protestantism, Paul seems in our days near the end of his reign: Jesus, on the contrary, is more living than ever. It is no more the Epistle to the Romans which is the recapitulation of Christianity, it is the Sermon on the Mount. True Christianity which will last eternally comes from the Gospels, not from the Epistles of Paul. The writings of Paul have been a danger and a stumbling-block, the cause of the chief faults of

Christian theology. Paul is the father of the subtle Augustine, of the arid Thomas Aquinas, of the sombre Calvinist, of the bitter Jansenist, of the ferocious theology which condemns and predestinates to damnation. Jesus is the father of all those who seek in dreams of the ideal the repose of their souls. That which gives life to Christianity, is the little that we know of the word and of the person of Jesus. The man devoted to the ideal, the divine poet, the great artist, defies alone time and revolution. Alone he is seated at the right hand of God the Father for eternity.

Humanity, thou art sometimes just, and certain of thy judgments are good!

THE END

www.ingramcontent.com/pod-product-compliance
Lightning Source LLC
Chambersburg PA
CBHW021239090426
42740CB00006B/601